"WE'LL ALWAYS BE PALS"

The last words of a dying father and a true hero!

A true story
By Tom McManus

First published by Dog Ear Publishing
4010 W. 86th Street, Ste H
Indianapolis, IN 46268
www.dogearpublishing.net

ISBN: 978-159858-768-5

This book is printed on acid-free paper.

Printed in the United States of America

TABLE OF CONTENTS

ACKNOWLEDGEMENTS

This all started out for my first daughter, Avery Ann, for I wanted the first born of my mom and dad's grandchildren to know about Grandpa Geno. It has grown into so much more. For my Kelsey, my little roaring lion, I love you. Harley Mae to be, we can't wait to see you. Your Grandpa is so proud of you all.

For my brothers and sisters and all of your children, this is for you, and although we all had different kinds of relationships with our Dad, our common thread is the love we have for him.

To my half-sisters, Linda and Sue, and our dad's grandchildren whom he loved and talked about so much: I know my father always wanted us to be closer. He would always say, "They're family!" This is for all of you and your families so that you will know these stories and how they have inspired me.

My mother, Joan, our "Joanie", we love ya ma! This book is for you too. You lived it with a first class ticket the whole way. You were and still are Dad's love of his life. You're the best. All I ask is that when your time is up and you step on that escalator that will take you up to the front of the Pearly Gates, would you put in a good word for me?

My Kristina, my wife, you are simply the best. From the time she was pregnant with our first daughter, and I was upstairs typing away, laughing and crying the whole time, she has been there for me. She is my soul. I know you have only seen my Dad in your dreams, but you are one of his. Thanks babe, for everything.

Special thanks also go out to the following people who helped make this book a reality:

George Harrell was one of the first real writers to look at my original story titled, "Geno", and he believed in it from the minute he finished reading it. He has been a "coach" and a friend, and a huge help in putting this book together.

To my crazy Boston attorneys, the Lakin Brothers, Kenny and John, you had faith in it from the start as well. Your representation is second to none and your friendship is the best.

Rick Bieber, Hollywood film producer, who wrote an adaptation of this story in a screenplay format. Thanks Rick. I know you have always believed.

Tom Brokaw, author of "The Greatest Generation". Your writings helped inspire me to write this story.

Glenn Strong, Jr., who is the son of my dad's co-pilot, gave me incredible information regarding the time my dad spent in the war.

Brett and Robbie and the rest of the staff at the UPS Store in Ponte Vedra Beach who were always very accommodating when delivering what I needed. Much thanks to all of you.

Dave White (Whitey), author of "Overcoming OCD & Depression: My Personal Journey & Recovery", and Bill Simpson, an author of many books and an editor. Two guys whom I never met before other than through the phone and e-mail conversations, thanks for the wisdom, and helping getting this book ready.

And last but certainly not least:

To The Good Lord, Jesus Christ, without you I am nothing.

LEARNING THE GAME, GENO STYLE

"You need to get that goddamn grin off your face, Tom. You didn't play the game as well as you think you did!" my father deliberately said to me after an eighth grade playoff game.

Stunned by his words, I responded: "But, Dad, I scored four touchdowns…."

I mean I was feeling pretty good about myself. I had received accolades from my teammates and my coaches, even the opposition and their coaches. However, my dad didn't see it that way. I knew he was unusually quiet in the car ride home, but I didn't see what was coming. When we arrived at our house, I went straight to my room, got changed, and met my father in the kitchen after he requested my presence. It was where he shook me out of my revelry.

"I don't give a damn how many touchdowns you scored. You didn't block and tackle the way you are supposed to!" he snapped back.

"But", I tried to reply in my defense.

He quickly interrupted: "Don't you 'but' me, Tom. You were not as physical as you are supposed to be, on every play. You've got to get mad at your opponent. Knock him down every single time!" he demanded.

"I thought I had a good game," I nervously muttered back, hiding the tears that were welling up inside of me.

"Football is about blocking and tackling, Tom! It's about hitting! I don't care if you scored ten touchdowns today, you didn't hit like you should have! And let me tell you something else. Don't ever let me see you help the opponent off the ground again! Do you understand me?" he asked as his volume continued to rise.

By now I couldn't control my emotions and I began to cry. Tears were dribbling down the sides of my face. I was both embarrassed and crushed. My dad was chewing me out for not being tough enough, which in our household was the benchmark for all of us three boys.

He never took a breath and continued: "There are no friends on that goddamn football field. You knock them on their ass and don't ever help them up! After the game, you shake their hands and are a good sport, win or lose. But during the game, they are the enemy! Do you understand?" he finished.

"Yes, Dad." I answered back, now sobbing.

"And quit your crying before I give you something to cry about!" he barked as I immediately left the kitchen and headed downstairs to my bedroom, shaken and hurt.

I really should have known better. I didn't play that great of a game, at least not like I was used to playing. Sure, I scored four touchdowns but they were easy scores. I think I was hardly even touched on three of them. And on defense, although I was in on a bunch of tackles, I didn't really drill anyone, not even close.

After I wiped away the tears of disappointment, I began to realize what my dad expected out of me. The lecture that night was about what it takes to succeed, there in sports and later on, in life: Toughness. Physical, mental, and emotional toughness. It meant that it didn't matter what level of athletic ability I had, it all had to do with my heart and my guts. I grew up learning that there was a lot more to an athlete than what meets the eye. What's inside is what sets people apart.

That same kind of philosophy went for other sports as well, whether it was rebounding in basketball, or blocking home plate as a catcher in baseball. No matter the case, just give it your all and never give up, and above all, be one of the toughest ones out there.

I started playing organized tackle football in the 4th grade. The home I grew up in was located in the parish of St. Mary's of Buffalo Grove, located about 30 miles northwest of Chicago. St. Mary's was a K-8 institution with a reputation of having great sports programs. We actually transferred from a different local Catholic school because it didn't have a tackle football program, just flag football, and Gene McManus' sons didn't play flag football. We played tackle!

Football was always a mainstay in our household. We played in the streets, at the park, or in someone's backyard, no matter what time of year it was. Hell, when you couldn't find any grass during the winter, snow football was an awesome substitute, whether in the streets using the plowed banks as the sideline, or out in a field. My older brothers played, and most of their friends all played as well. It was highly competitive, too. My two brothers, who were a year and a half to three years older, would make sure that I would get hit, and hit I was, often.

I was usually the youngest kid in the neighborhood games, unless I could recruit one of my friends to play, but that didn't happen too often. I was big for my age and although I usually took a beating, I enjoyed being out there. I was a natural competitor and wanted to be in the action, no matter who was older or bigger. We played basketball too, as well as, a little baseball, depending on what time of the year it was, but football was our staple diet in contact sports.

St. Mary's had a terrific football program filled with history and success. We traveled all throughout Chicago taking on other Catholic schools. Our home games were held on Sunday afternoons after the church schedule was over. We had big crowds, or so it seemed. It was like a ritual, every Sunday in the fall, to play football for our school and then all would go to a local eatery were the parents would drink and the kids would eat.

After the feast, we would go outside and play more football. We were all bound by the pride we had for our school in winning football games. I have such great memories of St. Mary's and the foundation that was built of faith, family, friends and competition. It was a great start to my young life and very significant in my upbringing.

At home games, with several hundred people in attendance, we would gather at the top of a hill, outside the rectory hall, where we would kneel and say the Lord's Prayer together before each game.

My first coach, Mike Flood, was a great influence. He worked us hard and taught us how to win. He molded us into a tough, physical team. He was a coach whom everyone looked up to, and whom the parents loved. He would also come up with unique ways to get us motivated for the upcoming games.

He would tell us to bow our heads as we recited the Lord's Prayer, and when we were finished, he would read a "mystery" letter from the opposing team that somehow he had managed to receive. It would get us all riled up. "McManus is a wimp!" he would proclaim was in the letter. I can vividly remember hearing that and staring at the ground, grinding my teeth and clenching my fists. I would silently promise to myself and to my school that I would make someone pay for that. I was in sixth grade.

The anonymous letter would have many insults in it for my other teammates and friends as well. We would really get fired up with venom to bust someone's butt on that football field. After his eloquent, passionate pep talk, we would all be jumping up and down ready to face our opposition. It was a moment we all eagerly awaited before each game.

After his speech and after we had calmed down at bit, we would walk in a single file line chanting fight songs at the top of our lungs, dying to get out there and beat up our opponents. It sounds so silly, but from 4th to 8th grade, it was everything to us as we looked forward to every weekend, rain or shine, to get out there, and win.

My dad chose not to coach his sons. He never wanted to for fear of parents wondering if he was giving special attention to us. He also believed in letting coaches coach his sons, not the other way around. He did, in fact, later on become a coach at St. Mary's but it was after I left to go to high school. He was always a huge presence, though, always critiquing my play. I took his critique very seriously and deeply yearned for his approval.

During my final season at St. Mary's, I was one of the top players on the team as three other teammates and I were recruited by private high schools to come play football for them. We were tough kids and our services were highly sought after. Our team had only been beaten once in a four-year time span. I was a running back on offense and a linebacker on defense. I played both sides just like my father had in his youth. That gave me a great sense of satisfaction and pride. Times were great, but my dad always made sure I had my head on straight, and he made sure that I knew what it took to be more successful out on the field of play every time.

I was thirteen when my football days came to a close at St. Mary's. My dad had by then retired from Prudential. He was 63 years old. He worked 35 years for that company, and received a pension from them. He began to work at a local convenience store to keep busy and earn extra income.

Eventually he became a golf ranger at a local country club, one of which he had helped get the financing while he was at Prudential. They loved him there, at the Lincolnshire Country Club. Everyone loved my dad, it seemed. He was a man's man, the life of the party, a great people person who was well respected in our community. I desperately loved him as well.

My older brothers both went on to a local Catholic high school called St. Viator. My brother Mike was a very good football player himself, garnering accolades and attention as a tough linebacker throughout his years at St. Viator. Bob, my oldest brother, played sports there too although that truly wasn't his passion. He was very well liked and made a great deal of friends, but he was more of the brains in the family. They were both popular students and let's just say cut from the same cloth as their father.

After my days at St. Mary's, everyone assumed that I was going to follow in my older brothers' footsteps and play alongside Mike on St. Viator's defense. I, too, thought that was where I was going until one day the coach from Wheeling High School, a local public high school, made a visit to St. Mary's. Rick Benedetto, the head coach of the football program at Wheeling, and his star quarterback, Greg Anderson, who was also a St. Mary's graduate, sat in front of me and my three teammates in a classroom one afternoon. After the meeting was over, I went home with the most unforeseen news, especially to my father.

As was usual when I got home from school, my dad was sitting at the kitchen table reading and waiting for his kids to come home. When I walked up the stairs he asked how my day went.

"It was a great. Wheeling High School came for a visit to talk to me, Brendan, Steve, and Rich. The coach brought Greg Anderson with him. It was real impressive." After a slight pause, I proudly announced, "Dad, I have been doing some thinking. I think I want to go to Wheeling."

"Why do you want to go there and not St. Viator?" he asked inquisitively as he put down the newspaper. I knew that he had thought, like everyone else, that I would follow my older brothers' lead.

"I want to go to Wheeling and make a name for myself, Dad. I want people to know me as Tom McManus, not Mike McManus' little brother," I uttered back.

I had never seen my dad light up so quickly. His reaction was somewhat surprising. I expected an argument, at least a debate about my announcement, but that's certainly not what followed. The news, although a bit shocking, was music to his ears and it showed. His youngest son had just made a profound statement, perhaps well beyond his innocent years. A broad smile lit up on my dad's face. He proceeded to tell me how proud he was that my reasoning was to stand on my own, to make a name for myself, all by myself.

I believe he saw me as a budding leader, probably because all three of my friends, who were all supposed to go to St. Viator, had also decided to come with me to be a Wheeling Wildcat. I remember that he had been listening intently to my revelation and decision. He slowly raised his head from apparent deep thought, smiled and said: "I respect your choice. Now you are going to have to prove to yourself that you made the right decision." For a moment I stood in stone silence. I couldn't believe that he would not have some reason to question my decision, but he didn't. It was a sign of his complete support for me, support that would endure throughout my life.

My parents did their best shuffling between seeing Mike's games and then coming across town to see me as much as they could at Wheeling. I was the younger one so Mike's games trumped mine, especially when he was a senior and I a junior, but my parents hardly missed one of my games, if any.

My dad would always stand in the exact same spot, at the top of the bleachers, with his arms folded, watching intently. His posture never seemed to change the entire game. He would cheer no doubt, but for the most part, he just stood there dissecting my every move. My mother, on the other hand, would be sitting with all the wives and mothers, a few rows down from my dad and his buddies. I could always hear her screaming: "Kill 'em, Tommy!" which was funny, thinking that my father would be the one who acted like that.

I was a good player at Wheeling and stood out on the team. I wasn't the fastest player out there but fast enough, especially for high school, and I could hit. I was a physical player who never gave up, and I knew my path at an early age, thanks to a conversation I had with my father when I was 15 and a sophomore.

"Tom, sit down, I want to have a word with you," my dad started off one night at the kitchen table. "You are doing a real good job out there at Wheeling, Tommy. I'm proud of you. You're playing the game the way it should be played and you're a natural leader. Those are great qualities to have."

He continued, "I want you to know something. I know that you have your heart set on going on to college and playing ball but you have to know that I cannot afford to send you. I couldn't do it for your older siblings and I can't do it for you. Now, you can do one of two things. You can go into the armed services like your brother Bob, or you can try and earn a football scholarship, if you want to. I think you can do it, if you set your heart on it and work real hard. You not only have to excel on the football field but you also have to have good grades, but I believe you have what it takes for a college to possibly want you," he added.

My heart raced as I took in what my dad was saying. He believed in me. He thought I could do it. It was all that I needed to hear.

After that talk, my whole life changed. Don't get me wrong, I was still your typical high schooler, doing, let's just say, high school things, but now I knew my path. I made sure that I always got my workouts in, whether it was running sprints at night, doing extra rope jumping, or working on my strength. I probably went a bit overboard, so much so that my high school coach sat me down to discuss my drive towards my goal.

Nothing he said registered, though, for I had already made up my mind. I was going to make a name for myself, go to college and play football. Sure, I had my naysayers telling me that I was "too small", or "too slow", but that just stoked the flame inside of me even more. I would prove them all wrong, I would say to myself over and over again.

They were somewhat right in the speed department, anyway. I simply wasn't overly fast. I mean I was certainly fast enough for the high school level, but I was more of a quick and very instinctive player and above everything else, a tough, hard-nosed kid, for which I took tremendous pride. And, I had my dad on my side and that was all that mattered. If the toughest and greatest man I knew said I could do it, well then dammit, I was determined to prove him right and accomplish my goals.

The support and encouragement along with his honest but tough critique led me on the path that I dreamt about from when I was a youngster when I would put on my long john pajama bottoms, roll them up to make them look like football pants, and wear my favorite Chicago Bears jersey right before every Monday Night Football game.

My dad was someone I constantly wanted to be like, especially on the football field, and his belief in me was crucial in believing in myself, which would lead me to fulfilling my football dreams. The lessons he taught me and what I learned at a young age stayed with me throughout my teenage years and really for the rest of my life. He was hard on me, no doubt about it, but through a lifelong journey of chasing a dream, above everything else, we became best friends.

And by the way, for the record, after that eighth grade playoff game, I never helped the "enemy" up after a tackle ever again!

EARLY MEMORIES, 1978

One of my earliest memories of my dad is an event that happened when I was about eight years old. It was an incident that I have never forgotten. It was a rainy weekday afternoon in the springtime in the northwest suburbs of Chicago. The nasty winter had finally become history and the first signs of spring were among us, with melting snow and frequent rain showers. You would have thought that we had just come out of hibernation during that long winter with the way my brothers and I were running around outside, like we had never seen rain before. We didn't need jackets, gloves and hats, just a pair of jeans and ratty old sweatshirts. They were the attire of choice for the day.

With all of the excitement around us, Mike and Bob and I had an idea of gathering up as much twigs, grass, or anything we could get our hands on to build a few dams near the sewer drain in the street. We lived on Downing Road, which was part of a huge subdivision aligned with numerous families. There must have been about thirty kids who lived on our street, ranging in ages from high school years on down to around my age.

We had a bunch of good times, playing kick the can or flashlight tag with the other neighborhood kids, but, as in most neighborhoods, there were a couple of families that we didn't exactly get along with too well.

My dad was known as a tough, but fun-loving man who loved his wife and kept his kids in line. My mother was seen as sweet and a very "hands on" type of mom who could hold her own.

The McManus boys and my sister were well known in our part of town of Buffalo Grove. We were all pretty athletic and somewhat popular on the playing fields, at school, and in our neighborhood.

My sister, Moira, the oldest, would have to stick up for her brothers from time to time, especially me, until I got older, that is. Bob and Mike would have to do the same when called upon as well. Case in point: I got beat up by an older neighborhood bully one day down at the local school. I came home with a black eye and my dad immediately sent Mike and Bob back down to the school to take care of that bully, who was more their size and age. They did, for the mere fact that they would have to answer to our dad if they didn't obey his orders.

My brothers and I weren't really into any serious mischief, but to say that we were choir boys would have been sadly mistaken. Being the youngest, half the time I just followed along on what they were doing. Sometimes a few neighbors didn't take a liking to our rambunctious antics.

One of those neighbors was a big man who lived a few houses up on the other side of the street. I don't remember his dimensions, but he was a tall and overweight man, perhaps in his late thirties. And boy he could yell!

He and his wife had two daughters, and he had a reputation as a loud father, always yelling about this or that. There were urban tales of him hanging his daughters upside down off their second floor railing whenever they got in trouble. He was somewhat intimidating, especially to the young kids in the neighborhood, not the very least of whom was me.

So, there we were, building these fake dams, not bothering anyone. To be honest, the dams barely worked, but we tried diligently to change all of that by adding more and more twigs and leaves. We were having a great time, home from school, homework done, enjoying the first days of spring. My mother was inside and my dad was on his way home from work in downtown Chicago.

I remember vividly this big man getting out of his car, and immediately yelling at us with something to the effect that we were going to back up the sewer system with our dams. We boys didn't think we were really doing anything wrong, but we didn't talk back. Our dad never let us talk back, whether it was to him, our mom or to elders in general. That was a sure way to get a crack on the butt or on the back of the head.

I talked back once to a different neighbor and she called my house to complain about something I was supposed to have done. My dad immediately called me in and gave me a good one for that, so it was instilled in us from a very young age: Don't talk back to adults. It's disrespectful. If you have a problem, you come to me.

All I remember is that this neighbor kept yelling as he walked briskly towards us. I was the farthest one down the street looking at him coming at us. I stood there, frozen in silence, wondering what was going to happen next. As I stared at this big, menacing man marching in our direction, I saw my dad's car turn down our street. The man kept getting closer and closer, flailing his arms in the air.

I don't remember what the man kept yelling about for I was now fixated on my dad's brown Cutlass Supreme coming down the road. The threatening neighbor didn't see him coming because he had his back to the direction of the street where my dad was heading from. The man was just past our drive-way in the street when my dad pulled into the drive. He screeched to a stop and I could see his eyes focused on us and the large man shouting and pointing his hands at us.

I stood there and watched my dad get out his car, calmly take off his tie, and roll up his sleeves. He then walked briskly towards us and the neighbor in the middle of the street. I was just a few feet away, standing by our mail-box. My heart was pounding as I could see that my dad became very upset in an instant. "You yelling at my kids?" he shouted with his fists now clenched as he approached the man. He had to look up to the taller and wider neighbor as they stood toe-to-toe, but the look in my dad's eyes was fierce, almost scary.

"Gene, they're building these dams and messing around with the sewers and..." he started to explain. My dad immediately interrupted and pointed his finger at the eyes of our neighbor and barked: "If I ever catch you yelling at my family again, I'm going to knock you on your ass and drag you up and down this goddamn street! You got that?" His face was so red I thought it was going to explode.

"I'm sorry Gene. I'm sorry. It won't ever happen again!" the neighbor said as he backed away with his opened palms near his chest. My dad quickly turned his look toward us and firmly said: "You boys get inside."

When we walked into the foyer, just inside the front door, he slapped the closest one to him across the back of the head and growled: "Why in the hell are you building those dams anyway?" He clearly wasn't looking for an answer. "Get cleaned up and get ready for dinner!" We just kept heading towards the stairs of the house that led us down to our bedrooms, knowing he would head to the upstairs part where the master bedroom and kitchen were situated. I went to my room and sat on the edge of my bed and recounted what had just happened.

I knew my dad was tough. I mean, he always seemed tough, from his tales of playing football with no pads, to his boxing days filled with lore. He lifted weights every morning to keep in good shape, baring wide shoulders and big arms. And although he was very affectionate, he also could be very intimidating, when the time was appropriate, which always gave me an underlying fear of my father. I had always looked up to him. I mean, he was my father, but soon after that encounter I realized that he was a bad ass, a force to be reckoned with in my eyes, who would do anything for his family, no matter the circumstances.

Another vivid memory that has always stuck with me happened when I was around ten years old. I got into a fist fight in front of my parents before one of my little league baseball games. It was the first time that had ever happened, except with my brothers, although they would usually just beat the crap out of me. My mom and dad stood among a small crowd overlooking the baseball diamond at the local park district.

One of my teammates who was a year older and quite frankly, a spoiled brat, tried to jump my position in batting practice. I stood my ground and made my case. He tried to bully me and push me out of the way. Before he or I knew it, I had socked him a good one right in the mouth. He fell down and I jumped all over him.

It was over in a matter of seconds and I knew I had won the bout, but I was immediately overcome with a slight fear for I didn't know how my parents were going to react, especially my dad. When I got off the boy, I looked up to where my mom and dad were standing as I shook inside with a bout of trepidation. It quickly dissolved though, because without hesitation, my dad flashed me an "okay" sign with his hand.

He had watched the entire encounter and thought that I was in the right with my actions. At that precise moment, it gave me a tremendous sense of satisfaction and acceptance as one of Gene McManus's boys. Later on in life, my mother would tell me that as the fight was about to take place, she made an attempt to walk towards the fence to stop it but my dad quickly reached his arm across my mom's body and told her to hold on a second for he wanted to see how I was going to handle the situation. I was ten years old!

My dad wanted his boys to be tough, whether it was playing sports, at school, or out in the street standing up for ourselves. He also made sure that we were good kids too. Behaving in school, getting good grades, being respectful to elders, teachers, and coaches and obeying him and my mother were all top priorities in our upbringing, but being tough was equally important. I believe he wanted to instill in us physical toughness in all walks of life which would in turn give us the mental toughness that it takes to succeed in the world, just like the toughness that he had to show on his way to becoming an adult.

It wasn't until years after, though, that I learned that his inner strength and toughness came from a lifetime of facing and overcoming adversity. He would impart those lessons on me as I grew older and, as I faced adversities of my own, those lessons would help get me through it all. Those life experiences that he endured and made him the man that he was, would help prepare me not only for the game I loved but also for the game of life.

THE BEGINNING, 1932

The day was going as normal as any other day. Young Gene McManus was on his bike nearing his home after another game at the park. But as he turned the corner to go down the street that would take him to his house he saw something very unusual. His father's car was parked in the driveway, which was normally a good thing. The problem was that his father was never home that early, not with dinnertime being a good hour away. Young Gene didn't know whether to be excited or scared as he rushed through the front door.

Being 12 years old and thoroughly filled with the natural optimism of youth, he chose excitement at the chance to spend a bonus hour with his busy father. Little did he know that the presence of his father's car in the driveway meant that Gene's life was about to take a dramatic and often painful turn.

"Mom, Dad, I'm home! Oh boy, we killed 'em today and I scored a couple of touchdowns!"

His excitement quickly drained as he saw his parents sitting in the living room, looking somber. A feeling of gloom mingled with the smells of that night's supper. "Dad, what are you doing home?" Gene asked apprehensively.

His mother answered. "Gene, sit down. Your daddy just got laid off. He lost his job today."

Gene didn't know the meaning of it all, but his eternal hopefulness immediately overpowered the sadness of the moment. "I'm sorry about that, Dad, but you'll get another one. You're really good at what you do."

"Why don't you go upstairs, get a bath, and get ready for dinner?" his mother instructed firmly as she realized that Gene was too young to comprehend the gravity of the situation. Reluctantly, Gene went upstairs. Already, his mind was spinning as thoughts of helping his family replaced thoughts of touchdowns and home runs.

The year was 1932, and the McManus family, which had avoided the pain of the Great Depression until then, had just become one more casualty of the nation's economic collapse. Gene's idyllic childhood had come to an abrupt end.

Eugene E. McManus (Gene, Geno, my father) was born on November 27, 1920 in East Orange, New Jersey. World War I was over, and Americans were living in a time of optimism and prosperity as the US assumed its new position as the most powerful nation in the world.

America's population was nearing 100 million people. The auto and communications industries were on the rise, the stock market was booming, and the culture was evolving with the rising popularity of professional athletes, movie stars, and authors. Life in America was very good in The Roaring 20s.

During the 20s, America witnessed the coming of age of the broadcasting and publishing industries. Radio became an integral part of American life. New magazines covered not just news, but sports and entertainment. Regular families were able to own automobiles. Heavyweight boxing became a new and frenzied spectacle, college football's attendance soared as rivalries formed, and Babe Ruth was the most famous person in the country.

In the McManus home, life was quite comfortable. Gene's dad, Edward, a devoted husband and father of three, held a good job as a regional tire salesman. The family had their own automobile, plenty of food on the table and a nice home covering their heads in a city just north of Newark, New Jersey.

On weekends, Edward and Claire hosted many gatherings with family and friends, good food and drink and fun-filled days. Yes, times were good, but dark clouds were looming on the horizon.

With the fall of the stock market in what is now known as the Crash of 1929, the economy of the United States was falling fast. 1300 banks closed, industries collapsed, and over four and a half million people were left without jobs.

Still, many people were working, and Edward was one of them. He had managed to keep his job for almost three years, and he thought that he would be able to make it through this terrible crisis. However, on that fateful day in the fall of 1932, his life and the lives of his family changed dramatically.

Young Gene, or Geno as he was so affectionately called, was the oldest of Edward and Claire McManus' three children. In many ways, he was a lot like the other young boys in his pleasant, middle class neighborhood. He went to school, sometimes got into a little mischief along the way, and always seemed to be playing sports. He participated in just about every athletic activity that was presented to him, but there was one sport that he grew to love more than all the others, and that was football.

On many autumn afternoons, he would sit next to his father in front of the radio and listen intently to the broadcasts of his gridiron heroes, legends such as Red Grange, Knute Rockne, and Bronko Nagurski. His love for the game started taking shape during those times with his dad, and it would run so deep that it carried over to his own style of play on the football field which would eventually travel through a generation.

Geno and his friends would gather regularly at the local park and play against the other neighborhood kids. They would don their high top black leather boots, knickerbockers and, in cold weather, wool caps. Then they'd emulate the plays that they had heard over the airwaves time and time again.

Yes, Geno was just like the other kids, except for one thing. When the games started, he was clearly the best athlete on the field. He could run faster and tackle better than the other kids, and he was tough. When he got hurt, he never complained. He just got up and went back for more.

On a typical afternoon after school, Gene and his closest friends, Chuck Grisham, Billy Czonka, Frank Wilson, and Eddie Knight, would all stop by the playing field looking to pick up a game against their neighborhood rivals. Their contests were always intense with bragging rights on the line.

In a scene played out hundreds of times, Gene and his friends would break from the huddle. Gene would play quarterback and call the plays, telling his team where to line up and whom to block.

On his favorite plays, he would take the ball himself, run straight at the other neighborhood boys, punch a stiff-arm into the face of one opponent and run right past the entire defense as he headed to the goal line.

The opposing would-be tackler would grab his nose as he felt the pain of Gene's powerful straight-arm. As Gene crossed into the makeshift end zone he would thrust his arms in the air, signaling another touchdown. His teammates would run down the field to join in the celebration. With an assured innocence among them, they would all end up in a pile. Then in a sportsmanlike fashion, just like they heard on the radio, they would shake hands with the other team.

When the game was over, the boys would jump onto their bikes for dinner was fast approaching, and they all knew better than to be late for their family dinners. Covered in mud, they would race each other home. Gene would lead the pack, and as each boy reached his home he would peel off into his own driveway.

"What a game!" they cheered in unison, as they each sped home.

"Yeah, we beat those guys' butts real good today, thirty-two to ten," Chuck said as he skidded into his driveway.

"Geno, I think you broke that boy's nose on your last touchdown run. He was bleeding like a pig," said Billy, as he pedaled beside Geno.

"Hey, football is a tough game, played by tough people! I heard that on the radio listening to the Giants' game with my dad," Geno spouted back as he peeled off to ride down his street. The other boys carried on towards their houses farther down and each waved as Geno disappeared around the corner.

Life was good for young Geno. He didn't have a care in the world. The weekend was approaching and he couldn't wait to get home and tell his mother what another good effort he had had that day. In his mind, every game was an all-or-nothing world championship game. He eagerly awaited his father's return from work, just like every other weekday, to tell him of another winning football game. He also couldn't wait to tell the tale of how he busted some kid's nose with a mean stiff arm on his way to another touchdown.

However, this was the day that would change his life forever. At the dinner table, as the kids were fidgeting in their chairs, Edward stared into space in a somber mood. After Claire delivered the dinner prayer, the conversation turned into the seriousness of the situation.

Claire said, "Children, listen up. Lots of fathers all over America have lost their jobs. We're in what is called a Depression. Times are going to be tough for a little while. Your daddy lost his job today and we all are going to have to tighten our belts until he finds another one. In the meantime, he'll be here at home and he will want some peace and quiet. I want you three to respect that and behave yourselves. We'll have to cut back on a lot of the extras that you kids are used to, like ice cream and candy."

"Aw shucks, Mom," Geno replied, as his siblings also expressed their disappointment.

"Now, listen. This may not last too long and we'll all get through this, but we are going to have to make some sacrifices around here!" she demanded.

"Yes, Ma'am," Geno responded, as he quickly felt that he too would have to sacrifice and help out in any way that he could.

Not knowing it at the time, Gene soon would have another big influence enter into his life: his Mother's sister, Aunt Lee. She was already a major presence in the life of Gene and his siblings, for she attended most of the family gatherings, but soon she would introduce Gene to a very critical aspect of his growth.

The next day Aunt Lee came over to discuss with Edward and Claire the possibility of moving in with them to help out. Aunt Lee had money, and she was pretty well off. She wanted to help out in these trying times because that's what families did back then. She stated that she had rented her house and that she chose to move out and join the McManus household and help Claire with the chores. Her income and presence could help her sister and brother-in-law get through their crisis.

That night as young Gene sat on the stairs to the upstairs of their home and out of sight, he overheard a conversation between his Mom and Dad and Aunt Lee.

"I have an old friend that I went to see. He owns the Cavalier Hotel. His name is James Steinman. Anyway, he owes me a few favors and I talked him into hiring you, Edward, as a busboy for the restaurant," Aunt Lee started.

"Are you kidding me, Lee? I'm a grown man. That job is for a child. I do have some pride, you know!" Edward spouted back.

"But, Edward, we need..." Claire stated as she tried to interrupt.

"Don't 'but' me, Claire!" Edward snapped. "I didn't work twenty years as a salesman for Goodyear Tires to become some cheap hired help. Let them find some child to do that!" he gruffly added as he stormed out of the room leaving Claire and Aunt Lee looking at each other in dismay.

The next morning, young Gene woke up early, got in a quick breakfast, and then headed out the front door abruptly.

"Where are you going, Gene?" his mother called out.

"I... I have got something I've got to do, Mom, I'll be home shortly," he responded back and out the door he went.

As Gene pedaled as fast as he could down Main Street, he truly didn't understand the magnitude of the bold move he was about to make. He only knew that he had to do something for his family because his father had always taught him that family came first. He came to an abrupt halt at the front door of The Cavalier Hotel, dropped his bike on the sidewalk and ran inside. He almost bumped right into a well-dressed man just inside the doorway.

"Whoa young man, where's the fire?" the gentleman asked Gene.

"Excuse me sir, I'm looking for a Mr. Steinway?" he asked breathlessly.

"The name is Steinman son, and you're looking at him," the man replied.

Gene whipped off his cap and clutched it to his stomach. "Yes, sir. I'm Gene McManus. You know my Aunt Lee. She said you need some kind of bus or something. Dad won't do it, but I can!" Gene paused and then continued, "I can do anything, Sir. I'm real strong and you can count on me, sir. Please, sir," Gene pleaded.

"You certainly have got the right spunk, kid. Do your parents know that you are here? Would they…" he tried to continue before getting interrupted by Gene.

"My Aunt Lee will tell them I can do it, I'm sure," he proudly stated.

"Well, I've known your Aunt Lee for many years now. She's quite a woman. Any one of her kin must be good people. Make sure your parents are okay with this and have your Aunt Lee drop by and see me tomorrow," the man replied.

"Yes, sir. Thank you, sir! I'll tell her to come by. Bye, sir!" Gene shouted as he ran out of the hotel. He immediately jumped onto his bike and quickly headed to tell his parents that he had gotten himself a job and that he too could help the family out. However, when he got back at home, young Gene was met with some resistance from Edward. Gene told his mother and father of his good fortune, but despite his mother's agreement with his plan, his father stood his ground: "He's only twelve, for Christ's sake! I told you before, we've got pride in this family. No son of mine is going to be working at his age," he firmly stated.

"Edward, many boys his age are working now. It's the times!" Claire jumped in.

"What's the Cavalier paying? A buck a week?" Edward sarcastically replied.

"No, they pay five bucks a week. Plus, Geno could get an occasional extra tip or two. It's a good job for a young man," Lee chimed in as she gave Geno a wink.

"That's a weeks worth of food for the five of us, Edward! It would really help out!" Claire stated.

"I can go to school, do my homework, and work afternoons, evenings, and weekends. And still play some football too, you know." Gene proudly announced.

"Edward, let him do it. It'll be good for him and frankly, we need the money!" Claire added with a sigh of desperation.

Edward soon realized that he had lost this battle and flung his arms in the air. "Aw, I give up," he conceded and exited the room. Young Gene jumped up and down excitedly. Aunt Lee and Claire hugged as Claire reached out and ruffled Gene's hair in an act of proud tenderness.

Gene had taken matters into his own hands and had showcased the leadership that would help take him through the rest of his up-and-down life. Over the years of Gene's adolescence, Aunt Lee would not only be a member of the family, but she would also serve as a sort of mentor to Gene. She helped instill in him the confidence that he could have anything he wanted if he worked hard and believed in himself. She coached him that while earning five dollars a week at the hotel, he could save a dollar a week and give the remaining four dollars to the family. That way he could buy himself things he wanted, like a new pair of football cleats, all the while helping his family get through these hard times.

These early experiences would help guide Gene through future adversities that were on the horizon and give him a great foundation for the enormous challenges that he would face throughout his life. He was determined to succeed in the world no matter what was happening around him, and he came to see a challenge only as an opportunity.

HIGH SCHOOL IN THE 1930'S

As Gene approached his teenage years, he and his family were still stuck in the middle of the Great Depression. His dad was performing government labor work and his mom was working odd jobs to help make ends meet, but it wasn't enough, so Gene maintained his job at the local hotel. He continued to give his share of his weekly earnings to the family, but he kept the extra money that also came from tips from the daily customers. He took his job very seriously as he knew how badly the money was needed at home and how important his role had become.

Gene was a very well liked, well mannered young man. He earned constant praise from Mr. Steinman as a hardworking kid who always put in the extra effort without having to be asked. He always made sure that the dining room tables were cleared and set back up in a timely fashion. He would run up the exit stairs to various floors to pick up the trays left outside the doors from room service meals. He figured that the more quickly he got his job done the better, and it was a good way to keep himself in shape for the game he constantly thought about.

Gene attended East Orange High School from 1934-1937. He was the youngest one in his class. He did enough in classes to maintain solid grades, and he also excelled in athletics, especially on the gridiron. He was a big teenager and a hard-nosed player who always did his best to showcase his talents.

He had a reputation on the street as well. He was known as a tough Irish kid who never backed down from a challenge. He wasn't a bully, by any means, but was always ready for a fight whether outside the school or in the alley. With tremendous pride, he also took on the role of protector for his younger siblings, making sure that anyone who messed with his younger brother or sister would have to deal with him.

Geno's mother was a big German lady who pretty much ran the house. She was proud that Geno always stood up for himself. She also reveled in the fact that he excelled on the athletic fields. He had a very close relationship with her, always aching for her approval. He was close to his dad as well, but his dad was never a fighter nor had he ever really been an athlete, so they had little in common in that regard.

However, Gene was very aware that his dad worked extremely hard, and he knew he was a man who always went about his business to provide for his family. Gene deeply respected his dad as the man of the house, no matter what.

When Gene would come home with tales of another scrap that he had gotten into, it often didn't sit well with his dad. Edward was always afraid that Geno would get hurt one day, whether by someone bigger and older or by a group of kids ganging up on him. Gene always responded to his dad in his normal sturdy and confident manner: "Pop, what're you so worried about? I can handle myself." Edward wasn't always so sure.

During these times of Gene's high school years, America was still recovering from the stock market crash. World leaders were plotting to take over the world as they saw a prime time to attack and overcome a nation that looked as though it was in disarray. America had tired of war after World War I and was in an isolationist mood.

Adolph Hitler and Japan's Emperor Hito were forming a treaty to support each other and had become enemies of the United States. The pickings looked ripe. "Take over the world and isolate America" was their apparent plan. It simply endorsed the old adage: "The survivor of the fittest always rules." As America looked like the wounded lamb licking its wounds, these leaders felt that the USA could be pounced upon by the much stronger lion.

President Franklin D. Roosevelt had successfully led America out of its terribly debilitating Depression with his "New Deal." European countries were being threatened by Germany's aggression. Japan had invaded China and was moving to take over all of the Far East. But, America was content to remain neutral as most of the citizens couldn't believe that either of these nations would dare make an attempt to invade American soil. It was in this uncertain climate that life in America assumed a mindset of promoting growth through hard work and an independence from the issues of the rest of the world.

In the McManus family, life was slowly recovering from the wrenching traumas of the Depression. Gene was by now a well known teenager in East Orange, New Jersey, not just as a tough kid, but also as a good football player, a really good one. His father was still struggling to make ends meet and Geno still had his job down at the hotel making his now $6 per week.

By the time Gene was a senior in high school, he earned himself a reputation as a legitimate high school football prospect for college recruiters. He had been named to a couple of All Star teams in the city and college recruiters were coming to East Orange High to scout Gene, the tough full-back and linebacker who never left the field. His stamina and toughness had become legend. The opposition not only feared him, but respected him.

Gene knew what he wanted. He wanted to go and play college ball so that one day his old man could hear Gene's name on the radio. He dreamed of going to somewhere new, somewhere where he could excel on the football field. He had big plans, no doubt about it, but unfortunately for him, the circumstances of that time did call for him to be a teammate and a leader, just not as a major college football player as he had envisioned.

On a cold gray overcast Thanksgiving Day in 1937, Gene was just about to turn seventeen years old. He led his East Orange team onto the field for the last game of the year and his last high school contest.

It was classic 1930's high school ball. Football players on the muddy field would wear leather helmets with no face masks, small shoulder pads and only high top black shoes. There was no tape wrapping their ankles, no mouth pieces to protect their teeth, no face guards to protect their eyes or braces to protect their knees. Thousands of people would line the sidelines or pack the stands.

Football had become a favorite spectator sport and a celebration of having come through hard times. It also presented an opportunity for parents to revel in the successes of their offspring, especially on the sports field. Gene loved that this was his last high school game, for he looked forward to what the future held. Although he didn't see it coming, he would end up demoralized when the conversation after the game didn't quite go as he had anticipated.

Shortly after the game had concluded, and Gene and his teammates had finished celebrating their victory, Gene was approached by his coach, followed by his father.

"Great game, Geno! It sure has been a pleasure to coach such a tough young leader," the coach said as he patted Gene on the back. He then continued, "Before you go, wait up a second. I asked your father to meet us down here on the field."

"Mr. McManus! How are you, sir? Geno played a whale of a game today." the coach stated loudly over Gene's shoulder as Edward approached the two.

"Yes, indeed coach. He played a great game. His mother and I are very proud of him," Edward responded, beaming with pride.

"Mr. McManus, I want you to know that if you and Geno have any questions about which college would be the best fit for him, I can help you with that," the coach said confidently.

"College? What do you mean, Coach? We haven't really even talked about college." answered Edward, who acted as if he was caught off guard.

"Mr. McManus, with all due respect sir, your son is one of the best prospects we have seen here in recent years, maybe even ever at East Orange High. There's a list of colleges that would love for him to suit up for them next fall. He's in real demand. He's a proven winner and we've been so proud to have had him on our team. He's got a real bright future." the coach stated.

"That's great to hear, coach, but there's a lot more to it than that. Gene and I will have to talk about that in private when we get back home," Edward replied firmly. He then looked at Gene and said, "Son, get cleaned up and I'll see you back at the house."

Gene and the coach both looked at each other in emotions confused by Edward's reaction. The coach seemed astonished that Edward didn't seem to be interested in any talk of a college education for Gene.

Back at their house, Gene, his mom, and dad sat down at the dining room table and had a heart-to-heart talk. Edward started the conversation in a very direct and somber manner: "Gene, your mother and I are very happy and very proud that you have done so well in football. It's great that these colleges have taken such a liking to you. But, we need you at home. You know that. Your weekly paycheck helps out the family. I know this isn't what you wanted to hear, but you are needed more here than anywhere else. I'm sorry but you'll have to put these plans on hold, for the family!" Edward announced as he rubbed his chin and looked toward Claire for support.

Gene looked anxiously at his mother, hoping that she would take his side. "Your father's right, Gene," she said. "I know it is very disappointing that college and football will have to wait, but we are a family and family comes first. We have bills to pay and we just can't make it unless you are here to help!"

"But, Mom?" Gene interrupted.

"Don't but me, Gene! We need you here at home!" Claire finished with a firm demeanor.

Gene got up from the table and abruptly walked out of the house, not knowing what to say. He spent most of that evening walking around his neighborhood trying to make sense of it all. He had thought and dreamed throughout his entire high school career that he was preparing for the next step in his life, to go and make a new name for himself in the college ranks. He had become an adult at a very young age and given his all to help the cause of his family. He had done all that he was asked to do. He worked his ass off to get to this point, to this great opportunity. It was his turn now to branch out and create his own life, he said to himself over and over. He was devastated and pissed off all at the same time.

After a little while he calmed down and decided that he would handle this setback in the only way that he knew how. He would take this stumbling block head on and make the best out of it. What the best would be was hardly clear to him at this particular point, but he knew he would prevail. He wasn't about to give up now. He had too many dreams and goals to attain. However, what he didn't know was that this was but one of many hurdles he would have to overcome throughout his adult life.

As the fates would have it, Aunt Lee would once again have a large presence in Gene's life, setting him up with a brand new opportunity. Gene would also play a big part in making his own opportunities, not only by keeping his gridiron dreams alive, but also by getting into an arena with which he really wasn't all too familiar, the boxing ring.

ORANGE TROJANS AND TWO TON TONY

After 6 years as a busboy, a job that lasted through all of his high school years, 18 year old Gene left the hotel for an opportunity that had the potential of becoming a full-time career. With help from Aunt Lee, he got a clerk's job at the biggest local bank in town.

Aunt Lee knew one of the main bank managers and did her best to sell Gene to him as a young man with tremendous potential. She was one of their best and most loyal customers, and if anyone deserved a favor, it was she. She always took a great liking to her nephew and wanted to help him out in any way she could.

Gene rewarded her faith in him. He showed the manager that he was a hard worker and was always willing to do any task to move forward in his position while learning the intricacies of finance. He turned out to be a quick study and he really enjoyed learning about finance, especially when it came to real estate.

He was a good people person, too, always able to adapt to any type of personality that walked through the front door. He started to garner the attention of upper management in a very short time. During the first year that he was at the bank, he started moving up in the ranks, bypassing the other clerks. Management started to ask him to join them in meetings with some of their top business clients.

Although Gene held a good position and was becoming a valued member of the bank's staff, the life of a banker wasn't enough for the young athlete. Banking simply couldn't supply the adrenaline rush that sports gave him nor could it fulfill his dreams. He still yearned for his chance to go to college, but, even more so, he missed the game he loved so much and thought about daily. If he couldn't play football at the collegiate level, he had to come up with another way to keep his skills up to par. So, he did just that.

He signed up to play football for the local semi-pro team, the Orange Trojans. He practiced during the week after working his hours at the bank and played games on the weekends. But, playing for the Trojans was not for the meek and feeble. The environment was that of club football at best.

There were no big crowds like Gene had enjoyed while playing for his high school team. There wasn't even a locker room. At the time, semi-pro football was just a bunch of grown men who enjoyed beating the crap out of each other, just for the fun of it, and for a little bit of money, if they were lucky.

They wore little, if any pads, and slim leather helmets. The uniforms were primitive by today's standards; full of patched holes from years of abuse. These were tough men, some who were ten years older than Gene. They were mostly "wannabes" who couldn't make it with the professional football teams in Philadelphia, Chicago and New York City. Some harbored ambitions to catch the eye of a pro football recruiter, while most just wanted to take out their frustrations of life on the gridiron and their opponents. Games were brutal. Rules were to be ignored. It was truly "smash-mouth" football at its most violent.

Gene was very popular on these playing fields, as he was known as the young kid with the all-star resume who could take anything dished out to him and still come back fighting. The older men made sure that their presence was felt with the young star as they gave him their best shots, often against the rules of football. A stiff-arm or a tackle in the face was common practice. Piling on after every tackle, followed by a knee to the groin was standard operation. Gene didn't care, he loved playing that game. He was always up to any challenge, on the field or off of it. He quickly showed these men and his coach that he could dish it out as well as he got it.

In the fall of 1938, his first season with the Trojans, Gene also took up boxing and trained at a local gym in Orange, New Jersey. He figured that after all the successful fights he had been in over the years, maybe it was time to see if he had the skills to be a real fighter in an honest-to-goodness boxing ring. Many men of the time saw boxing as a way to make a better life and get out of the situation they were all in: poverty. Gene, too, looked at it as a way to put some extra money in his pockets, plus, he liked to fight.

The gym in Orange, New Jersey was a classic boxing venue. It was an ancient, run-down, and smelly warehouse. It was the kind of neighborhood gym that housed legitimate fighters and street thugs alike.

Although all of his ambition and direction was to be that of a football star, Gene truly enjoyed the competitive nature inside the ring. He enjoyed being pitted one-on-one against another fighter, where it was all up to him and no one else. He eventually was convinced to join the New Jersey Golden Gloves and quickly earned himself a reputation as a tough, hard-nosed puncher with a nasty left hook that would send many of his opponents to the canvas in a heap. One day he found himself presented with a challenge that no one dared to take, except him.

There was a brawler named "Two Ton" Tony Galento who trained at the same gym as Gene. He was a bar owner by trade who used to challenge his patrons to fist fights out in the street every chance he got. He was a street thug with the reputation as a tough guy who would bust up your face just for looking at him.

The story goes that one night in his bar after beating up another one of his customers, a boxing promoter was there to witness the beating. He told "Two Ton" Tony that he should take up boxing as a career and allow the promoter to promote the bar owner as a "feared pugilist". Tony took up the promoter's offer and quickly established a reputation as a nasty fighter, using elbows and head butts, knees to the groin and raking of the eyes to intimidate and beat an opponent. Nothing was off limits for "Two Ton" Galento.

His fifteen minutes of fame came in June, 1939, when he took on Heavy-weight Champion Joe Louis, The Brown Bomber, in front of 30,000 people at Yankee Stadium. Prior to the fight, "Two Ton" Tony was relentless in making racial epithets towards Joe Louis and made it public that he was a bigot, a racist, and he didn't care.

Galento trained on "beer and spaghetti" and publicly promised that he would beat the shit of the heavy weight "nigger". After he knocked Louis down early in the fight, Louis, the great champion that he was, went to work and dropped Galento in the fourth round, opening a vicious gash in Galento's head that took over twenty-three stitches to close up.

"Two Ton" Tony Galento retained a reputation as one bad ass individual, but a pig as well. Louis later on said that Galento might have been the tough-est man he ever met in the ring. Ironically enough, Louis and Galento eventually became friends. In that Orange gym however, Galento was extremely feared as a very intimidating bruiser and a dirty fighter that no one wanted to mess with, especially after his bout with the famed heavyweight champion.

On one particular day, shortly after recovering from the fight with Louis, Galento was going through sparring partners as though they were bottles of beer. His trainer, Ray Arcel, was frustrated with the declining field of sparring partners and yelled out to the crowded gym to see if there were any more takers to train with the fat, dirty, and nasty bar owner who had once decked The Champ.

"All right, you faggots, I need one of you's gumbas to come into the ring and take on this fat fuck before he has to go back to his bar!" he quipped loudly. "I've got twenty five cents per round to give ya. That's if you can make it through a round," he added cynically, laughing after knowing that Galento had already sent a handful of wannabes to the locker room.

There were no takers. Not one fighter jumped at the chance of the offer. "All right, fifty cents a round," Ray continued on, "Which one of you pussies has got the guts to get in here? C'mon, he won't hurt you too bad." Again there were no takers. No one wanted to get in the ring, as they had often seen the beating Galento would dish out to other chumps in the gym.

"Aw, fuck it, ya bunch of pissass wimps. I'll give a buck a round and I'll try not to have ya's for lunch," Two Ton Tony blurted out.

From the back of the gym, a well-muscled now nineteen year old Gene was working on a heavy bag as his best friend Scotty was holding it in place. Scotty had acted as Gene's trainer for over a year and was constantly cheering him on. After barely hearing all of the commotion, Gene raised his arm and yelled, "I'll do it. I'll get in there with him."

His friend Scotty wasn't so sure. "Geno, what are you, fucking crazy? That's Two Ton Tony! He knocked Joe Louis on his ass in front of thirty thousand at Yankee Stadium!" he said, hoping to talk his friend out of this bad decision.

"You worry too much, Scotty. Look how fat he is. He's got a belly like a medicine-ball. He'll never catch me. Besides, Louis almost killed him. They had to practically sew his head back together," Gene responded with the same confidence he always had.

"Geno, this guy's a murderer. He's the dirtiest cocksucker in this fucking gym. Plus, he's ten years older than you! Don't do it! Trust me!" Scotty warned.

"Are you kidding me? A dollar a round? I'd do just about anything for that kind of money!" Gene countered back.

From the ring Galento chimed in: "You two faggots want to get a fucking room or are you going to get in here so I can get my workout in?" With that, Gene bounded across the gym with Scotty in tow, getting looks of shock and bewilderment from the other fighters. "Son of a bitch, Geno," Scotty added as he followed Gene into the ring.

"All right, kid. That's the spirit! Make this fat piece of shit move around a bit, will ya?" Ray asked with a snicker as he looked at the much younger and smaller Gene.

"Can I hit back?" Gene asked.

"Go to town, kid. Go to town," Galento replied.

Gene headed to his corner and gave Scotty a wink of his eye as he waited for the sound of the bell. The instant the bell rang, Gene met Galento in the center of the ring but was shocked at the brutal force that the much bigger man possessed as a right cross hit him so flush and hard that he thought that the blow had dislocated his shoulder.

Galento then shoved him into the corner and was about to deliver another big shot. As Scotty cringed, Gene quickly regained his composure and used his quickness to get out of that bad spot. He returned a few jabs, desperately trying not to let Galento grab him. Galento, of course, was up to his old tricks of eye gouging, elbowing, and head butting, but Gene was proving to be too quick and dodged most of his awkward, thuggish moves.

Then suddenly, Ray yelled "time", signaling that the first round was over. Gene was amazed that three minutes had already passed. Gene walked back to his corner and sat down on the ringside stool, breathing heavily and sweating profusely. "Damn, he's strong as a bull. What a big son of a bitch!" he said.

"Dammit Geno, let's go! I told you he was a fucking animal! Just grab your dollar and let's get the hell out of here!" Scotty petitioned.

"You mean give up? Naw, I don't ever give up. I can dance with this sack of shit for a few more rounds!" Geno confidently replied as he jumped out from the corner for round two without Scotty's words really registering.

"Geno! Don't do it!" Scotty pleaded.

Galento thundered across the ring and tried to block Gene into the ropes, but Gene deftly avoided him with a simple sidestep. Galento hit the ropes as Gene danced away from him. Gene began to use his jab to keep his opponent at arms' length. His speed and agility were beginning to frustrate Galento and his bullish tactics.

As the next few rounds continued on, Gene kept up his jab and counter punching, as Galento used his normal tricks of elbowing, hitting, even kicking, as he tried to overpower and exhaust the much younger fighter. After the fifth 3-minute round, Geno slumped in his corner, completely wiped out. He bowed his head as Scotty put a wet towel over his neck. He looked up and saw Galento was standing in front of him.

"You did good, kid. You did real good. I'll see ya around, okay. Looks like we found a new sparring partner, eh, Ray?" he announced, turning his head to his trainer/manager.

"Yeah, you're a tough kid. We'll use you again, if you're up for it," Ray added as he handed Gene his five bucks one at a time and headed out of the ropes behind the overweight and nasty Galento.

Gene and Scotty looked at each other and as Gene held up the five dollars, he gave one to Scotty, and then they both laughed. "Geno, you are one crazy son of a bitch! You just went toe to toe with "Two Ton" Tony Galento for five rounds. You're fucking nuts!" Scotty said as he shook his head in disbelief at what he had just witnessed.

"Sometimes, you just gotta tough it out, Scotty. Now, let's get out of here and get something to eat. I'm starving!" Geno responded with a great big smile on his face.

Gene soon became one of Tony Galento's sparring partners in that nasty Orange, Jersey gym, and he had upped the ante to six bucks a round. Ray gladly paid it as his fighter finally had a tough and relentless sparing partner who would help Galento get in shape for upcoming bouts, including ones against the renowned Baer brothers, Max and Buddy.

Over the next couple of years, Gene earned himself an even tougher reputation not only at the gym as his sparring sessions became legendary, but also on the football field with the Orange Trojans. He welcomed the atmosphere of playing with a bunch of rough and tough vagabonds. He was a relentless competitor, who stood out every Sunday no matter who the opponent was. Whether he was running for touchdowns, throwing lead blocks, or tackling on defense, Gene was recognized once again as one heck of a player.

Gene yearned for bigger things, though. He still held out a dream of one day playing for a university. He even had the Orange Trojans change his last name to Michaels, so he wouldn't challenge any eligibility rules. You couldn't play college football if you had been a pro, even a semi-pro. His name change would secure his anonymity. Even the local newspaper writer, who covered local high school football, as well as the semi-pro games, was in on the clever ruse.

He continued working at the bank and was still able to enjoy his extracurricular activities. He always dreamed of his higher goals, and although he was content with everything that was happening in his life, he made sure that he would be ready for the day if opportunity should come knocking. Unbeknownst to him, the opportunity of a lifetime was just around the corner.

TOO GOOD TO PASS UP

It was a chilly, but sunny afternoon during the spring of 1940. World War II was destroying Europe and Asia, but America was still focusing on its own activities, including football.

Gene's old high school football coach, who attended most of his Trojan games, stood on the sidelines with a man dressed in a black leather coat, corduroy pants, and a turtleneck sweater. Edward and Claire were standing on the sidelines as well and noticed that Gene's former coach was in attendance and nodded hello. However, they did not recognize the tall man standing beside him. This was Edward and Claire's first contest that they actually attended because Gene had not told them that he was playing for the semi-pro Orange Trojans until this final game of the year. The field had no grandstands or bleachers, just people standing on the sidelines and cheering for the hometown "pros".

Unknown to them and to Gene, the old coach had contacted the nearby Rutgers University football athletic department to invite them to take a look at the young man who ran around and through people in this semi-pro football league. Rutgers sent a recruiter to see this "standout" for himself. The people at nearby Rutgers had remembered Gene from his high school playing days and eagerly wanted to see if the older Gene McManus was as good as they had remembered. The recruiter had decided to ignore the fact that Gene was playing for a semi-pro team.

The Orange Trojans were up against the Plainfield Hawks, a nasty team known for their hard hits, especially after the whistle had blown. Gene was playing linebacker and wearing his old high school number - #31. He had a bunch of huge hits against the opposing team's running back throughout the game. He also had forced a fumble and returned it for a touchdown.

On offense Gene stood out even more as he lined up as halfback and took handoff after handoff and drove into the line time and time again. On more than a few carries it took a gang of players to drag him down as Gene showcased the same tough running determination that he had displayed back at East Orange High. Ed and Claire looked on in apparent amazement. They had no idea that this was what their Geno had been up to on Sunday afternoons throughout the past couple of fall and spring seasons. They had grown accustomed to seeing his weekly bruises, but thought they came from his boxing sessions.

Later in the game, as the clock was winding down in the final quarter, the quarterback lateralled the ball to Gene and he ran 45 yards around end for another touchdown, displaying the breakaway speed he always had. Ed and Claire turned to each other, smiled and applauded as they beamed with admiration while sharing tremendous pride in their son's obvious talent.

As the final whistle blew to end the game, Gene walked off the field, battered and bruised, but upbeat. His own teammates and players on the opposing team shook his hand and patted him on the back. Gene saw his mom and dad standing on the sidelines and rushed over to greet them as they stood next to the coach of the Trojans. The coach reached out to shake Gene's hand, but Gene excitedly said, "Hey, coach, this is my mom and dad, Ed and Claire McManus!" Gene proudly hugged both of his parents. Coach Belson replied back, reaching to shake Edward's hand, "It's my pleasure to meet you. You have one tough football player here. He's a natural. You must have done something right!"

"Well, thank you, Coach Belson, we are proud of him, too!" Edward responded, taken aback by the coach's complimentary comments.

"Shoot, he's the best I have ever coached and probably one of the top backs in the country. And, he's doing it against these grown animals! Damn, sorry Ma'am, he's still just a kid," Coach Belson chimed back. He proceeded to give praise for every play in which Gene had excelled. He was obviously in great admiration for the skills of his young recruit.

As Gene and his parents finished up their discussion with Coach Belson, Gene's high school coach unexpectedly approached the group, accompanied by the mysterious man who had been standing on the sidelines. Edward acknowledged the presence of Gene's old high school coach again and in his proud exuberance thrust his hand out. "Wasson! Did you know Gene was playing with this group of men?" Edward asked.

"Oh yeah, I have been following Gene for a couple of seasons now. He looks better than he ever has!" Coach Wasson turned and drew the man in the leather coat into the group and said, "Gene, folks, I would like you to meet Mr. Graham here. He is a recruiter with Rutgers University. I invited him to come down and watch Gene perform. Gene, I didn't tell you because I didn't want you to be pressured or anything like that. So, without further adieu, Mr. Graham, this is Edward and Claire McManus, and their son, Gene," Coach Wasson proudly stated.

Graham took off his hat and addressed the group, "Nice to meet you folks. Gene, you're a special talent. I like the way you play the game, tough but with integrity and sportsmanship. You are just the kind of player we need at Rutgers University. I would like to offer you a full scholarship to attend Rutgers, to get a great education and play football against some of the top teams in the country!"

"You mean go to college for free?" Edward asked in disbelief.

"Yes sir. Everything would be paid for. Tuition, books, plus room and board," answered recruiter Graham.

"Gosh, Gene has such a great job at the bank and they really like him there." Claire cautiously responded.

"What she is saying is that we really can't afford for Gene to go to college at this time. We need him at home!" Edward firmly stated.

Gene countered back in disbelief, "Dad, Mom, hold on a second. This is a great opportunity!" His eyes danced back and forth between his coach, Mr. Graham and his parents.

"Gene, we will talk about this back at home. Mr. Graham, we will be in touch. Thank you for such a great offer. Gene, I'll see you at the house," Edward said as he walked off the football field with Claire, holding her by the elbow. He did not look back at the group of people who were still standing in silence and disbelief.

Gene turned to the representative from Rutgers and announced: "I am real sorry about that, Mr. Graham. Ever since the Depression, all he worries about is if we'll have enough money. Thanks for the offer. It sounds great and I would be honored to be a member at Rutgers University. Can I get back to you on this?" Gene thrust his helmet back on his head and turned towards the parking lot hoping that the recruiter would not see the disappointment in his eyes.

"Yes, Gene. You go take care of your business and we'll be waiting to hear from you," Mr. Graham declared as he dropped his hand, having tried to shake Gene's. "Hey, by the way, you didn't accept any money from the Trojans, did you?" he further inquired as Gene slowly walked away.

Gene stopped in his tracks, turned around and replied with a wink of his eye, "Naw, I just did it for the fun of it. The writers call me Gene Michaels, sir. They played along with it. They know I want to go to college."

Mr. Graham responded: "Very clever, young man. You will do just fine at Rutgers. Hope you can work things out with your parents."

Gene hurried home to confront his parents. He was spitting mad and a little bit embarrassed, as well. He understood about the money and he respected the needs of his family, but this was his chance, the chance to finally make something of himself and to fulfill his dream at last. As he entered the house, he saw Edward standing out in the back yard. He burst through the back door and confronted his father with great determination written all over his face.

Before he could speak his mind, his father said, "There's no sense in getting all in a huff, young man. You know our situation. We need you here."

"But Dad, this could be my last chance to go to college, and it'll all be paid for, for Christ's sake!"

"Don't take that tone with me, Gene. We have all worked very hard through all of this. The family needs you. And where did you get that mouth? You will stop mixing with that Neanderthal crowd. You are too young to be playing against and hanging out with those men! You've got a good job at the bank and that's all you should be doing," his father proclaimed.

Gene, not to be intimidated, answered: "I have done everything you and Mom have asked of me. I've given up a chance to go to college and play ball before. I've done it all for you and Mom. Now I need my own life. Football is my ticket to get an education and it won't cost you anything!"

"You have a great job at the bank, Gene. They like you there. You will keep advancing if you keep working hard. Keep at it! I worked hard to be able to afford the house we live in, to have a car, to have everything we really ever needed. Football and college didn't make that happen. It was through hard work for a good company. We all gotta make sacrifices, son. You've made your share, but we still need you at home. That's it. That's all I have to say!" Edward turned and brushed by Gene as he walked back into the house trying not to slam the door.

Gene stood there in complete bewilderment, frustration and anger. He could hardly contain his emotions. He was so mad at the situation and at his father's stubbornness. He understood and his dad had a point, but he had dreamed of so much more than just working at the bank. "Dammit," he thought to himself. "When am I going to have a life of my own?"

To make matters worse, the next day at the bank Gene was called into the office of his manager. He was still upset about the night before. Every muscle in his body ached after the hard fought final game of the season with the Trojans. He also had a black eye and a Band-Aid on his cheek. Although Gene was progressing and doing a good job, his appearance was quite a distraction. Every Monday morning, Gene would arrive at the bank and have some kind of bruise, scrape, or bandage he was sporting from his Sunday games with the Trojans, not to mention his time spent at the gym sparring with "Two Ton" Tony. This day was no different. Not only did Gene feel bad emotionally about his conversation with his dad, but he also wasn't feeling very good physically. He entered his boss's office and was greeted with an outstretched hand and an offer to take a seat in a chair beside his boss's desk.

"Gene, you have done an outstanding job since you've been here. Your attitude and production are just what this bank needs. But, there is a problem," Gene's boss stated.

"Problem sir?" Gene answered back puzzled as to what his boss was going to say next.

"It's your appearance, Gene. You come in to work every Monday and you have a new bruise or cut on your face or on your hand. Quite frankly, you are making our customers feel a little uneasy by the way you look," the manager calmly stated.

"Yeah, well, I play football on the weekends with the Orange Trojans and do a little boxing on the side. It helps put extra money into the old pockets, you know." Gene responded in defense.

"Yes, Gene, you are making quite the name for yourself. However, I can't have you looking like you have been in a street fight every week. It's not good for business. We are beginning to get some complaints from some of our better customers. I am afraid you are going to have to cease your extracurricular activities or I'll be forced to let you go. I know it's what you like to do, but it's not good for the bank, son. You must put all of that behind you. You have a responsibility to the bank. I hope you understand. That's all for now!" His manager stood up and extended his hand for Gene to shake.

Gene left the bank manager's office and went back to his desk totally devastated by what he had just been told. It was all hitting him way too hard, first from his dad and now from his boss. They wanted him to stop playing the game he loved and he had been told to decline a full scholarship offer to go to Rutgers. No one seemed to care about what he wanted. He was very upset and contemplated walking out of the bank's office and telling his boss to stick it where the sun don't shine. But just before he got to that point he was interrupted by his boss again, calling out from the door to his office.

"Gene, I need you to go to lunch with a couple of clients of ours from Prudential. They will be here shortly and after they conduct their business, they would like you to join them at one o'clock. And by the way, it's okay if you come back a little late. Prudential is one of our top clients. They'll meet you at the Cavalier. Do you know where that is?" his boss asked.

"Yes sir, I used to work there. I know where it is." Gene somewhat sullenly answered back.

"Fine. Freshen up a bit as well, will you?" he finished as he turned to close his door.

Gene nodded at the man with a smile although deep down he would have liked the chance to change his boss's appearance. An hour and a half later, he saw two men ushered into the manager's office where they remained for about an hour. As they left the building, Gene grabbed his coat and headed out of the bank following at a distance behind them.

When Gene arrived at the dining room of the Cavalier, he was greeted by the two men from Prudential. They introduced themselves as John Kruger and Dick Grasso. The dining room was crowded with people dressed in nice attire, having lunch, some for business, and others for pleasure.

"Gene, it's good to meet you. We are excited to sit down and talk with you," said John Kruger, extending his hand.

Grasso also shook Gene's hand and said, "Gene, we have been hearing some real good things about you over at the bank. We at Prudential are always looking for good young prospects with the right attitude and you certainly fit the bill!"

"We've been told that you have been playing some football with the Orange Trojans and boxing a bit down at the gym. That's great and all, Gene, but you need to decide if that's the route you want to take or do you want to excel in business?" John Kruger followed up.

"I love doing it all!" Gene firmly stated and then added, "Football and boxing keep me fit. I believe if you're fit, you are stronger in the mind and that's good for my job. My job is great, but everyone has to have more than just a job."

"How about college, Gene? Is that an option for you? I know times are tough for a lot of people still, but if you can earn your college degree, it will clearly help you advance in our business! Have you ever thought about that?" Dick Grasso asked.

Before Gene could muster a reply, Kruger continued, "Gene, we can offer you part time work, sort of like an internship, at Prudential while you work on your business degree. What we are saying, Gene, is if you are committed to earning a college degree, you can work part time with us while you do so and when you graduate, you will be a Prudential man, so think about that."

Dick Grasso picked up the sales pitch, "Son, we've been assured that the bank will give you very good references and the two of us will do everything we can to introduce you to people at some of the local colleges to help you gain an admission. Would you like that?"

"I thank you both very much. You've given me a lot to think about. I actually have an offer from Rutgers which I've been mulling over. I think I'll be paying them a visit this week. Thanks. Your offer is very generous," Gene humbly responded.

Their food arrived at the table and the subject was changed. Gene was still trying to soak up the meaning of what he had been offered. Small-talk intermingled with the roast beef lunch. His mind was racing with thoughts of how he would approach his parents with all that he had been offered over the past 24 hours. He almost didn't hear the next question posed to him.

"Now, tell us about sparring "Two Ton" Tony Galento. Why, on God's Green Earth would you want to fight that animal?" Dick Grasso asked as he leaned towards Gene.

"Well, it all started when I had to put my future on hold after high school," Gene began. He was comfortable in his own element telling stories of his trials and tribulations, but also in the glory of sharing his successes on the gridiron and in the ring. The two men also continued to sell the benefits of working for their company. Gene was soaking it all in. His path seemed much clearer now. He knew he had to take the Rutgers offer to better himself.

He was being pulled in two different directions, but he knew where he wanted to go, where he must go. He had put his dreams on hold for far too long. He had learned that he had a future with Prudential, provided he had a college degree. He also had the offer to get that degree at Rutgers and to play his beloved game of football. It had all fallen into place. Now all that he had to do was to win over his parents.

After lunch was finished and thank you's were handed out, Gene walked back to the bank knowing the confrontation he was going to have with his parents was fast approaching. It wasn't that his parents didn't want him to succeed. They did. But, the way they wanted him to go forward and the way he wanted to go forward were on two different paths. Gene had his passions and they were to use his skills on the gridiron to better himself while getting his degree. His plan was now obvious: Rutgers, football, degree and then Prudential.

When he got home from work, he sat down for dinner as his mom brought mashed potatoes to the table. Gene took the plate his father had served and started what he anticipated was going to be a debate.

"Mom, Dad, we need to talk. I have been thinking about the fine offer that Rutgers University has put in front of me. I am going to take it. It's a chance for me to better myself on and off the football field." Gene spoke firmly. But before he could continue, he was interrupted.

"Gene, we have already had this talk. We need you around here. You are doing so well at the bank. Why disrupt that?" His father demanded.

"Because I have dreams of my own, Dad! I am good at what I do and that's playing football. It can help me get an education!" Gene added.

"You are not about to give up boxing, are you, Gene? I think that is where your future is and it's a great way to make some real good money. If you keep on that path, along with working at the bank, you'll be fine," chimed in Claire.

"Mom, I love boxing too, but the real story is my arms are too short to be a legitimate contender. I have the heart and the toughness but I do not have all the tools. With football, I have it all and I want to prove it every time I take that field."

"I think you'll make a big mistake if you give up boxing. You're good at it, Gene!" Claire said. Gene held his tongue and decided to eat some of his dinner while he collected his thoughts. He then continued:

"Maybe they'll let me box at Rutgers. I don't know. We'll see. If they let me, I'll take it back up, but football is my future, Mom!" Gene stated back with a smile, loving the fact that his mother had always believed in him.

"You don't need to go to college to be successful. You are doing just fine without some college degree," Edward countered.

"But, Dad, I don't want to be a clerk forever. I can advance even farther if I can earn a degree. Look, I met with two businessmen from Prudential today. They sat me down over lunch and told me that they like me and are looking for young prospects like myself. They told me that I needed to get my degree first, though. If I get my degree they'll have a job waiting for me as long as I keep progressing. And this is the best part, they'll let me work part time while I'm going to Rutgers, so I can send home some money to help out.

"Don't you see? I can go to college and get a degree so I can have a really good job with a really good company. I can play football, and think about it. It will all be paid for with a scholarship. You won't have to pay anything. And it's Rutgers. It's right around the corner. I can even come home and help around here if ya need me. Yeah, it might look like a sacrifice to you, but to me it's a tremendous opportunity and I am going to take it!" Gene finished defiantly.

"Now, you hold on there a second, Gene. I am still the man of this house and your father!" Edward blasted back.

Gene stood up and put both hands on the table and stared at his father as he said, "Dad, I put off college a couple of years back to stay home and help out. I did that. I put my dreams on hold for the family. I am not putting them on hold any longer. You can either accept it or not. I love you guys but this is what I have to do! I am going to accept the Rutgers offer. I'll make you proud. Trust me!"

Gene promptly got up, tossed his napkin on the table and walked out of the house. He had never confronted his parents in such a direct manner, but now was the time to stand his ground. He was wracked with emotion, but totally convinced that he was right to have made his decision.

Edward and Claire sat in total silence at the table. Claire slowly raised her eyes to meet Edward's and softly said, "You know, we might just have to let him go this time."

Edward looked at his wife and studied her expression for a moment, got up and left the room. They both knew that the time had come for their boy to become a man, on his own terms.

A DEFINING MOMENT

In the fall of 1940, Gene was a twenty year old freshman at Rutgers. He was playing football for the Scarlet Knights, and was also allowed to be on the Rutgers boxing team. He was a sensation the minute he took the football field. The time he spent with the Orange Trojans made him an even tougher player and an instant fan favorite.

He was having the time of his life, playing the game he loved, going to school and mingling with the attractive, admiring co-eds. He was in hog heaven. After the two years of hardship waiting for his opportunity while helping to support his family and battling adversity trying to get his parents to consent to his entering college, he had finally made it. He was making a name for himself on campus, even being dubbed "the fighting Irishman". His parents beamed with delight. Whether they went to see his games at the stadium or listened to Rutgers on the radio, they always had tremendous pride when they heard about their oldest child's success.

Gene was also making a name for himself in the ring at Rutgers. He had a vicious left hook, a sturdy chin and the attitude of not being afraid of going against anyone. His mother loved that part of Gene. He was the tough one who stood up for himself and others and never backed down from a challenge. His father wasn't so sure. He was still worried that Gene would someday meet his match in the ring and get himself hurt really badly.

When Gene came home from college one weekend afternoon, he had an announcement to make: "Mom, Dad, I have to tell you something. As you know things have been going real well for me at Rutgers so far. The football coach, Coach Harman, and the boxing coach are very pleased with my performances. I have gotten a lot of attention in the press and with the student body. So much so, that the heavyweight champ at the school wants to take me on. He's a senior and has held the title for some time now. I guess he doesn't like it that a freshman is stealing some of his spotlight," Gene announced.

"That's great Gene. I bet you can win that fight!" Claire proudly stated.

"I think I've read about that young man, Gene. He's a big Italian and has held that title for a little while now. Are you sure you want to do this? I don't want to see you jeopardize your football career for some silly grudge match!" Edward said with the worried look on his face that Gene had seen too often before.

"Dad, you worry too much. I'll be fine. I would love for you both to come down and see it. It should be a great crowd and I'll get you and your friends a great seat! Maybe even Aunt Lee would like to attend!" Gene boldly stated.

"I'll come to see you, Gene, but you better be careful. If this guy starts beating you up, I will probably close my eyes and hope that it is all over soon. He's bigger than you and he wouldn't be champ if he weren't a good boxer. Are you absolutely positive this is something you want to do? Maybe you should reconsider." Edward cautiously counseled Gene as if he would talk him out of this situation although knowing in his heart that wasn't going to happen.

"Just come on down to see me. I'll be okay. This guy can't be tougher than Two Ton Tony, and I went toe to toe with him many times. It's two Saturday nights from tonight. I hope you are there to see me in action!" Gene said confidently, finalizing the deal.

The buildup to the fight was tremendous on campus. The heavyweight champ didn't like Gene. He didn't like the fact that some unknown freshman was getting all the attention both on the gridiron and in the gym. The champ's intention was to beat up this Gene McManus and get all the attention back on him. Gene had other plans.

The crowd was a rowdy one. The school arena was packed with students and parents alike. Claire, Aunt Lee, Edward and his buddies made the drive down to Rutgers and sat a few rows back from Gene's corner. Scotty came too. Gene entered the ring first and although he looked impressive with his muscular build, Edward still harbored some serious trepidation. Then the heavyweight champ entered the ring. The crowd immediately went nuts, and Edward really started to worry. The champ was bigger than Gene and he looked as confident as a champ should, staring Gene down the whole time.

"Edward, your Geno might have finally met his match tonight. That guy is big as a house and he looks like an animal!" one of Edward's buddies lamented as he leaned towards Edward's ear.

"I know, I told him he should rethink this decision. I hope he's not in way over his head this time. Hopefully this will all end quickly!" Edward replied, nervously wiping a drop of sweat off his forehead with his hand-kerchief.

After the introductions of both fighters, the two pugilists met in the center of the ring.

"I'm going to kick your freshman ass and shut you and all your friends up!" mouthed the heavyweight champ as he gave Gene a shove, which got the crowd up on its feet. Gene took it in stride and went to his corner. He picked his father out of the crowd and gave him his usual confident wink. Edward flashed a look of despair back at Gene.

The bell sounded and Round One began as the older boxer stalked Gene and came storming after him. The Champ went for a quick knockout punch and Gene slipped it, jabbing the champ's chin as he moved around. The champ was bigger but he wasn't as quick as Gene and he quickly realized that he had underestimated Gene's speed and power.

In the middle of the first round the crowd settled down just a bit as the two men were feeling each other out. As the end of the round neared, the champ attacked Gene again and threw another roundhouse punch, packing it with all his might. Gene ducked and came up with a hard left hook to the body.

The Champ grimaced as he felt firsthand the mighty left of the tough Irish Mick. As The Champ bent down just a little, wincing with pain, Gene came up with a thundering left hook to the side of The Champ's head. The Champ went down in a heap, and lay on the canvas looking up at the lights. At the count of ten The Champ was counted out. Gene had knocked him out in the first round! The crowd went berserk, rising to their feet and cheering. Gene walked back to his corner with a grin on his face pointing to the crowd in the direction of his dad and mom.

"Well, I'll be damned! That's my boy!" Edward shouted as he rose with the crowd and cheered. He turned and hugged Claire who was standing in silent admiration of her son. With a display never seen before by any in attendance including his beloved Claire, Edward suddenly couldn't control his excitement.

It was a defining moment in Gene and Edward's' relationship. Gene had proven to his dad that he indeed could handle any kind of adversity thrown his way. He had overcome tremendous odds to win that fight and he had proved to his dad once and for all that he was in fact one tough son-of-a-bitch. After witnessing what happened that night, Edward finally felt confident that Gene was going to be all right in this world, no matter the circumstances. However, in the midst of all the excitement, Edward had no way of knowing that his Geno would be put to the ultimate test over the next five years in a series of life-or-death experiences!

PEARL HARBOR

On the bright and sunny Sunday afternoon of December 7th, 1941, in his sophomore year at Rutgers, Gene and some of his classmates were outside of their dorm playing a game of half-assed flag football. All were a little hung over from the night before and were dragging throughout most of that afternoon's attempt at getting some exercise to shake the cobwebs out of their aching heads.

Even Gene was a little under the weather and was just going through the motions, hoping that the game that didn't mean much would soon be over. As one side of the team lined up in their formation, one of their classmates opened the window to the upstairs dorm room overlooking the courtyard and yelled out, "Guys, you better come in here and hear this. This is really bad news!"

They all laughed and started the next play. The guy in the window yelled out again, "No shit, this is serious. You've got to come in and hear this."

Again, not really paying attention and trying to concentrate on the game while nursing their major league hangovers, one of the young men shouted back, "What, did you wet the bed last night? It's about time you got up. Get out here and play with the big boys!"

The kid hanging out the window shouted back, "I'm serious. I think we are going to war! It's on the radio, now!"

The stunned group, now sensing that he was truly serious, ran into the dorm to hear it for themselves. They huddled around the radio to hear the announcer report that Pearl Harbor, Hawaii, had indeed been bombed by the Japanese. Hawaii was American territory; therefore, the US had officially been attacked.

A few other classmates entered the room and slumped on the floor, totally riveted to the radio. Report after report was detailed vividly over the air-waves. Japan had attacked America and President Roosevelt had called an emergency session of Congress to convene the next morning. They all sat by the radio soaking up every detail. More friends and some who were not even known by the group arrived in the room and settled in, as they all knew it was going to be a long afternoon of bad news.

The room soon was filled with various young men. There was almost total silence as they listened attentively to the radio reports. Thousands had been killed. Hundreds more were injured. Ships were lying on their sides. Many were burning, out of control. It was "a travesty, a horror".

Then the announcer said words that shook every young person in the room: "War is surely going to be declared against Japan and most likely with Germany, as well. All young men are probably going to be called upon to defend our nation in this time of peril." Each of Gene's classmates, friends, and associates in the room looked at each other in silence, knowing that their lives were about to change forever.

Rutgers declared that the university's classes and all activities would be put on hold. Monday, December 8th, was to be a day of reckoning, prayer and patriotism. Gene and his friends had hardly slept the night before. Almost all of them had received phone calls from family, girl friends and others. At ten o'clock in the morning on that Monday, Gene found his dorm room once again filled with fellow students, eager to hear the report over the radio from the joint session of Congress.

"We are waiting for the president to arrive and address a joint session of Congress in an extraordinary and unprecedented emergency session called by President Roosevelt last night. Yesterday's events are just too horrific to imagine. Oh, here comes the President now. He's shaking hands with the leaders of the House and Senate and now is approaching the microphone," stated the radio announcer.

"Do you think the President will really declare war?" one of the classmates asked.

"He has to. Japan attacked us. He has no choice. I bet he'll declare war on Germany, as well," Gene responded softly. He swiftly put his finger to his lips to signal that all should shut up.

"December seventh, a day that will live in infamy," started President Roosevelt over the radio and in front of Congress. His brief address continued as each Rutgers student in the room strained to hear every word. Each man was filled with anticipation and anxiety about his impending future. They must have each heard at least his final words: "This form of treachery shall never endanger us again. The American people in their righteous might will win through to absolute victory!" FDR finished. The thunderous applause of Congress could be heard through the radio.

"President Roosevelt has called for Congress to declare war on Japan and they certainly will do so in just a few minutes. God bless America and its Allies," the radio announcer was heard saying as he wrapped up his narration of the speech. Gene's Rutgers classmates sat in stunned silence, each absorbed in his own thoughts.

Back at the home of Edward and Claire, they too were sitting in front of the radio listening to every word along with Aunt Lee, who had joined her closest friends and family. It was a moment in time when all Americans dropped all cares about anything else. America was going to war. Silence reigned in the McManus home, as well. Claire slowly turned away from the radio she had been staring at for seemingly an interminable amount of time and looked at Edward. Tears were streaming down her face. All she could muster was a weak question: "How does this affect our Gene? Our Gene may have to go to war!"

"Naw, he's in college now. He won't be called up...I hope," Edward quickly replied instinctively.

"Knowing our Geno, he will be one of the first to sign up. You mark my words," Aunt Lee proudly stated with conviction.

"God dammit. If I weren't fifty-five I'd go in his place," Edward responded as all three reached out to each other to give their hugs of support. Edward tried to display a manly demeanor, but was quickly overcome with his own emotions. He knew what the future held and he knew that his son would not stand by and let others take the fight to the enemies that were threatening America. Not his Geno.

They tried for hours to reach Gene by phone, knowing that their only means of contact was a pay phone hanging on the wall outside his dorm room. It was constantly busy. Edward tried to calm down the women and reassure them that he would contact Gene when he could. That night they all went to bed, but could barely get a moment's sleep.

Back at the dorm, Gene and his classmates were at first shocked, but as Aunt Lee had firmly predicted about Gene, he was the first to voice his intentions. "We're at war. It has been coming for years. We just weren't paying attention. It's Japan today. It'll be Germany tomorrow." Gene declared with solid resolve.

"Shit, Gene, I think you're right. Japan has a treaty with Germany. We'll have to declare war on Germany. You think they'll have a draft?" one of the classmates nervously asked.

When the attack on Pearl Harbor happened, the American civilians were in shock. Sure, they knew there were world issues going on in the East and in the West, but they never imagined that someone would actually attack U.S. soil. But what happened next inside Gene's dorm room and across our country was truly remarkable. Leaders emerged and vowed to defend their country.

"Forget the draft. I'm signing up tomorrow. Our country needs us. I worked too damn hard to get where I am and I am not about to let some foreign emperor or crazy Nazi ruin my future. I am going to learn how to fly and bomb the shit out of those Japs and Nazi fucks," Gene firmly and proudly stated as he stood up.

"Gene, you ever even been in a plane before?" one other classmate asked.

"No, but what the hell does that matter? Did you learn to ride a bike? Did you learn to drive a car? Well, I can sure as hell learn to fly an airplane. Throw your books away, boys, we're goin' to war and kick those Japs in the ass." With that college sophomore Gene McManus walked out of the room and became one of the first to enlist at Rutgers, leaving the rest in that dorm room to ponder their future.

Gene headed to his parents' home. Upon arrival he immediately announced his plans to join in the war. He was met with long, deep, and sincere embraces from his father, his mother, and Aunt Lee. Although, they didn't want him to go, they knew he had to go, like all of the rest of the great young men in America. Edward and Claire's oldest child, their beloved Geno, showed once again the kind of man he had become - a true leader and a respected American.

All across the great country, young men like Geno joined the armed forces and devoted their lives to the war effort. It was a time for drastic measures. The American people came together in a display of unity that was unmatched in the entire world. Americans dropped everything in their lives to go fight for our country's freedom, leaving behind family, friends, personal ambition, and loved ones.

Although none of these young men knew what the outcome of the second great world war would be, they all knew they had to defend their country and help secure its freedom. The women and family left behind would also have to play a major role in all of this by picking up the slack for their husbands and sons, and being the "rocks" of their respective families and communities, not knowing if their men would come back alive or dead.

It was an amazing era in the history of the United States of America. Despite having endured a terrible World War in 1917-1918, the people of our country came together once again, as a unit, as a country, to go and fight for something that everyone coveted: FREEDOM!

TRAINING

Affter deciding his fate, Gene immediately enlisted in the Army Air Corps, and like every other "newbie" went through boot camp. Over the next two years Gene was moved to five different bases as he went through various levels of flight training. At his initial flight training base, Gene was informed that he wouldn't be a fighter "jockey" but a pilot bomber instead.

At first he was bitterly disappointed, but that disappointment quickly turned to taking the challenge head on. If he couldn't be a fighter ace, he could focus on being a great bomber pilot, maybe even rise in the ranks and become a Group Commander. Gene was already setting goals for himself. If his football career had to be put on hold, he would become the best he could at his new calling.

He first went to officer training school and then to various flight schools for pilot training. He started with a slow training plane called the AT-6 in which the instructor sat behind the student pilot. Gene was an excellent student, always being praised for his aptitude. His boxing and football background gave him an advantage in the physical department, but the mental side of it came easily to Gene, as well.

He greatly enjoyed flying the single engine trainers and could imagine he was on the tail of a Jap Zero or a Nazi Messerschmitt 109. He was soon flinging his trainer airplane around, taking it to its limits while his instructor held on, amazed by Gene's newly found skills.

He complimented Gene after one training flight, "Son, you've taken to flying like a duck takes to water. You're gonna be a good one." Gene hoped that the Air Corps would change their mind and assign him to fighter training, but they informed him that there was great need for good bomber pilots. American fighter planes in 1942 had limited range and were being used mainly for defense, whereas bombers had much longer range and would be used for offense. This made sense to Gene, so he accepted their decision for him.

After his initial flight training, he moved on to flying twin engine planes, similar to the kind that Amelia Earhardt made famous. After he passed that training phase, he was moved to training on the big boys, planes with four engines.

Gene was in his element once again. Studying hard and keeping in shape, he always had a plan. He wanted to achieve, no matter what the task. After the hardships he endured during his teenage years, he was in a good place, feeling very confident in his abilities as an officer and a bomber pilot.

He did get the chance to make a decision on which bomber he would fly, the Boeing B-17 or the new Consolidated B-24 Liberator. He chose the B-24 bomber. The "24" (as it was commonly called) was a "truck to drive" and required a pilot with strength and stamina. The "17" was much more forgiving. The 24 was like driving a 16-wheeler without power steering while the 17 was more like driving an SUV with power-everything.

The Liberator was a big, gawky bird and very tough to fly. It was heavy and a struggle to get off the ground and maneuver in the air. It quickly gained the reputation of having finicky engines. The manufacturer had to tweak them throughout the war.

There were other dangers. One out of every four B-24's crashed during training in the United States. Keep in mind that there weren't any air traffic controllers keeping the peace in the skies. Pilots were taught to always keep alert and constantly know where they were so that they didn't accidentally collide in the air or on the ground. Young men were crashing into each other and into mountain sides during training. But somehow Gene mastered it. He had the skill and the demeanor to handle the 24 and keep it safely flying no matter the adversity he faced in the air.

One day he was descending out of the clouds for a landing on the airstrip. It was a bright, sunny afternoon with thick cumulus clouds at about 3000 feet. As he dropped just below the cloud cover and into sight of the field, he saw another 24 closing straight in line with his path, head on.

In flight training, every pilot was taught to make a violent dive with a starboard (right) turn to avoid a collision. The 24 was a slow, lumbering tank and was extremely difficult to yank up, so all pilots were trained to put it in a much more manageable quick dive. For some reason Gene instinctively in a flash pulled back on the wheel and forced his plane to make a sudden ascent instead of a dive. He also turned the wheel for a stressful bank to the right.

The maneuver demanded enormous strength and lightening fast reflexes. The pilot of the oncoming 24 made a fatal mistake and yanked his plane into a dive but banked it to his portside (left). Had Gene put his plane in a dive instead of the climb, they would have certainly crashed into each other.

Gene quickly caught his breath and muscled his 24 into a steep dive for an approach on the airstrip. As he had the landing area in sight, he got on the "blower" (radio to the control tower) and angrily shouted, "Who the fuck was that idiot? He coulda got us all killed. Ground that son-of-a-bitch before he kills someone. If I find out who it was, I'll rearrange his face. Jesus, that was close!"

When Gene walked into "Op's" for a debriefing, he was met by the commanding officer and told to immediately go to his office. Gene thought he was going to get a chewing out. Instead the officer praised Gene for his quick thinking and the action he took. He also added that only one in one hundred pilots of a 24 could have pulled off Gene's maneuver. That so impressed "the brass" that Gene later received a promotion to 1st Lieutenant well before most of his fellow pilots.

Gene's acumen carried him through navigation, flight formation and bombing training. He graduated with top honors at every level, showcasing his abilities, and displaying his tremendous work ethic and moxie. He was ready, ready to go to war for his country. He eagerly anticipated the day when he would be assigned his crew. He looked forward to being their leader. But the Army Air Corps had other plans for him.

It was July, 1943. Gene was anxious to receive his orders to enter the war before it ended. He had never anticipated that it would take almost two years of flight training before he could see action. He was getting very antsy. He was summoned into the office of the base commander. Gene stood in front of his commanding officer, Major James McFarlin, in his office at the stark and bleak Tarrani Field just outside Fort Worth, Texas. Gene stood at attention as Major McFarlin rifled through a number of file folders.

"McManus, you have shown outstanding leadership and skills. You came to us with a record as one of the highest graduates of pilot training at Foster Field, Texas, top of your class in bombardier training at Concho Field at San Angelo and you have excelled in mastering the B-24. We would like for you to stay on here and become an instructor. We need men of your caliber to help train new pilots," the officer firmly stated.

"Sir, with all due respect, sir, I joined up to become a pilot to bomb the crap out of the enemy, sir," Gene replied, astounded by the offer.

"I understand, McManus, but you would be a great asset to the war effort if you can help train more pilots to become as good as or even better than you," Major McFarlin countered back.

"Sir, I thank you for the offer, sir, but really, sir, I believe that my duty is to take it to the enemy. I hate the bastards, sir, and I owe it to my country to use my, as you say, skills to take it to them, sir!" Gene countered back.

"Well, McManus, I'm not surprised, but I am disappointed. You'd make one hell of an instructor. I won't force you to take my offer, but understand I could. Instead, I'll honor your request. But, you better bomb the shit out of the enemy and never forget about Tarrani!" finished the Major.

"Yes sir, thank you sir." Gene delivered a snappy salute and left the office.

All that awaited Gene now was to get his orders. He desperately wanted to take what he had learned in practice and put it into battle. The problem was that the only way he was going to get called up was through a sort of lottery.

One night, a young pilot, and a friend of Gene's, drew a winning card. Gene did not receive a lottery number that night, but he knew that this young pilot had two daughters and a wife at home. He would see their family together from time to time on the base. Gene too had been recently married, like so many other officers and soldiers did, with thoughts of not knowing if they would ever come back from their war efforts. Gene could have stayed but his desire to defend his country was much more powerful than to remain back in the States. He would ask himself time and time again, "What kind of man would I be if I didn't go and fight for my country?" Gene convinced the young pilot to allow him to have his lottery number and be sent off to war. When Gene presented his lottery number to his commanding officer, he was met with a little resistance once again and he had to convince the other officers to let him fight.

"Let that young pilot stay and be an instructor, sir. He has a wife and two kids at home. Let me go fight this war. I am ready and I want to go fight for my country!" Gene stated defiantly.

With that, Major McFarlin yelled to one of his officers, "Sergeant! Take McManus, get him on the next flight to Clovis so he can meet his crew and see to it that he gets into combat soon." demanded Major McFarlin. "Yes, sir!" the Sergeant proudly shouted.

The following morning Gene took off for his final training base at Clovis, New Mexico, to finally meet his crew and meet the men he would lead into battle!

THE CREW

Gene arrived in Clovis, New Mexico and was immediately directed to a Nissin Hut to hear his orders and to meet his crew. Gene entered the room and was directed to join several hundred other men. There were long tables in the room lined with folding chairs. Most of the men were standing and talking to each other.

Gene noticed a few faces from his past travels in pilot training and walked over to greet each one. He also noted the ever increasing din as each man met a familiar face. When a sergeant yelled out "ten-hut", the whole room went silent as the men snapped to attention and focused their eyes on the podium. A full-bird colonel entered the room and took his position behind the podium. Behind him a large blackboard was wheeled in. It was filled with lists of names.

"At ease, men, and please be seated," the officer started out. "Welcome to Clovis. Posted on the board behind me is the name of each pilot and the crew assigned to him. Pilots meet up with your crew, get them together and start the introductions. We will be briefing you as to when your training as a crew will begin. Pilots, we'll meet here at thirteen hundred hours. Non-coms, you will muster at building number ten at the same time. Until then, pilots, get acquainted with your crew. You all have worked very hard in your respective training programs. Now's the time to put those skills to work. Good luck and go get 'em!" finished the Colonel.

After the Sergeant belted out his ten-hut again, signaling the conclusion of the debriefing, the Colonel walked out of the room and the pilots raced to the blackboard. Gene found his crew one by one and once they had all been rounded up, he said, "Let's go outside out of this noise and get to know each other." Gene led the way to just outside the building. He then directed them to congregate by a Jeep for the "meet and greet."

As they gathered around the Jeep, Gene began the introductions, "I know my name on the board reads 1st Lieutenant, Eugene E. McManus, but you can call me Gene, although sometimes I go by Mac, or Geno. I'm from East Orange, New Jersey. My background is football and boxing with a little bit of business. Let's go around and introduce ourselves and our position on the team. Second Lieutenant, Glenn Strong is our co-pilot. Glenn and I were at the same training facilities together. Good to have you on board, Glenn." Gene started the introduction.

"Thanks, Gene. It's a pleasure to be flying with you." Glenn replied back. The men then each took their turn, announcing who they were, and proudly stated their specialty.

"1st Lieutenant Bill Van Horn. Navigator."

"2nd Lieutenant John Spargo. Bombardier. I'm from beautiful San Francisco."

"My name's Julius Moses. Engineer. I call Altoona, Pennsylvania, my home. Most folks call me 'Moe.' I'm gonna keep our bird flyin' high and strong."

"Sergeant John Folcik. Radio Operator. Long Island, New York. I can also handle a 'fifty' (fifty caliber waist machine gun). You can always count on me. I'm damn good on both. Pleased to meet you's."

"Vincent Marimpietri. Waist Gunner and damn proud of it, sir!" the youngest member of the crew confidently stated. "I was born in Italy and still have family over there. My home now is in Pittsburgh, P. A. Everyone calls me 'Pete'."

"I'm Robert Hendrix and I'm a waist gunner, too." echoing the enthusiasm of his gunner mate which he displayed with a high five to Pete. "I hail from Sequim, Washington. You can call me Bob or 'Gunnie'."

"Marvin Guthrie. Ball Turret. Wichita, Kansas by God. Call me 'Gus'." The others in the crew noted that he sounded like a cowboy from the movies. A man of few words, but busting with a confident swagger.

"I'm the craziest son of a bitch out of all you. I'm Val Bleech. Tail Gunner. I'm from Kalamazoo zoo zoo. Glenn Miller's favorite town. You can count on me to protect your ass." he said with a big grin from ear to ear.

As they finished up introducing themselves, Gene wrapped it up. "Great to meet all of you. We are going to be together for a long time. We've got some serious training to do before they send us overseas. I'm all for a good time and as you'll soon find out I'm pretty good at that, but when it's time to work, when it's time to be on our marks, we have got to be focused and prepared every time.

"I won't settle for anything but your best effort. All of us have had our own individual journeys to get here up until this point. But starting today, 'I' becomes 'we'. Understand? We are a team now. I will fight for you and protect you to the best of my abilities. You can count on that. Let's all combine our strengths and be a formidable crew and survive this goddamn war!" Gene firmly stated.

"I also want you to be aware when we finally get stationed, we will be throwing the football around and challenging other crews to some games. We will work as a team and strive to win every time we take the field. There is nothing like the game of football when it comes to show how teamwork is so vitally important to win in the heat of the battle." Gene added.

"Now listen, now that we got that business out of the way, let's get down to the important stuff." Gene said with a grin on his face.

"Fellas, only a few of us can get into the officers' club, but I was told of a place called Rosie's Bar in town. I hear it's a happening joint. Everyone make your own way there. Discretely please! About seven thirty? Capeche? We'll have a toast or two to our new friendships." Gene finished.

It was Gene's first of many discussions to show his crew members that he would take care of them, to show them that they could lean on him as he led them into battle. He took that responsibility very seriously and felt confident his skills would show them all that they were in good hands.

EUROPE, 1944

When Gene and his crew were given their flight plans for their first mission, they were told first to fly to the east coast of America, stopping in West Palm Beach, Florida. From there they made overnight stops in places such as Port of Spain and Trinidad in the Caribbean, and traveled to Fortaleza, Brazil, their last stop prior to crossing the Atlantic Ocean.

There they refueled and had a long, bumpy, and rainy flight as they headed for the western African coast where they would have a two-night layover in Dakar, Senegal. After making a couple more stops, in Morocco and Algeria, they would eventually head up to their new home base, an airfield near Cerignola, Italy. All in all, it took Gene and his flying crew a couple of weeks to get to Cerignola.

Half of the crew, the officers and a couple of non-coms, including John Folcik, Bill Van Horn and Julius Moses, would fly with Geno and his good friend and copilot Glenn Strong in their brand new B-24 Liberator, which was equipped with the latest version of the top-secret Norton bomb sight.

The plane might have been new, but the accommodations were rudimentary, Spartan and very confined, but they were used to flying this bear of a "truck". Nowhere in this bird could you get comfortable for a long flight. The fuselage of the 24 was narrow and there was no such thing as heating in these monsters of destruction. They were only built to carry bombs, and the crew was expected to suck up to the inconveniences.

The flight suits were plugged into ports that supplied electricity generated by the four engines of the plane to heat elements built into their suits. If these elements failed, a crew member could suffer severe frostbite, and even possibly die. Also, they were flying so high that it was necessary for each crew member to wear face a mask that supplied oxygen to his body.

Otherwise they would faint or suffer a heart attack. There were no comforts of home onboard a 24.

For the most part, during their two weeks since leaving the States, the crew with Gene was having the time of their lives. Most of them had never touched foreign soil and now there they were in far off exotic places in the desert heat, biding their time, watching belly dancers, drinking all the booze their bodies could consume and seeing some of the world.

Their last stop was in Algiers, where they spent five days on a mini-vacation, waiting for their plane to get refurbished by the maintenance crew before they were to tackle the Nazis and the dreaded Luftwaffe. They were treated like conquering heroes, ate three square meals a day, and had a good solid bed to sleep in.

The problem was that during the two and a half years that they trained for this great war, they envisioned days and nights of bombing missions, of being in heroic battles, of making a difference, and here they were, finally overseas to defend their country, and they felt like a bunch of truck drivers delivering goods.

"Can you believe this shit, Mac? We spend the past two years in high intensity training, getting ready for battle, and here we are deliverin' fucking toilet paper for crying out loud!" Glenn Strong joked one day as he sat next to Gene in the copilot's seat as they taxied down the runway.

"Aw, what's a matter Bud, you feeling underappreciated? Not enough action for you yet? Trust me, we'll see all the action we can handle very soon. Besides, put yourself in the troops' shoes. Toilet paper to them is like rubbing your ass with hundred dollar bills!" Everyone on board heard the exchange and burst out in laughter.

Their "Taj Mahal" way of life came to a screeching halt upon their arrival at their new home base. Cerignola was located near the eastern coast of southern Italy, where they were greeted by rainy and cool weather. The accommodations weren't in the nice barracks that they were used to, but instead, a blanket, a hard canvas bunk and a leaking tent.

They finally met up with the rest of the crew there. They flew out of a makeshift base called Guilia Air Field. It was occupied by hundreds of pilots, crew members, maintenance men and officers, all part of the 757th squadron. The field was strewn with hundreds of tents, personnel in soggy uniforms all milling about, having daily jobs on the makeshift base while others were preparing to fly their next missions.

When personnel were not on duty, games of football, baseball, softball and other activities would be common on the base. They did whatever it took to keep a positive outlook, away from thoughts about their next mission, to keep their minds off loved ones they had left behind in the States or friends they had recently lost over enemy territory.

Soon after Gene and his crew arrived, they were debriefed by their commanding officer and immediately found out that they would have to give up their brand new bird that they had flown over from the States and were assigned an another "old crate" that had seen a lot of combat action.

There was no way a crew with no battle scars to show was going to fly a brand new bomber in the war. They would be reassigned to an old war-torn bird named, "The Naughty Angel". She had already gained a reputation for her longevity of service, ability to endure heavy damage and still maintain her good looks. At least that's the way her former crew tried to valiantly sell her to the new virgin crew.

The Naughty Angel was one of the original contingent of "24s" remaining with the 459th Bomb Group. She sported a shiny new starboard wing tip that glinted in the sun because it had not been repainted in the drab gray paint of its fellow aircraft after a part that was shot off had been replaced.

Many crews had flown her before. She had a reputation of shooting down German fighters and unloading tons of bombs on enemy targets without major damage and she had almost always brought back every crew member without a scratch despite severe flak, fighters shooting at her, and that troublesome engine fatigue that was common with the 24.

Members of the squadron found her easily recognizable because of her shiny wing tip, and she was often used as a lead plane in a formation box on missions. The Naughty Angel was a unique old bird and Gene was honored to be able to take over her controls. He immediately said to himself that he was going to see this ole lady through to the end of the war, come hell or high water.

Gene and his crew also found out, upon arrival at Guilia, that Bill Van Horn was needed on another crew, one which had just lost their navigator in a recent fight with the enemy. The crew's life of luxury was quickly replaced by the unsettling conditions and reality of where they now were.

"Lieutenant McManus, you are to report to Ops with Lieutenant Strong, over there. (Pointing to a large tent) Welcome to the 459th Bomb Group. Van Horn, come with me. You've been assigned to another group!" were the commands stoically given by a sergeant, as he saluted Gene and his crew.

As another Sergeant approached, Gene and his crew were introduced to their new crew member. "Lieutenant McManus, this is Lieutenant Lindberg. He'll be your new navigator," snappily stated the Sergeant.

At the same time Van Horn turned and saluted Gene, "Lieutenant McManus, Mac, it's been a pleasure working with you. I'll see you around here from time to time." Gene then immediately shook the hand of Van Horn after returning his salute.

"Bill, you've been one of the best and we'll sure miss you. You were a great halfback too, but know that if we meet out on that field again I'm coming right for ya!" Gene mused with a slight grin and finished, "Fellas, say so long to Bill. He's needed on another crew." Gene then turned to his new crew member, Lindberg, and shook his hand while making a warm greeting: "Good to meet you. Welcome to the crew. Do you know what was with the change?"

Lindberg tentatively replied, not wanting to offend his new pilot and leader: "Sir, my name is Fred Lindberg, but everyone calls me Freddie. Pleased to meet y'all. Seems Van Horn was needed on another crew, probably had to do with that new piece, the bomb thing you had on your bird. Sorry 'bout that, but I'm your guy and ready to do whatever it takes."

Lindberg then confidently stated, "Looks like you'll be mostly flying The Naughty Angel. She's one of our grand old ladies here. She a tough old bird and has taken her fair share of beatings. You can't miss her either, look for the 24 with the shiny starboard wing tip. She's yours now flashing her newly fitted adornment," Freddie proudly boasted.

"You mean ours, Lieutenant. Don't ya, Freddie?" he purposely corrected his new navigator. "You are on our team now and we are glad to have you on board. We work as a team and succeed as a team at everything we do. We left the States rated as the number one crew from Clovis and we take tremendous pride in carrying that status with us. I am damn sure you will add to it. By the way, do you play any football?" he asked the Lieutenant.

"No, sir, not really, but…" Freddie started to respond, but was quickly interrupted by Gene: "Well, we do play, as much as possible. I am expecting you to be in good shape and help us be the number one team in the air and on the ground. They do play some ball around here, don't they?" Gene inquisitively asked.

"Oh, yeah, sir. You'll see plenty of action whichever way it comes. A bunch of different crews get together and beat each other up." Lindberg enthusiastically responded.

"Good. We look forward to it. Just make sure you can keep up. Now, let's go take a look at our "old lady". Where is she? Take us to her!" Gene responded as he motioned Freddie to show them the way.

They all climbed in and stroked her with affection, each offering her a silent prayer that she would bring them home after every mission. She was going to be their womb and protector throughout most of the remainder of the war. That night they bonded with their new crew member and shared lots of stories about their training experiences. The jovial interchanges blocked out some of their individual fears about the following day's first mission. They were now comrades in war but had their own demons to deal with.

Fear was all pervasive for some. Gene, although he had not faced combat, knew that he had to be stoic, rock solid and fearless in front of his crew. They had to believe in him as their leader.

Before they retired to their respective tents, Gene had them all group together and put their fists together over the tin pot that contained the last embers of a fire warming their tent and softly proclaimed: "Remember gentlemen, we are a team. We will take this fight to the Nazis in the air and we will win on this field on the ground!"

They all punched their fists together and parted. It was a similar scene that he had experienced on the football field over his years. Now it was a symbol of unity and comradeship to the death with his crew.

Gene and his crew in all flew twenty-two missions, mostly with the Naughty Angel, when she wasn't getting repairs after the many bullets she took on. They bombed sites all over Europe, including Northern Italy, Austria, France, Hungary, Yugoslavia and Romania. Over Romania, their raids took them to Ploesti, which was known as one of the most dangerous missions to go on. Attacking Ploesti was very important to the US and Allied forces for it housed oil refineries, aircraft factories, and communication targets of the enemy.

It was very heavily guarded as flak was thick and the Luftwaffe airbases were always on alert to protect these great assets for their own war effort. Also, the 24's had to make low level passes to make sure that they were on their marks for the many targets, which made it easier for the ground forces of the enemy to shoot them down.

Dozens of aircrews lost their lives on these missions to Ploesti. Gene and his crew made the trip to Ploesti twice. The Naughty Angel always brought them back like she did with many other crews before Gene took her over, even though just getting her off the ground was a challenge.

Being a heavy "bird", she needed to be muscled the entire flight, which took tremendous stamina. She also seemed to be having engine trouble all too often, but she always came through in the clutch. Gene's physical strength was what made him such a great B-24 pilot and a great "driver" of the big "truck". The Naughty Angel, however, was always a handful.

Gene and his crew knew how to handle her and very quickly got to grips with her many idiosyncrasies. Gene and Glenn were always talking to her and giving her confidence as they raced down the airstrip on each takeoff, encouraging her with a "that's a good girl" as they successfully lifted off.

The flight crew became very attached to the Naughty Angel. She took care of the crew, too, and never came back from any of their missions with one injury, despite dealing with flak, enemy fighters, freezing conditions and fatigue. They always wanted to be the crew that flew her and they swore that they would never trade her in, when she was flyable, of course. After every successful mission, each member of the crew would affectionately give the old lady a pat on her nose before they went into a debriefing session.

When they weren't on assignment, Gene and his boys took pleasure in playing pickup football games on the base and drinking beer together when it was appropriate and in ample supply.

There were a lot of tough men in the war. They had to be, which led to very competitive, very rough, tackle football games. The daily unpredictable weather of southern Italy in the spring of 1944 made their makeshift football field a soggy mess, offering more sticky mud than lush grass. They all had to wear their standard issued boots, which made it even harder to move with any speed and agility. Nevertheless, the contact was somewhat brutal, but they knew that they had to avoid injuries. If a crew member was hurt playing football, there would be hell to pay from the colonel.

Missing loved ones and wondering when the war would be over consumed their minds daily, so these kinds of distractions were badly needed. Gene loved those pickup games. He was always directing his crew to line up in the right formations, to play tough, and of course, to win. It brought them closer together more than ever. Matter of fact, those games made the entire base as upbeat as possible, whether crew members were actually involved playing or just rooting their respective crews on. They often gambled on their favorite team with their packs of smokes or sometimes even goodies sent from home. It was a welcome diversion.

Gene never second guessed his decision to stay with his crew when he declined the offer to be an instructor over in the States. Sure, that would have been a cushy job, but if he accepted that position, in his mind, he would have felt like a total sellout. He wanted to lead and he told his team from the beginning that he would be there for them. He would take care of them as best he could and he would bring them home. If he had taken that job, he wouldn't have lived up to what he stood for, and to Gene that meant everything. He also soon found out in a letter from his wife that he had even more to live for: a daughter was on the way. He now had even more to prove, not only to his crew, but something even more important, being a good father himself.

He missed organized football, though. He had worked so hard and had beaten so many odds to achieve his dream of playing major college football. He had stayed with his family because they needed his help, but he had also made the most out of every opportunity, sometimes even making his own luck. But he wouldn't have traded anything for his patriotism and his call to defeat America's enemies. His passion was to be a leader at all times and to have people counting on him, as he had always held that status for most of his life. He was built for it, both mentally and physically.

After their twenty-second mission, he and his crew knew that they were lucky to have survived so far, not only because they had seen first hand fellow crews being shot down, but also seeing a few crews lost by simply not being able to handle the 24.

Although twenty-five percent of B-24's perished during training back in the States, the ratios weren't as high over the skies of Europe. However, when they did crash it was because the mountainous terrain always brought an added dimension to the dangers of flying a bomber, especially when flying in the dark. Also, many planes lost power after being shot up and couldn't make it over the mountains or just ran out of fuel and crashed.

The men were smart enough to know that the end of the war was soon near because the United States and their allies were gaining ground on the enemy. In addition to that, the crew knew that they were gaining ground on their required number of missions that warranted a ticket home.

To give them even more assurances that that goal would be reached, the Naughty Angel was soon due a much needed engine change. Gene and Glenn Strong also looked forward to a promised week-long escapade of R & R, rest and relaxation, on the Island of Capri, something that was due to happen after their next mission, which figured to be their toughest one yet. The two men were tremendously excited and looked forward to their much needed break from the seemingly endless doldrums and terrors of the war. Their bags were packed and sat on their respective bunks awaiting their return.

On the morning of June 9th, 1944, three days after the D-Day invasion, they prepared for their next mission in the briefing room. Most members of the 459th saw D-Day as just another day in the war, not realizing its significance until after the war was over.

June 9th was described as a perfect summer day. It was beautiful and clear, a great day for flying. As Gene and his crew readied for their twenty-third mission, each man talked to the "old lady", said a silent prayer and strapped himself in for another long flight.

Thirty-nine B-24 bombers of the 459th Bomb Group took off on that morning, including the Naughty Angel with Gene's crew onboard. They were situated in the D-7 position in their formation box, which was in the back left and a little bit lower than the front. The Naughty Angel was already experiencing engine trouble so they put her in the back of the formation and hoped that she could keep up. She always could be easily spotted by everyone, including enemy fighters, as she was still sporting her shiny silver, unpainted starboard wingtip.

They gathered up over the Adriatic Sea and flew in formation as they headed towards Munich to bomb industrial marshaling yards. It was a major rail yard with trains ready to supply Nazi troops. It was their specific target. It would be the farthest penetration of the group into Germany. All knew that it would be their toughest mission to date, for Munich was heavily defended and they would have to be prepared to deal with many enemy fighters and a ton of flak. They had been in similar situations during previous missions, most notably the two runs they made at Ploesti.

However, this particular flight to Munich would be their longest one yet as well, over four hours each way. They would have to fly over the Bavarian Alps to get there, which meant they had to deal with below-freezing temperatures during the entire flight, to and fro. Gene and his crew knew they needed to be at their very best for this mission. Anything less would court disaster, especially if they wanted to make it back alive. They all had to be consciously aware of the fact that frostbite was an ever present danger and could prevent a gunner from being able to handle his machine gun while defending his ship.

The huge contingent of American and allied bombers of the 459th that day was also expecting an escort of American P-47 fighters. At the designated rendezvous point in the air where they would be meeting up with the fighters, one of the crew members would always shout out that he could see the "little angels", which they were endearingly referred to by the bomber crews. The Naughty Angel and her tired engines were straining, but Gene and his crew were able to keep with the formation as they took the position of tail end Charlie.

"We're now over the Udine, fellas. Keep a lookout for our little friends. They should be linking up with us very soon," Gene calmly announced over the intercom. "Yes, sir!" the crew responded in unison.

"Hey, Mac, I think I see them coming now. Eleven O'clock, portside!" declared an excited Sergeant John Folcik, the radio operator of the crew.

"Yeah, I see 'em Sergeant. Good eyes. There's our little angels! We should have no problems now!" Gene announced confidently.

"Who in the hell is firing at them, Sir?' shouted Julius Moses, the engineer.

"Nobody's firing at them! Shit! The bastards are firing at us!" shouted back Freddie Lindberg with his heart in his throat with fear. The tail gunner blurted out over the intercom: "Christ! They ain't ours, they're the fucking FW's!"

Gene, trying to be calm, passed on an important reminder: "Okay dokey, boys, short burst, save your ammo, we still got a long way to go." In seconds came an excited shout: "Bandits, two o'clock" and before he could finish his words, several fighters roared past The Naughty Angel, guns blazing. They passed so close that the plane violently rocked. This time Gene was fighting mad. "Give 'em Hell, boys!" he shouted defiantly as the Naughty Angel's machine guns erupted.

Members of crew in Algiers;
Gene is 2nd from left

THE RECRUITING GAME, 1987

In late fall of 1987, I was finishing up my senior year at Wheeling High School. I was just shy of six feet two and weighed nearly 220 pounds. I had made a name for myself on the football field, becoming an All-Conference, All-Chicagoland Area, and All-State linebacker. I was getting a lot of attention from the local papers, parents, coaches, award ceremonies, etc. I was also starting to get more heavily recruited by Division 1 football programs. It was an exciting time in my life and very rewarding after all the hard work and belief in myself.

Despite my so-called local fame, my dad always made sure that I kept my head on straight by critiquing my play after every game. I would first go home after every game before I would head out to meet my teammates and friends. After I cleaned up and got dressed, I would sit across from my dad, like I always had, and we would talk about my performance. There was no sugarcoating anything. He told it like he saw it without holding anything back.

One night at Wheeling, I had the best game of my high school career. It was against the eventual state champions. I had an interception, a fumble recovery for a touchdown and over a dozen tackles. It was a huge upset for our team, and a highlight reel kind of game for me. All the students stormed onto the field after the game. I knew I had played well and felt great afterward, so much so that I eagerly awaited my dad's "critique" at the kitchen table that night. However, when I got there I was immediately humbled.

"What happened to you in the third quarter when you missed your block and your quarterback got sacked?" he asked intently as he critiqued my play as an offensive tackle, the position I played that night when I was on offense. I thought I had had a pretty good game at tackle too, but Dad obviously had other thoughts.

"Dad, I don't even remember that play," I stated back truthfully.

"Sure you do. You had a great game, Tom, but you've got to play the whole game, every time you are out there. You understand what I am saying? These colleges are going to look at how you play, every play, whether it's on offense, defense, or special teams. You must be at your best every single time!" he said with tremendous conviction.

I was a little stunned, no doubt, but it was another set of lessons learned: Always play your heart out, don't rest on your laurels, and never take a play off, meaning give your best effort on every single play and not when you just feel like it. He meant that I should have a high motor the entire game. Show the college recruiters that no matter how the game is going, whether you are blowing the opponent out and beating them decisively, or you're in a "nailbiter" that is coming down to the wire. Play every play the same - all out.

He was always instilling me with these things. He wasn't abrasive when teaching lessons, just very direct. I learned to take his critique like a man and although I didn't always like hearing it, I knew it was good for me. One night the downstairs phone rang and I just happened to be the one to answer it. I was the last one at home, so by the time I was a senior, I was never fighting my brothers or sister to see who answered the phone first.

When I picked up the phone, a sports writer from the local paper was on the other end, wanting to do a story on me. I obliged and was excited to do so. My dad must have heard what I was saying from the upstairs kitchen as he came downstairs in a little huff. He wasn't too thrilled that I was doing an individual interview, a one-on-one, so to speak. Obviously his old school mentality instilled in him made him believe that, "You do your talking on the field". But, I knew how to handle it.

During the interview, I gave all the praise to my teammates and team and never made it seem like I thought I was some big shot. When the story ran the next day, my dad gave me some good praise for reacting and answering the questions as a leader should. He actually thought it was a really good article. His lessons were getting through and I am sure that made him happy.

When my season was over, the recruiting from Division 1 colleges and universities really picked up. One day I was called out of class and was told to go the coach's office. When I pushed the door open, there was a slew of head coaches waiting to talk with me, mostly from Big Ten schools, including Indiana, Michigan State, Purdue, Minnesota, and Northwestern.

It was a great feeling as I entered the locker room and saw about six or seven coaches standing there. One by one, they came into the office and made their pitch about why I should come play for their respective programs. My high school coaches did all they could for me, something I will never forget. I later learned that they sent out almost 300 letters on my behalf, along with a couple of other teammates. They always made sure that the recruiting was done the right way and it always made them feel good when one of their players was garnering consideration for an athletic scholarship.

I wasn't hugely recruited, though, most likely because I wasn't the greatest athlete in the country. Don't get me wrong, I made a lot of plays and stood out on the team, but my athletic measurables (size, speed, athleticism, etc.) on paper didn't exactly jump out at anyone. But as news got out about a tough, hard-nosed linebacker in suburban Chicago, I started to get more and more attention. The funny thing about recruiting is that once you start getting that kind of notice, other schools start snooping around. It's like a domino effect. Certain schools will wonder why they aren't looking at you if their competition is, so they get in on the action.

My mom and dad loved the recruiting process. We always had the visiting coach over for dinner. That was a must. My parents' routine was that if you wanted to talk to their son, then "Come over to our house and break some bread with all of us." One night this really nice coach came to the house from the University of Minnesota. He was a very jovial man and a pretty big guy, to say the least, and man could he put some food away.

He sat at the kitchen table and kept eating and eating. Even after all the other plates were cleared from the table, he was still eating whatever was left over. Of course, Mom was flattered that he liked her cooking so much, but Dad and I thought we knew better. He was your quintessential chow hound. Oh yeah, I forgot, he had two helpings of dessert. My dad and I just winked at each other and smiled the whole time.

My dad really loved it all. After the meal, he always offered a beer or drink to the visiting coach. Whether the coach obliged or not, he always made one for himself. He loved talking football and always wanted to hear what the respective school had in store for his youngest son.

On another particular night, Bill Kollar came to our house. He was a defensive coach from the University of Illinois, the fighting Illini. He was a fiery guy and had done really well recruiting in our area. After dinner, we all watched Monday Night Football, but after a while I was getting really tired.

There I was, thinking, "Okay, this guy has made his pitch and the night is over, right?" Wrong. I shook his hand, said good night and went to bed. Coach Kollar and my dad stayed up until God only knows when telling stories. My dad's storytelling was second to none, everyone loved to hear them and, of course, he had a lot to tell.

My dad's and my personal relationship started to enjoy very subtle and positive changes during my senior year in high school. Obviously, the great thing we had in common was our love of the game. But I also earned his growing acceptance as a tough ballplayer, which meant everything to me.

No coach could come close to the impact my dad had on me in football and in life. I was playing the game like he thought it should be played. He was really excited about the recognition I was earning and the prospects of what was lying ahead for me.

I had accomplished a goal. I set out to make my own name for myself at Wheeling and earn a scholarship, and here I was being courted by colleges and universities with full scholarship offers. He would always tell me how proud he was and say, "I love ya." I would remember all the times that I had feared him or all the times that he was hard on me as I was growing up. But those three little words always made up for it all. That's why I guess it's called "Tough Love".

He was starting to mellow out a bit too. Maybe it was because his youngest kid was going to be moving out of the house, and he and his Joanie were moving to Florida to live the good life in his welcomed retirement. He was longing for days filled with golf, sandy beaches and nights of Happy Hours.

Don't get me wrong, though. He still could have whipped my ass, even at age 68. He was in good shape, lifting weights almost every day. He might have always been the older parent in their circle of their younger friends, but he could hang with the best of them. He was always the life of the party, with his Joanie by his side. The old war hero and football star telling stories about the "old days", including his rounds with Two Ton Tony. "The bigger they are the harder they fall" he would tell them.

He also got heavily involved in coaching at St. Mary's while I was in high school. One of his defining moments in that regard came when he led a group of 5th and 6th graders to a comeback victory in the city championship game. I would stand on the sidelines and watch him kneel down in the middle of the huddle telling the young kids that he believed in them and that they could do it, even as they faced adversity and needed extra effort to win an important game.

"It's a war out there", he would tell the kids. Watching him coach always brought a big smile to my face. I believe that if he had chosen to go the coaching route, he would have made a great one. All the kids loved him and Mr. Flood. They were a good coaching team, along with their friend "Murph", who also coached me at that age along with Mr. Flood. All three of the men were very close and really good friends. You could always tell that they genuinely loved those kids and taught them how to win.

Yes, everyone loved to hear Geno tell his stories. He was looked upon as a genuine, giving mentor to kids and a lovable soul. When my parents left Buffalo Grove for good for their retirement, there were a couple of parties thrown for them by the St. Mary's crowd, as well as the Wheeling bunch. They were saying goodbye to good friends they had made along the way. They were a great group of people and my dad and mom really enjoyed being with them. Oh yeah, and the parties were pretty great, too.

When I finally made my decision and accepted a scholarship to play football at Boston College, my dad was in heaven. He beamed for weeks telling anyone who would listen about my choice. He was funny about other things at the time, too. He would always ask if I needed a couple of bucks to go out with, especially if he had a couple of drinks in him. Like clockwork, he would pull out his cash, lick his thumb and offer me money, whether I wanted it or not, which I, of course, always obliged.

It must have been because any pressure of his having to put me through college, which he and I both knew he couldn't afford, had totally subsided when I received my scholarship. He must have felt good about being able to give me a little cash here and there, so I could have some fun, especially during my last few months at Wheeling.

He always wanted to know where I was headed and where the party was. He liked the fact that his sons and daughter were well known, young, popular adults in our community, good kids for the most part, but let's face it;

the apple doesn't fall too far from the tree, and he knew his kids liked to have a good time.

He also knew we were leaders and although we weren't error free, we knew how to conduct ourselves, for the most part, anyway. Shoot, being the youngest of four, I was pretty well rounded and mature in that regard, meaning I knew how to handle myself and knew what not to do, at the very least knew how not to get caught.

Heck, I was even a bouncer at a local nightclub at age seventeen, although I lied about my age. I and two of my buddies, who both went on to play college ball, would be tossing guys out of the club who were five to ten years older than us. It was great fun. If the owners only knew how old we actually were! One night, one of my Wheeling coaches showed up in line and I actually carded him. When we both looked up at each other, my mouth busted wide open. I asked him to not give up my true identity or to tell anyone else about it. He never did. Thanks, coach.

I, myself was looking toward my next step in life. I was ready to be out on my own, even if it was 1000 miles away from what I knew. It was time for me to go and try to achieve even bigger goals and realize more of my dreams. My dad gave me the only advice he could before I left, "Give 'em hell."

Oh, he could have gotten all sentimental and given me a long speech about becoming a man, striking out on my own, working hard, being a gentleman, busting my ass on the gridiron, avoiding getting into trouble, doing the right thing, and taking full advantage of your opportunity and graduating. But, when he said those three words, they were all what he needed to say for I knew exactly what they meant.

I hugged my mom and dad and said my goodbyes at Chicago's O'Hare Airport. I knew as I boarded the plane that it would take me to a place filled with new and exciting opportunities. What I didn't know at the time was that the journey I was about to set forth on would lead me to an unforeseen path to my future and for the rest of my life.

DAYS AT BC

To say that I made a name for myself during my first three years at BC would be far from the truth. I was a popular and respected member of the team and when given the opportunity I had made a little bit of an impact. However, it wasn't exactly what I had in mind when I left Wheeling High School for Beantown. I had a couple of older players in front of me. They were good players, but I felt that I was equally as good. I had faced a different kind of adversity for the first time in my life; not being THE guy.

My linebacker coach, Red Kelin, and I would battle quite a few times about my lack of playing time. He was always a stickler on how fast I could run my 40 yard dash. He felt as though I needed to run at least a 4.7 second 40 to be one of his starters, which was a good time for a linebacker in college back then. A couple of guys at my position of inside linebacker could run that fast and were good players, hence their starting roles.

I was never too subtle in my argument with him, either. I felt as though it shouldn't have been how fast I could run a 40 yard dash in a straight line. In my mind all that really should have mattered was my overall production on the field.

Plus, it wasn't like I was terribly slow, (as I usually posted around a 4.9 second 40 at the time), although at the same time I wasn't terribly fast either. When given the chance, my play spoke for itself, not some sprint down a track with a stopwatch time. I had showed during spring football practice and at live scrimmages that I could make a bunch of plays. I could always hit, especially near the goal line.

I earned my toughness label not only through those tests but also during my first year in spring ball following my "redshirt" freshman season. "Redshirt" means that I didn't play in any games, along with the entire freshman class, but practiced throughout my first year at BC. When you do that, you are given four more years of eligibility.

On a shitty rainy and cold afternoon (that's Boston in March for ya), we were in full pads performing a live contact drill. I smashed into one of our senior offensive lineman on a running play and next thing I knew he threw a punch that hit me in the facemask after the whistle had blown.

Well, I snapped and starting wailing him back. We went at it, going toe to toe for a minute or so before the coaches broke it up (they let us slug it out for a little while). It was quite silly really. We each had our helmets on and kept whacking each other in the facemask. He had these padded gloves on like most offensive lineman would wear. All I had on were equal to wide receiver gloves that offered no padding. He outweighed me by a good 50 pounds or so, but I stood my ground and was much quicker than he was, so I got in about three times as many punches than he hit me with.

We laughed about it in the locker room after practice. At least he did. I was still kind of pissed off, but you understand very quickly that at that level that kind of stuff stays out on the field. It doesn't overflow into the locker room. The senior leaders wouldn't allow that.

It was pretty dumb of me really. I could have broken a knuckle, or worse, but at the same time I wasn't going to take any shit either. That incident gave me an early reputation as being a tough kid. The funny thing about it was that the offensive lineman and I actually became really good friends. Football players really can be kind of weird in that way. I can't really explain it, although some would call it a kind of Neanderthal mentality.

I got my first chance to start during that next football season due to an injury to the starter. We played against Army and their vaunted wishbone attack. I hated playing them because their offensive linemen wouldn't try and hit you up high, rather they'd cut your feet out from under you. It was always a pain in the ass, to be honest.

I ended up having 15 tackles that game. I made plays all over the place, but then I didn't see the field again that entire year, other than on special teams and on goal line stands. It drove me nuts feeling that I finally got the chance to show I could play but then it didn't change my status at all. Sure, I might not have been the fastest linebacker on the team, but I was always around the ball and never felt overmatched by the speed of the college game.

The next year, then a "redshirt" sophomore (my third year at BC with two more years to play after that), the same thing happened. I was relegated to backup duty and got the chance to start a game again due to another linebacker's injury. I made twenty-two tackles that game, the highest "hit" total in one game by any player that year, but again never saw the field after that. It was extremely frustrating. I felt like I was never going to get a fair shot at the starting job. As they say in slang in Boston, "I was bullshit!"

I remember one of my roommates, who was two years older than me, telling me, "You're only a sophomore, Tommy Mac. You gotta wait your turn." I didn't believe in that crap. Just because someone was a senior who happened to be playing the starting position for a year or two didn't mean that no one was better than him. I know that sounds so self-absorbing, but I did showcase my abilities when called upon. When given the opportunity, I made the most of my time.

I didn't help myself by always challenging Coach Kelin about why I wasn't playing. Those debates got pretty heated. Look, I was always taught to stand up for myself. I was taught to respect my coaches, too, but they were also human and humans sometimes make mistakes. I truly felt that I was in the right and I was becoming really unhappy being there. However, the starter in front of me was a good solid player and a senior, so it wasn't as blatant as I saw it, but it was killing me inside.

To make matters worse, I got so fed up that I went over Coach Kelin's head and pleaded my case to the head football coach. That really wasn't a good idea, but I was young and didn't know any better.

Unfortunately for me, I learned a valuable lesson that day. A head coach will never undermine one of his assistants, especially one that has been with him for so long, as was the case with Coach Kelin. It backfired on me big time, to say the least, for I hardly ever saw the field again that entire year. My frustration got so bad that I wanted to transfer to another school where I thought I would get a fair shake. My dad squashed that idea very quickly.

"You're not going anywhere, Tom! You're going to have to tough it out," he said to me over the phone one night when I asked for his advice on the matter.

I knew he would have never really let me transfer anyway, but I was strongly considering it. I was pissed off and feeling a little sorry for myself. Transferring, in my dad's eyes, would have been like giving up. There was no way I was giving up and to be honest, there was no way he would let me. Don't get me wrong, I was having a great time at BC and had made great friends, but I was becoming very discouraged with the way my football career was going. I had big plans when I got to BC and up to that point I hadn't accomplished anything, at least in my mind. I always felt that I was facing an uphill battle. I just couldn't seem to win the coaching staff over no matter how well I played when I got my opportunities.

They weren't bad coaches. They were actually real good guys. Jack Bicknell was the head coach and he had a lot of success, especially when Doug Flutie was there. He was what was called a "Player's Coach". A "Player's Coach" means that he would listen to his players and not always have the attitude of "it's my way or the highway" kind of coaching style. I did like him a lot and above all, I respected him. He always stood up for his players, no matter what.

Case in point: One night, I got into a fight. I was acting in self-defense for the most part, and the guy deserved everything he got. It all started after he and his friends peppered a car that I was riding in with snowballs. I was in the back seat behind the driver's side as we came home late from the bars.

A nice co-ed, whom I didn't really know that well, was driving her dad's Mercedes. She wasn't drinking and was just trying to get me and some friends back to campus, when these guys opened "fire". The snowballs must have been hard-packed because they hit the vehicle pretty damn hard. She immediately shrieked saying, "Oh my God, this is my father's car!"

I had a few brews under my belt, to say the least, and was feeling no pain, so I told her to stop the car. When I got out, this guy popped out from behind a tree near the side of the street and made some smart-assed comment like, "What the fuck are you going to do about it?" Well, knowing the tales of my father, you probably guessed it right. I took off my jacket and staggered towards him. With that, he whipped a snowball at me and it hit me right above my left eye.

I immediately wiped off the snow, moved up towards him and decked him. Really good, too! His nose splattered and he hit the ground. I had these "boat" shoes on and I slipped in the snow when I hit him and fell forward, almost landing on the guy. He never got up and just lay there writhing and holding his nose with blood coming out through his hands. The wimp just lay there, crying. He wasn't some little guy either. He was as big as I was from what I can remember. Thoughts of, "Where did all that tough talk go?" instantly rummaged through my head.

Out of nowhere, his buddy came up and kicked me in the side of my head. Man, that hurt! Now I had the whole tunnel vision thing going on and I was steaming. So, I grabbed that guy's jacket collar and whacked him, too. Then out of the corner of my eye, I saw another guy coming at me at a fast pace and I knew he was trying to hit me, as well. I turned and hit him with a left cross so flush that it stopped him dead in his tracks and he crumpled like a sack of potatoes: best left-handed punch I had ever thrown.

A couple of seconds later, two offensive linemen teammates of mine, who had seen the whole thing as it unfolded, arrived on the scene. One of them picked me up from behind to stop me. The problem was, he grabbed me around my arms and left me unprotected as one of the guys I had decked came up and punched me in the face. I saw the punch coming the whole time. It felt like it was in slow motion. I winced and ducked the best I could, but he caught me just above my right eye.

The campus police came just as the big O-lineman put me down. I turned to him and said, "What in the hell are you grabbing me for?" He replied, "Sorry, Tommy Mac, I just didn't want you to get into any more trouble!" Fair enough, I immediately thought. Well, the cops had to write out a report and they charged me with battery. I got off on the criminal charge, but I ended up getting sued by this 24 year old punk, who shouldn't have been on our campus anyway.

Hey, I was 19 and young and dumb. But he did throw the first punch. Actually it was a snow ball, but it hit me in the eye at close range and it kind of hurt. Plus I felt bad for the girl who was driving her daddy's car. That really got the whole thing going. I was standing up for her! Okay, I have to admit, I was pretty drunk, so the snowball didn't really hurt, but it was the damn principle of the whole thing!

I went to court and I ended up being served with a $1,500 judgment against me. I didn't have a pot to piss in so my dad had to pay it. I didn't tell him until I absolutely had to, which took about eight months, due to continuances in the trial.

I was scared shitless, to be honest. My poor mother knew the whole time what had happened as I had told her the story months before after she was sworn to secrecy. She never told on me, which held true to the label of her being the "rock" of our family and always protecting her kids.

I picked the time to tell my dad when I was home from break one afternoon as we were walking down the beach, and the money was soon due. I was literally shaking inside. But, he understood, although he wasn't happy about the money he had to shell out. I felt really bad about that, but I think he could have seen himself in that same situation, probably had been at some point during his lifetime. Plus, I didn't start it, and being a bully was never tolerable in his eyes. "Never back down from anyone, but never start a fight" was what he always instilled in me. "There's always someone out there tougher than you," which was something that I always adhered to.

Anyway, back to Coach Bicknell. He never wavered from his loyalty and supported me through the whole ordeal. When I told him how it had all happened (minus my "judgment" at the time, of course, although he wasn't naive), he said, "I would have done the same thing, too!" He stood by me and that meant a ton at the time. I never have forgotten that.

After my third year ended, Jack Bicknell and his staff were fired, let go by the administration. I felt bad for them to a certain degree. I really did. But I also looked forward to starting with a clean slate with a new staff. Incidentally, years later, I became really good friends with Red Kelin.

I finally had the chance to show what I could do. Little did I know at the time that the next coach at Boston College would have such an impact on my life forever. When Tom Coughlin was named the new head coach at BC in the winter of 1991, no one on our team really knew who he was.

I remember comments that were made by a couple of older alumni that I knew, guys who had played at BC back when Coach Coughlin was the quarterback's coach when Flutie was there. They told me that he was just what we needed, a tough disciplinarian who would turn the program around. After the story I just told, I guess they were right on. What he was though, was one hell of a cultural shock. Whew, he was tough, right from the get-go!

We had been in our winter conditioning program for about two weeks when he was hired. We didn't even know what he looked like or anything like that, but he made his presence known when he first stepped on campus. Early one morning, we were doing our usual running, performing 200 yard sprints around the oval of the Fieldhouse track.

One of our defensive backs, Mike Reed, let's just say, had a stomach problem that morning. While he was making his way around the track, he bee-lined it into the nearby bathroom which was located about midway up the side of the track. Little did he know that our new head coach was hiding behind the Fieldhouse curtains, watching what was going on.

Next thing we knew this silver-haired man in a suit that no one had ever seen before came storming up the side of the track and hurriedly went into the bathroom. The next thing we saw was Mike Reed being thrown out of the bathroom door. He started running right away and still had some residue left over running down his leg.

Coach was seen by all of us just standing at the door of the john with his hands on his hips, frowning. We knew right then and there that our new coach wasn't going to take any shit. Hell, Jack Bicknell would have just said "Finish your business and get back out here as soon as you can." It was a shocking moment for all of us and a huge difference to what we were used to. I think my jaw dropped and stayed open for at least a minute. I barely looked at him as I went by when it was my turn to sprint around the track.

Enter Tom Coughlin. It was actually kind of surreal. Coach Coughlin came in with the old General's attitude and was clearly on a mission to "weed out the weak." Man, those mornings sucked. They were the hardest thing I ever had to do in my life, and not only physically either. The mental anguish of anxiety the night before each running workout would kill me inside. Thinking about what he had in store for us the next day was sheer torture and would keep me up for most of the night.

He had these big barrels filled with garbage can liners placed on each corner of the track for guys to throw up in. Guys were dodging in and out of those things all morning long. We'd never seen things like that before. Puking didn't get you out of anything, either. The coaches had no problem if you had to puke, just get it in the garbage can and make sure your ass was back on the line in time for your next sprint.

They didn't give a rat's ass if you had puke running down your shirt either. I think I threw up every morning we had to run. It didn't matter what I had in my stomach either, if anything at all. I was yakking. On top of that, the Fieldhouse had an indoor pool in it, and the smell of chlorine always made me queasy to start.

The coaches would be yelling at us all the time, too, challenging us to go harder and to dig deeper. I had never been through a "military style boot camp", but I bet it was close to that. They crushed us constantly - physically, mentally, and emotionally, breaking us down every day, as much as humanly possible. It was awful. I regularly would call my mom and dad and tell them about what was going on with the new coach.

"Dad, he's killing us. Guys are throwing up all over the place! They're yelling at us the entire time. It's crazy!" I reported to him one night after he asked me how it was going. I won't lie, I was looking for a little sympathy. I should have known better.

"You guys need it!" my dad would reply back laughing. He was right too. We did need it. Coach Coughlin came in to find out who his players were going to be. He wanted to know who was willing to go the extra mile to make himself and the team better. That's what he needed to find out.

I was determined to show that he couldn't break me. He actually reminded me of the tough love my dad brought me up with, although the "love" part didn't come into play until much later on in this story.

I eagerly awaited spring ball when we would finally start playing football again, in pads, with none of this "who can run around the damn track the best" stuff anymore. But, as the old saying goes, "Careful what you wish for" rang absolutely true that entire month of his first spring practice, because we hit and hit and hit some more. We were in full pads the entire program! And he continued to run the shit out of us too. He never let up.

I ended up having a really good spring and won one of the starting inside linebacker jobs alongside Stephen Boyd, a sophomore who turned out to be one hell of a ballplayer and an eventual Pro Bowler in the NFL. However, like the rest of my teammates, I eagerly awaited the spring game, which would signal the end of the offseason. Thank God!

In the fall of 1991, our first season under Tom Coughlin, we lost our opening game on the road against Rutgers, of all teams. My mom and dad made the trip up from Florida, and my dad had a small reunion with some of his former teammates from his alma mater, Rutgers. I had a decent outing and ended up with 25 tackles. I chided my father after the game and asked who he was really rooting for, knowing all along the answer, as he would never betray his own blood.

The next week, Michigan, the #2 team in the country, came to Chestnut Hill, Massachusetts. We held our own for three quarters and then the plug got pulled out of the drain and we went down the toilet, fast, as the eventual Heisman Trophy winner, Desmond Howard, scored three touchdowns to lead the Wolverines to victory.

It was a nationally broadcast game on ABC, and Brent Mussberger and Dick Vermeil called the game. With my parents once again in attendance, I ended up having another big game with 19 tackles and received a ton of adulations from the legendary ABC announcers, which to me was a big time honor. However, a conversation back at my apartment with my dad was even more rewarding.

We always headed up to my on-campus apartment after the games. I say up because BC is built on a hill, hence the name of the town where it sits, Chestnut Hill. It is such a beautiful place. We first would head out to the tailgate parties right after, and BC had some pretty great tailgates, not huge mind you, but good quality partying with good people, tons of food and endless drink.

The festivities would then continue back at my place. I lived there with three other students, two of whom were teammates. We also let another student live in our oversized closet. He was not a "Jock" but a good guy anyway. His requirement to stay with us rent free was that he had to make sure that my parents got a great parking spot when they were in town. He would wake up early on Saturday mornings for home games, secure a spot and wait for my parents to arrive. My mom and dad loved those games at BC, and so did my brother Mike, who happened to be in town that weekend, too.

We would go to the apartment and have a bunch of people over, drinking beers and eating some more. My dad, of course, was always the life of the party. My friends and teammates loved to hang out with "Mr. Mac", as they called him. He would return the favor, telling his stories and showing them how he used to knock guys down in the ring. The more he drank the more exuberant he became. He was 71 at the time and always won them over.

In the middle of the get-together after the Michigan game, I felt my dad grab my arm and lead me out of the apartment and down the hallway. We stopped near the end so he could have a private word with me. My brother Mike saw what was going on and followed us to join in the conversation.

"You really stood out there today, Tom. You made a ton of tackles and some really big plays. I'm real proud of the way you play this game," he said as he touched his finger to my chest.

Mike chimed in, "That was fucking Michigan, Tommy. You guys almost had 'em. Those big hits on Ricky Powers on third and two and fourth and one in the third quarter were awesome!"

Dad piped in, giving Mike a quick, little sneer for he was miffed that he had been interrupted, "You're reading the plays before they develop. You are a leader out there. If you keep this up you will have a chance to play in the NFL, if you want it. I think you can make it!" he finished.

"Hell, yes, I want it. More than anything," I responded.

Lifting his glass in his hand, he saluted me, "Cheers, Tom. We are all real proud of you. I love ya, both of you boys." Dad wrapped up as we all shared a big hug and turned back towards the door to the apartment.

"Now, enough of that, where are we rocking tonight, Tommy?" Mike jumped in, as he usually did, always looking for a good time, as all of my friends and I were, as well.

That moment of acceptance from my father, the former tough two-way collegiate player, was the most gratifying to me. To hear my dad tell me that he thought I was good enough to play with the elite, in the NFL, was all I needed. I was smiling from ear to ear inside knowing that I had earned his approval once again.

I thrived under Coach Coughlin and his staff during my last two years at BC. When my college football career ended, I had the honor of being named a two-time, 1st team All-Big East linebacker along with two great linebackers from the University of Miami, Michael Barrow and Darrin Smith. I led the conference in tackles for two years and finished my college career as BC's all time leading tackler. After my senior year at Boston College, I was also named a third team All-American by one publication: Football News.

Although it started off a little rocky, my goals that I had set prior to my arrival on the Boston College campus had finally been met. I believed in myself and proved all of the naysayers from back home wrong. I had set out to make a name for myself while I was at BC and I had done it.

At the same time, if it wasn't for Tom Coughlin getting the job as Head Coach in my junior year, I don't know what would have happened to my career. His hiring gave me a clean slate, a new chance to impress, and I took full advantage of that opportunity. It was tough, no doubt, probably one of the toughest things I had ever experienced, but it was all well worth it.

Up until that point, everything had worked out. All of my hard work had paid off and I looked forward to what lay ahead for me and my football future. I knew what I wanted, something every young ballplayer dreams about: to make it into the NFL.

Too bad, I didn't realize at the time that the road to my dream would take an unexpected turn that I wasn't quite ready for. Nor could I have foreseen that later on down the road that Tom Coughlin would not only once again play a major part in my football career, but also play a major role in my life!

MY FIRST BOUT WITH ADVERSITY

I played my final game for BC in the Hall of Fame Bowl in Tampa, Florida on New Year's Day. We lost to the Tennessee Volunteers that day, but overall that year was a great experience. We had gone 8-3-1 in Tom Coughlin's second year as head coach. It was the only successful season as a team during my stay at Boston College, and my only bowl trip, so it ended on a positive note overall.

I made a ton of great friends and went through so much during my tenure, from a guy who was struggling, to being named one of the top players in the country at my position. I had also graduated with my business degree in Marketing from the Carroll School of Management, which made my parents even more proud that I accomplished that.

After that game, I focused on what my next goal was - to play in the NFL. Unfortunately, the NFL didn't see my future as clearly as I did. The NFL saw me as an overachieving, good college football player, but not some hot prospect for the next level.

I was not invited to the NFL combine, a yearly event held in Indianapolis in late February that draws the best college talent and all of the representatives from around the NFL. Every year it is a chance for college football players to showcase their skills, physically and mentally. It is the first leg in the evaluation process of getting drafted by an NFL team. They didn't feel like I was one of those prospects, so I stayed back at BC during that time.

Although I was disappointed, I took it in stride. "Screw 'em," I said to myself. I figured that I would just be ready when they came to our school for our annual "Pro Day", a day where juniors and seniors got tested in speed, agility, and strength at their respective schools.

I trained with my strength coach from BC for a good four to six weeks, working on all facets of what Pro Day testing would bring. I tested out okay that day. I came out of it feeling pretty good. I didn't run any kind of blistering 40 yard dash time, but it wasn't a slow one either. The 40 yard dash seemed to be the benchmark for the NFL to judge whether you were good enough or not. I never figured out why it was so important to run on a track in a straight line when football was so much more than that.

I thought it was about making plays, which I made plenty of, but I was wrong. The NFL is all about "potential" and "upside" when looking at the next year's crop of talent. It seemed like production didn't mean anything, which isn't totally true. You had to be a decent football player to be looked at, but you could be an average player who runs a fast 40 time for your position and all of a sudden your draft "stock" would go up.

Now, there were players who were excellent college players and who also fit the bill as to what the NFL was looking for. For example, Marvin Jones out of Florida State was a hot linebacker prospect, not only for his production on the field, but he also was extremely athletic and fast. He was rated as one of the top guys at his position, same position as mine, for the upcoming big day and rightfully so. He had tremendous "upside" and was a hell of a player.

I was a realist when it came to thinking about where I would end up in the NFL draft which takes place near the end of April every year. I knew I wasn't going to be a high round draft prospect, but I thought that I would get drafted in the later rounds during the second day of the NFL draft weekend. So, my expectations weren't extremely high, but I did anticipate being drafted at some point during the eight-round draft.

I went down to my parents' house in New Smyrna Beach for the big weekend. I didn't hold any kind of big party, but a couple of my family and some friends were over. My mom and dad were excited, wondering about all the possibilities for their son.

Mom had laid out chips, dip and lots of snacks. Dad had made sure that the fridge was full of beer. Me? I just wanted some team to draft me, to give me a chance. I was eager and anxious, hoping that a team had seen my play on the field as the benchmark of whether I could play in the NFL, rather than what some stopwatch read.

As Chris Berman of ESPN brought to a close the first day of the draft on the TV and my name had yet to be called, my dad got up and quickly announced that "Tomorrow is another day. Tommy's name will be called tomorrow."

Although I knew I wouldn't go in the top two rounds, I had wishful thinking that maybe I would sneak into the latter part of the fourth round, which would end the first day. I would be lying if I said I wasn't disappointed, but the next day would bring new hope and possibilities. I thought that some team had to feel that I was a player and could be an asset on their team.

The following day we all sat around the TV eagerly watching the final rounds of the draft. Time and time and time again names were called, but not mine. The mood in the house began to change. I was becoming somewhat dejected. Why didn't anyone recognize my talent and my skills? What the hell are they looking for, I thought to myself.

I started to pace around the living room as everyone was still riveted to the TV. More names were called and still I had not heard mine called or even received a phone call. Guys were being drafted that I had never even heard of.

For crying out loud, I had been on national TV making a name for myself. I had set records with a nationally recognized football team, and I wasn't being drafted. I was becoming crushed, devastated, and eventually totally demoralized. My whole life I had beaten the odds and had shut the naysayers up, but on the biggest day in my career I was being shown the door. I couldn't believe it.

When the last pick on the second day of the draft was called, thirty-seven linebackers had been picked in the 1993 NFL draft and #53 from Boston College wasn't one of them. Thirty-seven linebackers! Whew! That was a tough one to swallow.

The NFL threw a brick wall that smacked me right in my face and knocked me into a daze. It hurt. It hurt really badly. I was distraught, pissed off, you name it. My play on the field didn't amount to anything in their eyes. I averaged almost 15 tackles a game my last two years at BC as a fulltime starter, even ranked seventh in the country in the most tackles in a season at 165, a record that would hold at BC for over a decade. I was the defensive leader. I was smart, had great instincts, and was a tough, hard-nosed hitter.

To me a linebacker needs to have great instincts. Sure, you can make up for bad instinctive play with great speed, but I was the kind of player who recognized the play almost immediately as it was unfolding. Most of my tackles were done near the line of scrimmage, which is what counts in the game of football. Sometimes you'd see guys rack up a bunch of tackles in a game, but if the running back had made 10 yards down the field, then that defensive player wasn't doing his job.

I was so distraught and pissed off, I could have taken on the world. I continued to think, how could the NFL overlook what I had accomplished on the football field, and select some unknown linebacker because he ran a great 40 yard dash time and jumped to the moon in his vertical leap test, another test that wasn't exactly my strength?

Did that mean he was going to be a productive player in the NFL? The league's coaches and scouts apparently thought so. Don't get me wrong, you do have to be able to run in the NFL, but you don't have to be the fastest. Quickness, smarts, and toughness are more important than what you can run on the track, especially for linebacker's play.

I mean, it wasn't like I had to run a pass pattern 50 yards down the field like some wide receiver. That was for the cornerbacks and safeties to cover. But the NFL didn't see it that way. You either had "upside" or in their eyes you tapped out all of your potential from college and it seemed based on some stupid, ridiculous sprint. Do I sound bitter? I was, no doubt about it.

When the draft ended, I couldn't control my emotions in front of my family and friends. I had to go take a walk that night through my parents' neighborhood after it was all said and done, fighting back tears of disappointment, trying to gather myself.

When I returned to the house, I was greeted by my dad with a message saying that the New Orleans Saints had called and wanted to offer me a rookie free agent contract. My mood quickly changed to one of excitement for at least someone was going to give me a chance. I called them right back and gladly accepted their offer.

Again, I said to myself, "Screw 'em"! I would prove them all wrong and prove that I did in fact belong in the NFL. I told myself and my dad that the New Orleans Saints would not ever regret their offer. I was going to prove that they had made the right choice.

For the few weeks before I would have to report, I trained as hard as I could, working on my speed and quickness. I went to training camp in 1993 with the Saints, but before I left, my dad had some choice words of wisdom for his youngest child, "Keep your mouth shut and play your ass off! You are going against real men now, not some college boys. I know you can do it, Tom. Just be yourself and play the game the way you have always played it!" Dad said as he dropped me off at the airport, and once again let me know that he believed in me.

The Saints were loaded at linebacker with the late Sammy Mills and the great Vaughn Johnson starting on the inside and Ricky Jackson manning the outside. Their backups had been there a couple of years and were good special team players. Their defensive playbook was heavily weighted on linebacker strength. If I was to make this team, I would have to beat out the rest of the rookies and be the fifth linebacker on the roster.

Training camp was a tough slog, but I have to admit that it was nothing like what Coach Coughlin put us through at Boston College. My confidence was growing every day and I felt pretty positive that I would make the team. It all depended on how I played a real game on the field, not just in practice and drills, and I got the opportunity to play quite a bit in my first preseason in the NFL.

We traveled to Japan for our first game. The NFL had agreed to open the season with a preseason game in Japan to spotlight its "international appeal." I hated that trip. We flew fifteen straight hours into Tokyo, and being a rookie free agent, I held the lowest spot on the totem pole on that team.

I sat in the last seat in the back of the plane and hardly talked to anyone. The veterans only talked to you when you had made their team, which was a unique way of being accepted. It was a lonely trip, but once game time came, I got the chance to get in there and make some tackles, one of which came on a critical 3rd down, which proved to be a big stop.

I played in all five of the preseason games, the last of which was on Monday Night Football against the Chicago Bears in my new home base, the New Orleans Superdome. A couple of injuries to the starters gave me more playing time as I was moved up on the roster. I had a good game against the Bears, making a handful of good, solid tackles. I felt pretty good after that game, especially after some of the veterans came up to me and asked if I wanted to join them for a night out on the town.

It felt great thinking I was now being officially inducted as a part of the New Orleans Saints. We stayed out late in New Orleans that night celebrating with a bunch of "cheers" and offers of congratulations from some of the veterans for making the team. Unfortunately for me and my hangover, the Saints coaching staff didn't see it the same way.

The following morning the phone rang in my hotel room and I rolled over to pick it up. I ached from head to toe and in more ways than one. "Coach needs to see you and bring your playbook," was all I heard on the other end of the line.

I struggled to dress and shave without cutting up my face and took a cab to the stadium. I naively thought that they were going to tell me some really good news and that I had made the team. The meeting was brief and frankly impersonal. The Saints informed me that they were going to keep only four inside linebackers that year and I wasn't in the top four.

I was thanked and shown the door. My knees could hardly keep me upright. They were mush. To say I was devastated would be a huge understatement. I was crushed, ground into little pieces and spit out. I had done everything I could do. I had broken up key plays in almost every game I played in and I was cut. It was my first real bout of adversity in my life and in my football career. For the first time in my life, a goal had not been reached. I had failed in my quest.

I called my parents at their home. My dad was elated to hear from me. He excitedly reported that he had stayed up to watch the entire game with some friends and he had boasted that he could now say that his son was a member of the National Football League. When I told him the bad news, he was crushed too.

I could almost see his face over the phone as he let out a deep sigh. He truly felt that I was going to make it and that my play answered all of the questions that were laid in front of me from the start. I, too, had felt that I had done well, especially after the way I was greeted after my last performance by fellow members of the team. We were both wrong.

"What are you going to do now?" he asked immediately, somewhat tentatively.

"I'm going up to Chicago, Dad, and live with Mike and hope that my agent can find me a spot somewhere else," I replied. Dad just grunted: "Good luck." He was speechless, like me.

That call from my agent never happened. After a couple of weeks, I didn't receive any interest from another team, which later brought the weekly response from my dad, "Well, you better get a job."

I had my business/marketing degree from Boston College, but I wasn't quite ready to go into the real world. I became a professional bartender at two establishments in downtown Chicago, one that a BC alum had owned called The Fieldhouse, and another in the tourist district, Shenanigans, an Irish sports bar at Rush and Division Street.

I did have a little tryout with the Washington Redskins in the summer of 1994, a 10 day mini-camp. It came to no avail and I actually ran a pretty good 40 yard dash for them but it wasn't enough, so I went back to Chicago to get my old jobs back.

It wasn't a bad life. As the 1994 NFL season approached, I had just turned 24 years old. I had somewhat put to bed my dream of getting into the NFL. It just wasn't going to happen. I reunited with old high school friends, got to hang out with my brother, Mike, a bunch, and did what most 24 year olds did: party! I rebelled a bit, no doubt about it. For a little while, anyway. I worked out a little, as much as I needed to keep in some semblance of shape, and other than that, just had a great time.

But, I wasn't truly happy. Every Sunday, I worked a double shift at Shenanigans. They had televisions everywhere. It was a happening spot with always something going on. There were eight NFL games on those Sundays. I would see guys on the screen that I had played against in college and played with in a couple of All-Star games after my college career was over.

It killed me inside, not that I would let anyone else see it. But, my dream was dead. Sure, I had an impressive resume as a good college football player, but that was the highest accolade that I would ever receive.

I talked with my parents over the phone every week. I would also see them during the holidays whether we celebrated Christmas down in Florida or back up in Chicago.

Florida was great for my father. He woke every morning, did his weights, played golf, and hung out with his Joanie, either in their own living room with friends, or at some local establishments. After all he had been through in his life, it must have been a glorious feeling to have him pull up a beach chair, place his feet in the sand and fall asleep to the sounds of the ocean. He deserved it. They both did.

My relationship with my parents blossomed over those couple of years. In their eyes, I had bounced back from not realizing a long-held dream, taken it like a man and kept my view of life as glass half-full, not half-empty. I was ready to move on.

My dad's and my relationship made us more like buddies, good friends, although I always respected and honored his status as my father. We always had a bunch of laughs when we were together, whether it was wrestling around, talking about football or life, or just sitting and knocking a few drinks back. He was fun to be around, just like one of the guys.

My siblings and I enjoyed our time with mom and dad, either as a family or if we had just them to ourselves. Geno was like a magnet. He was easy to be drawn in to. He was the embodiment of what family is all about. And Joanie? She was just simply the best and Geno adored her!

At the end of summer in 1994, I made a decision to move back to Boston and use my BC connections to get a job. Yes, a real job in the real world.

The old college football star went back after failing the ultimate opportunity. I moved in with an old college girlfriend. She was a good girl and a good friend, who later on in life, after college and after we had broken up, succumbed to leukemia at the age of 29. God rest her soul.

Upon my arrival I started setting up interviews and also took a side job as a bartender at an old hangout. The Boston College Alumni Association was awesome. They had me set up with a half dozen interviews in no time and I eventually agreed to join a company that specialized in home health care and fitness products. It was a good sales gig, as I was to go to area colleges and pro sports teams and sell them products of the company. I had just recently verbally agreed to come on board when, early one morning, I got a phone call out of the clear blue sky.

"Tom, Coach Szabo. How are you doing?" asked my former linebacker coach under Coughlin at Boston College. My immediate thoughts were: "What the hell is he calling me for?"

"I'm doing all right. I'm living in Boston, about set to start a new job. How did you find me?" I asked as I tried to shake the cobwebs out of my head from my night's sleep.

"The athletic department at BC helped me track you down. Listen, I'll get right to the point. I don't know if you heard yet, but Coach Coughlin has been named the head coach for the new NFL franchise, the Jacksonville Jaguars. He's taking most of his staff from BC with him, including me. I called you to see if you might have interest in coming down for a workout. I can't promise you anything, but I think I can get you a look. Are you in any kind of shape?" he finished.

My heart began to race. "Sure," I responded, lying through my teeth.

"We'll be holding workouts in December. Can you get down here?" he asked.

"Yes, I can definitely get down there," I replied as I was now trying to control myself from busting at the seams.

"How about a place to work out? Is there anywhere you can go to get your workouts in?" he inquisitively asked.

"Yeah Coach, I believe I do," I responded, still trying to remain cool.

"Get in the best shape of your life, Tom, and we'll see you in December. I'll call you to let you know what date your workout will be on." Coach Szabo continued.

"I will, Coach, I will. Thanks for thinking about me," I responded, still in a state of shock over the news.

He added, "It's just a small shot, but it's a shot. I'll see you in a couple of months," and he hung up the phone.

"Holy shit," I said to myself. I was totally caught off guard by that phone call. I just sat there with the phone dangling in my hand. I wasn't even dressed yet, for crying out loud. I had long since thrown my cleats in the trash heap of football history and now, out of nowhere, there was a glimpse of light coming through a crack? I immediately called my parents' home in New Smyrna Beach.

"Hello?" my dad's voice answered on the other end of the line.

"Dad, it's me, Tom." I started off.

"Tommy, how are you? Did you get that job you were going after?" he asked.

"I did, Dad, but listen, you are not going to believe this. I just got off the phone with Coach Szabo from BC. He told me he's joining Coach Coughlin for the new coaching gig down in Jacksonville. He asked if I wanted to come down and work out for Coach Coughlin and the other coaches. It's only a workout and there's no guarantee that they'll sign me, but the offer is there," I stated, almost jumping out of my skin.

"Wow, that's great, Tom! I read that Coughlin was getting that job and wondered if there would be a connection for you. Coach Szabo must have really gone to bat for you," he responded back.

"Yeah, I guess he did. I was totally shocked. What do you think about me coming down there to stay with you and Mom and work out? I'll help around the house and do my part, but I'd really like to get out of here and come down with you guys and just concentrate on training and getting back in shape. What do you think?" I tentatively asked while trying to mask my excitement.

"What do I think? What do I think? Get your butt down here, boy. We've got a lot of work to do. Do you have enough money to make it down or do I need to send you a plane ticket?" he roared.

"No, I can make it, Dad. I'll see you in a few days." I finished saying as I hung up the phone. If anyone had seen me moments later, I would have been profoundly embarrassed as I raced around the living room in my underwear pumping my arms and shouting: "Yes, yes, YES!!!" like a five year old who had just opened his most coveted gift at Christmas.

I sat back on the couch in a tiny apartment in Lynn, Massachusetts, and time stopped for a minute. I had to catch my breath. I couldn't believe what had just happened. My dream had died, and now I was sitting there with one little sliver of a chance to make it happen. The challenge would be one that would be greater than any other I had faced in all of my 24 years of life.

In addition, although I didn't realize it at the time, my journey down south was much more than just getting in shape. It was also another opportunity to impress my father and grow even closer to him.

ME AND GENO TOGETHER

When I arrived in New Smyrna Beach in October of 1994, my dad was almost 74 years old. He wasn't your typical 74 year old, though. He still worked out every morning, right next to where I slept in the living room. When I had lived with Mike up in Chicago, he never had an extra bed, so I slept on his wooden floor, out by the TV. As long as I had a good pillow, the floor was fine with me, which is where I took up residence in my parents' home at night.

Geno was the kind of man who got up at the crack of dawn no matter what had taken place the night before and there was plenty that took place at Geno and Joanie's home. Every afternoon at 5 o'clock, it was time for "Happy Hour." Geno drank Canadian Club Whiskey with a "just a splash of water", as he would say, and my mom would join in with her own glass of scotch.

The funny thing was, when I arrived, Geno always wanted me to make the cocktails, no matter what I was up to because, in his mind, I was the "professional" bartender. Hey, he was right. I had been pumping beers and mixing drinks for any and everyone who pulled up a chair in the bar in Chicago for damn near two years. It was my "profession" at that time.

I was awakened every morning by the clanging of his old metal weight barbell, the same set he had when I was a kid. Oh, and he loved to grab my big toe and shake it until I woke up. He then would announce, "We've got a lot of running to do today, boy." I would always chime back, half asleep saying; "You've got a mouse in your pocket. What's this 'we' stuff?" That always got his big belly laugh to come out of his shorts.

He was a sight to be seen, really. Imagine this older gentleman, standing at about five foot eight inches tall (yes, he did shrink or maybe I just grew a lot), weighing about 220 pounds, with big arms and massive hairy fore-arms, wide, still strong looking shoulders, and this big, round hard belly like a "medicine ball" of old.

I'm sure a big part of the belly was from the nightly drinks, but he never passed up a meal either. He did work on his stomach, not that he was try-ing to get buff abs, just making sure he was strong and in reasonable shape. He would balance himself on his butt, cross his arms across his upper body and do these scissor kicks until his face turned purple. He would be wear-ing a pair of pajama bottoms, a v-neck T-shirt, unlaced high top gym shoes, and a pair of old garden gloves.

He would also, like clockwork, have these peanut butter and coffee stains on the front of his shirt. You see, he would wake up so he could get an early "snack" in while pumping his brand of iron. He thought he was fooling my mom, for when she would wake up, he would tell her how he was going to make "a little breakfast." She knew full well he had already had his first course of the day. She would call him out on it every time, and he would just give that laugh, time and time again. It was a daily routine that was always so funny.

So, there he would be, grabbing the old, fat barbell, and he would hoist it in front of his head and then in back of his head, military press style, time and time again. Then he would do a few sets of arm curls, and then finish with the scissor kicks.

As I woke up, I would sit up on the couch and watch him. I couldn't help but grin in amazement that he could still throw that weight around. Jeez, he was damn near 75 years old! He had about fifty pounds on the bar, which isn't a ton, but at 74 it sure was impressive to me. He was such a tough son of a gun, always pushing himself. I would head into the kitchen to get my day going and he would eventually follow me in there, always looking to be horsing around. It happened the same way, it seemed, every time.

At over 6'2" and about 250 pounds, I was much bigger than he was, so at his height he was always coming up to just under my shoulders. I would be holding the refrigerator door open looking for breakfast when he would come in. He would nuzzle his head under my arm, like a big old lion, and give me some soft rabbit punches into my side. Of course he was feeling good from his workout, and he would say every single time with his belly laugh, "I used to run through guys like you in the ring," or "You're lucky it's not me you're going against."

I would turn into him and we would start to wrestle. We were always wrestling around, always laughing through it all. And you know what? He was strong! He would give me all I could handle. Not that I would try my hardest, but he wasn't very easy to move. We would move all across the kitchen, banging into the counters, the table, the fridge, whatever was in our way.

Then my mom would wake up, come out to the kitchen and cry out, half in jest, "Will you two knock it off? Gene, he's much bigger than you. Leave him alone. Tommy, let go!" she demanded. "Aw, I'm not afraid of him. I used to chop down guys much bigger than him. Plus, he started it!" he would counter back with a big smile on his face, along with some peanut butter still smudged on the edge of his mouth.

Then we would do it all over again until Joanie's tone was one where we knew it was time to really knock it off. He would always get the last word in: "You're lucky she was here to save ya," laughing the whole time.

I loved it. I loved it all. It was like two old college buddies messing around. We would hang out quite a bit during my stay with them. In between my workouts, whether running or lifting, or both, we would play golf, go out to eat with my mom and brother Bob, or just sit at the local pub and down a few brews. Plus, he loved to announce to anyone who would listen: "This is my son Tom, the football player." He was a proud father and I reciprocated that feeling as his son at every moment I could.

I would also accompany him to his doctor's visits. When we would arrive he would introduce to me to anyone who would listen, showing me off, so to speak, although in my mind there wasn't that much to show other than an unemployed football player. He had skin cancer for years from sitting in the sun throughout years in his earlier life. He would literally have to get the cancer cut right out of him. It was in his head, his hands and arms, even the tops of his feet. It looked so awfully painful. But he never complained. He never let anyone see if it really bothered him or not.

We played a good bit of golf. My parents loved the game, especially Geno. He would play almost every day. Their rented duplex was located on the first tee box of a public golf course in sunny central east Florida. He could literally walk out of the back porch and tee it up. To him, it was like he was at some beautiful Caribbean resort.

We would have some memorable times out there on the course. One time I hit a nine iron on a par three and the club flew right out of my hands. It went farther than the ball and out of bounds over a bordering fence. Geno took off down the side of the fairway, in disbelief, saying, "How in the hell do you do these things?" My mom would just sit there in the golf cart and laugh. I was always breaking something in the house or out on the course. I was a "bull in a china shop" to the fullest extent.

One day I came out of the bathroom at their house and informed Geno that I had broken the toilet seat, not at the attachment to the toilet but the seat itself. It had snapped right in half. I told him it was "on accident", and he shook his head and pounded his fist on the kitchen table and barked: "Tommy, how in the world did you do that?"

He laughed most of the time, but I am sure he wasn't pleased with me messing around with his supposed quiet and peaceful retirement. I would always make him laugh and say: "Dad, sometimes you've got to adapt and improvise," one of our favorite lines from an old Clint Eastwood movie.

Geno loved what golf stood for; the honesty and integrity it took to play the game the right way. He was a stickler for etiquette, always was, since I was a teenager joining him on the course. He made sure his boys knew what kind of etiquette was required on the golf course.

At his advanced age, he was still a pretty good golfer. He couldn't hit as far as he used to, but it was always down the middle of the fairway and his short game and putting were better than average.

Me? Oh, shit, I was a meathead by trade. Geno would always tell me to swing easy and I would try to do it that way, but a switch always clicked from the top of my backswing to the time I would try and connect with the ball and then "bam". I just wanted to see how far the ball would go, even if it flew into the neighborhood or on another golf hole. He would just shake his head and walk down the fairway.

"This is a game of finesse and skill, not how far you can hit a ball. Will you get that into your thick head?" In his later years, I would outdrive him, but his game of chipping and putting was his forte. It was a classic tale of the tortoise and the hare. He would always catch up and beat me with his lower score.

Mulligans? He would bust my balls if I tried to take one. Dropping a ball out of an unplayable position without taking a penalty was completely unforgivable, unless he did it for himself. That somehow was acceptable.

Although I loved being with my mom too, I cherished the times when it was just my dad and me out there. We would talk about life, family, football and, of course, the opportunity that lay ahead for me. I really didn't care if I played well or not. I was focused on getting my body into the best possible condition, plus I never thought that lifting heavy weights and golf went together. At least that was my excuse and I stuck with it.

It was an interesting, dynamic reality. We were fifty years apart in age, but we had so much in common and I could connect with my dad in so many ways - as my father, my friend, my mentor, and sometimes my friendly competitor. He was always telling me about "life's lessons", and I always enjoyed hearing about them. However, just like our golf games went, our generation gap was the polar opposite.

"Aren't you going to look for your ball?" he would ask as I duck hooked another ball into the woods.

"Naw, I've got a bunch more in my bag. I'll just hit another one up here," I would respond.

"That's the trouble with you kids today. You are so spoiled. Everything is handed to you on a silver platter. You never would have made it in my day," he always proclaimed.

"Dad, it's just one ball. It's worth about a dollar. I'll just hit another one," I would reply.

With that he would grab one of his irons and take it with him into the brush. He used it for a little protection, just in case a snake or another critter was hanging around in the weeds. This is the same man, who would crawl under his house and throw moth balls at pygmy rattlesnakes to get them out of there.

The whole time he was in the woods I could hear him quipping to himself, "One dollar you say? You'd think it was worth a penny for Christ's sake. Back in my day we used to get a sandwich and a cup of soup for five cents!" After a few minutes, where I couldn't see him but could definitely hear him, he would emerge with about 10 balls nestled in the basket he made with his golf shirt stating, "Like I said, you kids would have never made it my day."

We'd laugh along the way back to the clubhouse to grab our 19th-hole brew, which was a staple in our golf outings. When my mom did accompany us out there, she knew he and I had something special going on.

GETTING TO WORK

My running workouts were held at a local high school football stadium that was located near my parents' home. I tried to run in the hottest part of the day in order to get the most out of my workout, and the heat would help me get in tip-top shape. Although it was October, the sun was still very hot. The field was run by the park district and was in reasonably good condition. There would be no one around except for a couple of maintenance workers. They agreed to let me run there pretty much any time I wanted. And run I did!

My dad and I would arrive right before noon on most days. Geno would wear his usual Florida attire: a golf shirt with his sleeves pulled up high, khaki shorts, and pair of hi-top sneakers with the laces undone, of course. He would also wear his favorite flimsy, cloth floppy hat, the kind that you could get wet to cool you off. I would park his car, open the trunk, and grab his beach chair and umbrella, along with my cleats and a handful of screw-drivers.

I carried most of it, so Geno wouldn't have to, not that he couldn't. I just felt like he was doing me a favor, sitting there in his chair, timing sprint after sprint, in the hot sun. I used the screwdrivers driven into the turf as yard markers. I had a long measuring tape that would help me mark off 10, 20, 40, and 60 yards. The plan was for Geno to sit at the finish line and bark out my times after each run.

A good "40 time" for a middle linebacker in the NFL was around 4.7 seconds. Now, there were plenty of guys who could run a lot better than that. A 4.6 was considered ideal, while a 4.5 or lower would be considered really special.

For me, a realistic goal was to run around or under a 4.8. Keep in mind that we trained on grass, which would be the surface for my workout with Jacksonville. Running on grass added around a tenth of a second or so to your real time (that on a track). If I could consistently get to a 4.8 on grass, that would be a great time for me. It would be faster than Coach Coughlin would have ever seen me run at Boston College. There, I usually ran around a 4.9, and that was on BC's track at the stadium.

I could run and I was quick, but I didn't have what they call in the NFL "closing speed", meaning that I wasn't going to run anyone down from behind. However, one thing I never did quite understand was the fact that if I had to run 40 yards to make a tackle, then the defensive line and I weren't doing our jobs. But, the 40 yard dash was a gauge for the NFL, and still is. So be it, that's the business and some unknown, out-of-work linebacker wasn't going to buck the system.

I had grown physically since Coughlin and the BC coaches had last seen me. I was a little bit taller, heavier and also stronger. I had read somewhere that some athletes don't hit their athletic prime until around the age of 25-29. That was definitely true in my case. It's a great feeling too. The easiest way to explain it is this: it's when you mature physically and just carry your weight a lot easier. You get bigger but also faster, naturally. Of course, you have to train to achieve it, but once you get there, you feel it every day. Some guys reach it earlier and some keep it going later, into their early 30s. And then there are the guys who are just freaks of nature and are born with tremendous natural ability and keep it for most of their entire athletic career.

Me, I was two years removed from playing ball, but I felt good where I was at, athletically speaking, but my hurdle was that I had to break the label of being too slow for the NFL. It was something I was eager and determined to overcome. The only way of breaking it was to run an impressive 40 for the Jaguars. Without breaking that label, I would be certainly sent home. Of that there was little doubt.

I would run a series of the shorter dashes first, the 10 and 20 yard dashes and finish up with a ton of the 40s and 60s. The shorter ones were used to get off to a good start and the longer ones, especially the 60s, were so I would run through the 40 yard marker with no problem. It would make the 40 seem shorter physically and psychologically.

The 40 yard dash had always been a weird thing for me. In the past, I would psyche myself out of it. It felt like the finish line was a mile away and I wasn't going to make it. It might have been a lack of confidence, probably was. I never lacked confidence while I was on the football field playing, but when I lined up for the 40, my mind would start racing. But that was in the past. My confidence grew every day for I was seeing the results of all the hard work I was putting in. The best part about of the whole thing though was having my good buddy Geno out there with me.

My running workouts lasted for over an hour each and every time. Geno would sit there at the end of each sprint and tell me where my times stood. He would cheer me on and, as usual, the old coach would come out in him.

"We need to do one more," he would repeatedly say after each sprint, especially towards the end of a long, arduous workout, having pushed me time and time again.

I would be gasping for air, sweating profusely, and would breathlessly respond back half jokingly: "What's this 'we' stuff you keep talking about? You've got a mouse in your pocket?"

He would bark back: "Watch it, boy! I'll get out of this chair and fill the air with a bunch of left hooks!"

"You're going to need some help," I would spout back in a smartass, but friendly manner.

"Just get back up there before I knock you on your ass," he would grumble jokingly.

I would turn around and half jog, half walk, back up to the starting line, cursing under my breath about the heat, the sun, and the fact that I was the only son-of-a-bitch working out here. When I would reach the starting line and turn around, I would see Geno sitting there in his beach chair and it would always bring a smile to my face.

He presented quite a sight for sore eyes with the bottom of his belly sticking out of his shirt. He always held the umbrella in one hand, blocking out the sun's rays, while holding the stopwatch in the other hand. Dammit, he was right the whole time. It was "we".

He wanted success for me as much or even more than I did. It may be hard to believe, but I know it was true. Maybe it was because he never took his game to the next level although he certainly had the skills to do so, from what I read and was told. I remember him saying that there wasn't enough money in the pro game back in his day.

He chose to go into business with Prudential instead. I don't know, maybe he had some regrets, or maybe he was reliving some of his past while watching his youngest son attempt to capture a dream for the final time. Whatever it was, it didn't matter. He supported me and cheered me on the whole time. I loved him even more for that.

He would raise his hand that was holding the stopwatch to show me that he was ready for me to take off. I would try to stay low in my start and finish strong at the end. I could tell over time that I was getting faster, but still not where I thought I needed to be.

He would read me my times, and if I wasn't happy with what the stopwatch read, I would question him on his timing technique. This was a source of constant ribbing and sometimes genuine frustration. I was always reminding him, "Start the watch when my hand leaves the ground and stop it when the first part of my body touches the finish line."

He would always shout back mocking anger: "I fought in the Great World War, for crying out loud. I've got years of pilots training. Don't you tell me how to work this thing!"

When my workouts were finished for the day, I would grab all of our belongings and we would head back to the car.

"You're looking real good, Tom. Keep working hard and good things will happen for you. I'm real proud of you." he said many times. And then he would follow up by trying to ruffle my feathers again by saying: "You'd be no match for me though." That would always end up with me dropping everything and we would playfully wrestle for a bit again and again.

I was becoming more and more focused as my workout date for Coach Coughlin grew closer. I was very encouraged as I was seeing the results from all of our hard work. My body fat was decreasing. I was feeling stronger and faster than I had been before.

My flexibility was second to none, as I continued to stretch every morning and evening. I was feeling good, but still not good enough in my own mind. I was always thinking about my next workout, my next meal, anything and everything that would make me better prepared for the fast approaching chance of a lifetime.

The evenings at my parents' home were a typical McManus family night. I would make the drinks, we would have dinner, and then retire to the living room to watch some television. In all honesty my mom and dad would retire, but I always had more work to do. While they were watching TV, I would sneak out to the street and get in some more wind sprints. I liked being out there by myself in the dark of the night. It was refreshing and it allowed me to be reflective on what was about to come.

I would talk to myself and push myself. Self-discipline was never a problem for me. I credit that to my upbringing. I never needed some coach or someone else to get me going. My motor was going all the time. I knew what it took and I didn't need any motivation from anyone. All of my motivation came from wanting to succeed.

When I was in high school and later in college, success on the field came somewhat easily, but I always had to work for it. I wasn't the kind of athlete who could just get up and fly down the track, or dunk a basketball at any given moment. I was a good athlete, just not an elite one, so everything that I achieved was pretty much through hard work.

Case in point, when I was in high school, my coach gave me a jump rope to better my athleticism. It didn't come easily right away. I had to work at it. I'm not talking about just jumping up and down with both feet like a girl skipping rope. It was more like the kind of work that a boxer would do, like hopping on one foot and changing to the other simultaneously, running sideways while jumping rope, or performing jumping jacks and scissor kicks while whipping the rope over my body.

It took me a while before I could master it, and I had to endure the many welts it would leave on my back when I would mess up, but I worked and worked and worked at it and until it eventually became very easy. From that point on I could always jump rope with impressive speed and precision.

My flexibility didn't come naturally, either. That came from a lot of hard stretching which I learned from an old Tae Kwon Do master who taught me how important flexibility was, especially with Tae Kwon Do, "his sport".

While in college, I had joined a local martial arts school to better myself as an athlete. I can remember being told that my hips were too tight, meaning that when I changed direction, it wasn't with a fluid motion. It looked more like a struggle. Well, the only way to fix that was to loosen them up. One of the ways I had to do that was taught by my instructor.

Imagine sitting on your knees and then lying back, with your butt eventually resting in between your ankles and then laying your back on the ground. At first, it hurt like hell and then little by little I would get farther and farther back. It wasn't pleasant, but it was something that I was determined to accomplish. Before too long, I was watching TV in that stretching position. I must have looked like a contortionist all twisted up while watching the tube.

I could eventually also perform the splits as well. My dad would always commend me on that accomplishment. It loosened up my hips and made my Tae Kwon Do kicks pretty impressive too. I actually ended up receiving my first degree blue belt, which was about half the way to a black belt. I remember my instructor telling me, "When you're done with football, come back and see me." He thought I had a future in his sport. That wasn't my path, of course, but I welcomed that training to better myself, and I enjoyed the competition against the other students.

The nights working out on my parents' street had become almost spiritual. When you are facing an uphill battle or ready to take on something that seems to be against the odds, reflecting and feeling like it's you against the world is a very powerful emotion. I reveled in that feeling.

The fire in my belly came from having been told I wasn't good enough. It was something that I always had to overcome, from high school all the way up until this seminal moment. It was like "I will prove them all wrong" was inscribed on my forehead, or at least that was my attitude. Fuck 'em, I would tell myself over and over again. No one could measure my heart, only I could, and I was ready to take everything on and prove everyone wrong.

The street outside my mom and dad's house was very dark at night. Other than a couple of dim street lamps and the stars and moon in the sky, there wasn't much light. I loved it. I would mark off my 20, 40, and 60 yard markers using neighbors' mailboxes as estimated distances, and I used my parents' mailbox as the finish line.

There was a light post just across the street from my parents' home so the finish line could just be seen. I would perform sprint after sprint. I could run forever in that night air. It was a lot more refreshing than when the sun was out and it didn't take as much out of me.

After a little while, like clockwork, my dad would come out. It was usually about nine or ten o'clock so he usually had a few in him. He would have his drink in his hand, grab a chair, and sit down at the end of the driveway.

My brother Bob, when he was around, would occasionally join us with his Bud Light. He thought it was funny how Geno would sit there and watch and make comments. I would perform some agility drills in front of the driveway and Geno would say, "Good movement, good movement," something my brother would ape, which always gave us a good laugh.

Geno would rattle his ice in his empty glass, a sign that he was finished, and hold it up. Of course, being his "professional bartender", he would ask if I would go make him another, which I always obliged.

I would run inside the house in between sprints and fill up his glass, which always resulted in my mom giving me the 'rolling of the eyes' look. It was all good fun, though. The man was 74 years of age and he deserved whatever he wanted. Although his drinking sometimes bothered me when I was younger, at this point in his life, he could drink as much as he wanted for all I cared. He earned that right, at least in my opinion.

The memories from those nights are priceless. There I was, working my ass off and enjoying it, and I had a peanut gallery watching my every move. But even more than that was what went on during those nightly workouts. I'll always remember one particular evening. I was in the middle of my workout. My dad was in his chair as usual and my brother Bob sitting on the back bumper of his car. Geno had more than a few in him and was feeling no pain.

"You want me to time you?" he asked with a wry smile on his face.

"Can you actually see the stopwatch?" I countered in a smartass kind of way.

"I've got pilot's eyes, unless you forgot. Just get up to the starting line, before I get out of this chair," his common rebuttal, especially when he was in this particular state of mind.

I grinned and snickered, "Yeah, yeah, yeah", as I headed to the starting point, a few mailboxes up the street. I raised my hand to signal I was ready and Geno did the same back to me to signal that he was ready too. I took off and headed down the street in the dark of the night. I ran through the finish line and jogged back to where he and Bob were sitting. I was eager to hear my time for it felt like it was going to be a good one. After all, with all of the sprints I did, I could usually tell what felt fast and what didn't. This particular one felt really, really good.

"What time was that?" I asked excitingly as I approached. It took Geno a couple of seconds to get the light just right before he blurted out my time.

"Four point two five," he proudly proclaimed.

With that I threw my arms up in frustration. "Dad, I don't run anything close to that. I'd be one of the fastest wide receivers in the NFL with that kind of time. Dammit, I thought you knew how to run that thing," I blurted out as I looked at Bob in disbelief.

"Hey, that's what the stop watch says, Tom!" Geno countered back defiantly.

"Dad, I don't run anything close to that. Are you doing it right, like I've told you how since day one?"

"The hell I am, and don't you go telling me how to work one of these things. I flew to hell and back working things like this. Just get your ass back up to the starting line and run another one!" he roared, laughing so hard that some saliva dribbled out of the side of his mouth. Then as I turned to go up the street muttering obscenities under my breath, he asked with a big smile:

"Hey, but before you do, will you run inside and make me another? And hurry up will ya? We've got some more work to do!"

"There you go with that we shit," I rapidly replied as I grabbed his glass and ran inside. In an instant I was back out there handing him his drink and pleading, "Would you please get it right this time for crying out loud? I need an accurate time, Dad!"

"You worry about getting back up there and I'll worry about the timing. And watch your tongue boy, or I'll get up out of this chair and fill you with left hooks," he declared with a smirk on his face.

"Oh, yeah? You're definitely gonna need some help with that!" I responded back, still a little miffed, but also seeing the humor in it all.

"Bob will help me, won'tcha Bob?" he jokingly pleaded as he turned to my older brother.

"I'm not messing around with that horse," Bob exclaimed putting his hands up.

"Yeah, you're probably right", Geno said with a laugh. "Now Tommy, get back up there and let's run another one."

I finished that workout with a 4.85, which was pretty decent considering it was around my twentieth attempt. I jogged back and grabbed Geno's chair and as we all walked into the house Geno said, in the fashion only he could deliver, "You're working real hard, Tommy. If you keep pushing yourself like today and tonight, we are going to make it this time, I just know it," he proudly stated.

"Now, don't you go all mushy on me, Dad," I said back as I put my arm across his broad shoulders as we all headed into the house. My workout in Jacksonville with the Jaguars coaching staff was fast approaching and I felt like I was ready.

I really believe I earned my dad's respect that fall. He saw how focused I was and how hard I had worked, but we both knew that may not be enough. I might have impressed my father, as well as Bob, but the one man whom I had to impress and who held all the cards to my fate was Tom Coughlin.

ONE WORKOUT, ONE SHOT

My parents let me borrow their car for the hour and a half ride up to Jacksonville, Florida. I was not familiar with Jacksonville, never having been there before. The farthest north I ever traveled from my parents' home was Daytona Beach, and that was usually during Spring Break, during its heyday.

As I approached the city limits off I-95, I saw the small skyline that the city presented. I can remember thinking that I "didn't even know there was a city up here." The city glistened in the sunlight reflecting off the St. Johns River, which runs through the middle of downtown.

I arrived at a local high school called Bishop Kenny. When I parked the car and headed into their athletic locker room, it felt like a small reunion. Coach Coughlin had brought a good part of his staff from Boston College, including the man who had apparently created this whole chance going for me, my old linebacker coach, Steve Szabo. I hadn't seen most of these men for over two years, so it was great to see them all. After our initial hellos, it was time to get to work.

There were about twelve other hopefuls that day at Bishop Kenny, but no one I had known or heard of, for that matter. But, they were there just like me trying to capture a long-held dream. People don't realize how hard it is to actually make it to the NFL. Many who leave high school leave with the status of being the best player on their team, or even in their conference, or in their respective hometowns.

Everyone knows you from your hometown and everyone thinks you are a stud on the field, and that your future is already set. Hopefully you get to go to college to play football, if you're lucky. Some are even fortunate enough to garner a football scholarship. But when they get to the collegiate level, they are surrounded by guys who came from a similar situation, guys who had achieved very well in high school.

Many of them become your college teammates. They were All-Conference, All-City, All-State, just like you were. Then when they try to go to the next level after a college football career, the NFL, they're playing and trying out with the best from the collegiate ranks.

Just in Division 1-A alone, the highest ranking division in all of college sports, there were 119 teams in 1993. There are approximately 85 players on each team, with about ten percent of those being what people consider elite college football players. But then, many of the guys get hurt, don't make acceptable grades, or in some cases get into trouble or just fall out of favor.

Out of all the players in Division 1-A football, approximately 10,000 players throughout the country, and that's a conservative number, do you know how many players got drafted in the NFL in 1993? Only two hundred and twenty three college players!

When looking at the odds and the percentages of how many college football players get to the next level, it is quite astounding, at least for those who were drafted. It comes to about two percent. Two percent of all Division 1-A college football players get drafted by the NFL! Two percent! Then you have to factor in the guys who don't get drafted and are trying to make the team as an undrafted rookie free agent, like I was when I tried out for the Saints.

Typically, there are 85-90 guys who go to an NFL training camp every year. Most high round draft picks end up making the team, for sheer politics. A team that drafts a player in the early rounds and invests money in him with a significant signing bonus, (the only money that is guaranteed to that player), is going to give that player the most opportunity to not only make the team, but to also play a significant role on that team. No owner is going to shell out big money to have a guy sit on the bench, especially in the first couple of years. Out of those 85 players who enter training camp, only 53 actually make the squad.

I had an even more difficult a challenge to overcome. Now, think about my situation. I had been out of football for two full seasons. I was labeled a "street" free agent, meaning I had been out "on the street", and not recruited or signed on anyone's team, which meant I had even greater odds to make it than even the undrafted rookie free agent players. That was also pretty much the same song and dance for those other players that were at Bishop Kenny High School that day.

The odds were stacked against me. I knew that going in, but I had one thing going for me. I truly believed that I should have been playing this whole time. There was no uncertainty in my mind. I knew I could play this tough and physical game. What I didn't like about that day's tryout was that there was no hitting involved.

No one was going to meet the running back at the line of scrimmage and get the chance to knock the snot out of him. We would just be running around in shorts, something that was never my strength up to that point, but I was ready. I was older, more mature, and felt better physically than I ever had before. The workouts that I had with Geno, all the hard work, were about to be put to the test.

After being measured and weighed, which I was six feet two and 247 pounds, the Jacksonville Jaguar staff put all of us hopefuls through a series of agility runs. Agility tests consisted of the 20 yard shuttle, where you straddle a line that was situated in middle of 10 yards with your hand on that yard line. You had to run 5 yards one way, touch a line, run 10 yards back through the starting point to another line, then touch that line and run back to the starting point. It was a measure of quickness and change of direction, something that I was always pretty decent at, but this time around I felt even better thanks to my months of training with Geno.

We also had to perform agility drills that were pertinent to our specific positions. For linebackers we had to do more change of direction drills, on the coach's command, like dropping back into pass coverage and seeing how we broke on the football when it was thrown by the quarterback.

They were important drills. They helped measure how fluidly you ran. Football is a game where you have to change direction on an instant's notice. If you are too tight in the hips, then you will have trouble changing direction at the speed of the NFL level, which is ultimately very fast.

All NFL football players are good to great athletes, even when some body types don't look like it. A big ole defensive tackle might have a huge belly and weigh up to 340 pounds, but watch him move in small spaces. If a defensive lineman only had to move about 10 yards (which is on average the most they should have to move on any given play) you can see just how quick and athletic he actually is. When you get him out into the open field or watch him try to chase down a running back, most of them don't get there. The best do, but most don't. However, in that short distance between the tackles, he will show some very impressive athleticism and surprising speed.

These drills were important, but the test that I needed to really impress the coaches was the 40 yard dash time. On the last occasion where I was timed by these former Boston College, and now Jacksonville Jaguar coaches, I ran around a 4.9 to a 5.0, which is considered pedestrian for a linebacker in the NFL. I was eager and very anxious to see where I stood against my fellow competitors. I got in my sprinter's stance, and I do use the term "sprinter" very loosely.

As I was poised to run on the grass field, anxiety crept into my mind. "This is it" raced through my brain. It was now or never. My whole life had come down to 40 yards of grass in a city where I had never set foot before.

The key to the start in the 40 yard dash is to come out low and fast much like you may see in a 100 yard dash. I always tried my best to do just that. The other key is to push through the finish line, not just run to it. The thinking there is if you just ran to the finish line, you might pull up before the full 40 yards are covered, which would give you a slower time. You also need to try to relax your body and not tense up.

I took a big deep breath and on the signal took off. I pumped my arms and legs as fast as I could. I ran through the finish line and pulled up from my sprint about 20 yards down the field, where all the coaches were standing with their stopwatches. I turned around and walked up to their spot, wondering, hoping, and praying that I had run a good time. When I arrived at the scene, one of the coaches looked at me and said, "4.83".

A 4.83! On grass! That equated to a mid-4.7 on a track! My heart skipped a beat. To me it was like winning an academy award. I had never run that fast before, which to be honest was only average for a linebacker in the NFL, but for me it was huge! A sense of satisfaction raced through my body.

All the work that Geno and I had done came racing into my mind. I couldn't wait to get home and tell him the news. However, there was something I had to face next. Like with any job, I had to have an interview with the boss. This boss, of course, was Coach Coughlin, and much to my surprise, this interview was equally as important as my 40 yard sprint time.

He commended me on my speed and agility tests, but it wasn't like he was giving me a bunch of "high-fives" or anything like that. He was impressed that I had kept in shape over the past couple of years, although I knew it was more like the past couple of months, but he didn't need to know that.

He also expressed concern at the same time. He wanted to know what had happened to me. Then he asked some very penetrating and difficult questions for me to answer. Why wasn't I playing in the NFL? Why should he give me a chance when all other NFL teams sealed my fate as not good enough and rendered me unemployed?

"Coach, I don't know those answers. All I know is I hoped for one more shot, one more chance to realize my dream of playing in the NFL. If I am not good enough, I will take it like a man and there will be no hard feelings, no regrets, just a sense of gratitude for having been given the opportunity," I firmly stated to my old college coach.

He sat there for a couple of moments and just kind of looked at me. I couldn't tell what was really going through his mind, but I knew I had come to impress and on some level I felt as though I accomplished that goal.

"Let me think about it. I've got to see who else we have coming in here and evaluate more talent. I'll give you a decision in the near future," he stated as he wrapped up the interview in his typical stoic manner. His poker face never gave a hint about what he was really thinking. It used to drive me crazy. Nevertheless, I had to think of a calm, relaxed response.

"Fair enough," I responded, not showing the disappointment in not being offered the chance for a job right then and there.

We looked each other in the eyes and shook hands as I walked out of his office. After I said my goodbyes and thank you's, especially to Coach Szabo for giving me the opportunity, I walked to my parents' car and headed back down south, eager to tell them all that went on.

I had a sense of achievement, however small, for I knew I ran well, not a blazing time by any means, but I had left an impression. I could tell that. I was bigger, faster, and more athletic than what they remembered from my days at BC, but the question remained churning in my mind: Was I impressive enough to earn a chance to be invited to the first ever training camp of the new Jacksonville Jaguars?

I arrived home to tell my mom and dad all that went on. They had a zillion questions, but when I told Geno what my 40 time was, it brought a huge smile to his face. He gave me a big hug and said,

"Well, Tom, you did all that you could. You had a goal, you worked your ass off to reach that goal and I'm damn well proud of you. All you can do now is wait and see if you get a phone call. How about a beer? You deserve it!"

He was right, as usual. It was out of my hands now. I did all I could possibly do to fashion my fate as a professional football player. The only thing I had to do was to keep working out and wait to see if I would get that call.

But, as the old Tom Petty song says, "The waiting is the hardest part". For me it seemed an eternity.

THE CALL OF A LIFETIME

The next couple of weeks were exasperating. I awoke every morning, as always, to the sounds of Geno's metal weights clanging on the living room floor. The noise that came from his daily workout sounded like a construction pile driver. One of his exercises was similar to what was called the "dead lift", which is where you start with the barbell on the floor, pick it up by bending your knees and lifting the weight off the ground.

He then added his own exercise along with it and turned it into a military push press over his head, which also made a rattling noise of the weights on the barbell. He then would let it drop back down to the floor again with a loud clang!

Imagine this; Chink bang! Chink bang! Over and over again. I could always hear the first couple of clangs, but I was still somewhat asleep. I think it was around midway through his set of this specific exercise that I would awaken. Can you imagine hearing that every morning as your alarm clock? Geno was the same as he had always been, upbeat and positive, clamoring to spit out his favorite words every time he saw one of my eyes partially open: "We need to do some more running," for that day's portion of my workout.

I wasn't as positive. I mean, I kept my spirits up because my nature had always been to hold a "glass half-full" look at life, plus I knew Geno wouldn't ever let me get down. But I didn't feel confident that I was going to get a contract offer. I went to the gym and to the field every day and still worked my butt off, but I felt like I was in purgatory. I didn't know my fate, which had never been something that I was good at handling. It was tough not knowing what was going to happen. I had always had a mission, a goal, a task, a future. At this time I really had nothing.

To add to my frustrations, New Smyrna Beach was a small beach town and everybody seemed to know everyone's business. I remember when my parents first moved down there. Mike and I always had the same winter, spring, and summer breaks from college. He and I would work out together and on many a night head down to the local taverns with Bob and Moira in tow.

And on occasion, Geno and Joanie would come, as well. There was one gym and about three bars in the whole town. I remember our first time in the gym. People were staring at us like "Who the fuck are these two new guys?" Being from Chicago and having the kind of upbringing that Geno instilled in us, I always gave the same look back.

Most of the people we got to know turned out to be really good people and we made a bunch of friends. They knew that I played football at Boston College, and they always kept an eye open when I was on TV, which frankly wasn't that often. Every time we came back we went to the same gym and the same bars and over time people got to know the McManus family.

When I came back from my travels to Jacksonville without an offer, it felt like I had kind of failed again. Not like I did with the New Orleans Saints. It was on a smaller scale, but it still sucked. It also seemed like I was asked daily if I was going to get a shot by someone, somewhere in the town. At first I tried to be polite and say something like: "Thanks for asking but I don't know anything, yet." But, after dozens of similar scenarios, I was getting kinda grumpy and I felt like taping a cardboard sign on the front and back of my body that read, "No, they didn't offer me shit".

Once again, I took it in stride the best I could. All I could do was what I'd done my whole life, to keep fighting until the end. I knew that this would be my last attempt, whether the Jaguars signed me or not. The days seemed long and at night I had a hard time getting to sleep. I often stayed up half the night. When the mind races like my mind was racing during those weeks without a phone call, it was tough to lay my head on a pillow and just crash.

I was performing my normal routine one day shortly thereafter at the local gym when the owner came up to me and announced, "Hey, Tommy, your dad is on the phone." I was into my workout, so I didn't really think that much of it. I thought he needed his car back, which I always borrowed, to take care of an errand or go to a golf game or to a doctor's appointment, or something of that nature. When I pulled the receiver up to my ear he told me some interesting, but uncertain news.

"The Jaguars organization just called. They're trying to track you down. Coach Coughlin wants to speak with you," he announced.

"Well, did they say anything?" I asked.

"No," he replied. "They didn't say anything. They just gave me a number to give you to call up there. He's expecting your call."

Just like during my interview, typical Coughlin, never wanting to tip his hand! I didn't know what to expect. Anxiety, nervousness and wonder all came rushing through my body at once. I hung up the phone and paused for a moment. This was it. What was he going to tell me? Would I be let down or given the chance of a lifetime? I asked the owner if it was okay to make the call up to Jacksonville. I didn't have any kind of cell phone or any computer. I had no money anyway, so those things weren't any kind of priority. He led me into his office, showed me the phone and shut the door to give me some privacy.

I gathered myself, wanting to play it cool, and dialed the long distance number. A sweet friendly voice from his secretary answered the phone and after I announced who I was, she said, "Oh, yes, Coach Coughlin is expecting your call. I'll put you through." I can't remember if there was some cheesy music I had to listen to while I waited or what, but it felt like it took forever.

"Hey, Tom thanks for getting back to me." he said first. I was standing up with one hand on the phone and the other pulling my hair back as hard and as tight as I could. I was hanging on for what he was going to say next. I was squeezing the phone so hard I thought I would snap it in half.

"I've thought about this long and hard, Tom. It wasn't an easy decision, trust me," he continued. Shit, I thought to myself, it's over.

"After much deliberating, I've made a decision to give you your shot. However! We must have an agreement that if you aren't good enough to make my team, I will have to let you go. There are no guarantees here. If we can agree on that, I'll sign you to a one year free agent contract with a $5,000 signing bonus." (That was peanuts in the eyes of the NFL, but to me, it was a great surprise, and badly needed.) He finished, although to be honest, I didn't hear anything after "going to give you your shot."

My heart screamed inside, but I kept my composure with my initial response, "All I want is a shot, Coach. Thank you for this great opportunity. I won't let you down!" My response was so collegian. It felt so rehearsed, but that's all I could come up with at the time.

He finished, "Hang on the line and my secretary will give you all the pertinent information. Our strength and conditioning program begins in March. I'll see you then."

We said our goodbyes and I threw in another "Thank you" and another "You won't regret it", as we both hung up the phone.

I immediately called my parents' house. My dad answered the phone after one ring and I told him the good news.

"That's great, Tom. You did it!" he shouted loud enough so my mom could hear. Then he turned into the Geno that I have always known and loved, "Now, that's only the beginning. You better get home so we can get some more running in," he stated.

I hung up the phone and opened the gym owner's office door. My normal weight lifting partner and good friend, Mark, who was a school teacher in New Smyrna, and the owner were standing just outside the door.

"Well?" they asked in unison.

"I got it. The Jaguars are going to give me one last shot of making it to the NFL!" I proudly stated with a smile from ear to ear. They both offered their congratulations. I quickly told them about the conversation and Mark and I headed back into the gym to finish that day's lift.

I had about a month and a half before I had to report to Jacksonville. I used the five grand to buy an old beat up CJ-7 Jeep with a soft top. It wasn't anything spectacular, but it got me around and I didn't have to ask for my dad's car anymore. I was 24 years old and it was about time I had my own wheels.

I attacked my workouts with even more fervor than before. I was extremely determined to put everything into this new opportunity. The odds were stacked against me, no doubt, and once again I would enter a professional football team at the bottom of the totem pole, but I didn't care. I was going to show the Jaguars' staff and the NFL that I did in fact belong in their league.

Geno was in all his glory. Every chance he got, whether to his golfing buddies, the nurses, even the grocery bagger at the local supermarket, he would always find a way to tell someone, "This is my son, Tom, he is a member of the new Jacksonville Jaguars team." He would beam so proudly.

I always would say to him after each encounter that I actually hadn't made the team yet, but that in reality I was only trying out.

"You're on the team!" he would declare, defending his statements, even to his son. He had the right. He was a proud parent and I was happy to bring a smile to his face.

But the real story was that I would have to pull off a colossal achievement to make the Jaguars' inaugural team. I was very focused and determined, but there were also those moments of self-doubt, wondering if I could really do it. However, those feelings were miniscule compared to the fire I had in my belly.

I felt like Sylvester Stallone in "Rocky", the guy who no one thought could pull off the greatest upset. To me it was such a parallel to my situation, but like a fistfight in the alley, I was ready to square off against the biggest and baddest opponent I had ever faced, which didn't have a face, but it did have a name. It was the National Football League.

SPRING OF 1995

In early March of 1995, I moved up to Jacksonville to take part in the off-season conditioning program. The 12-week program consisted of four workouts per week, with Wednesdays and the weekends being my days off. The workouts were pretty demanding, but I was in pretty good shape when I arrived so I was not intimidated with the prospects of a grueling schedule.

We did a lot of running that spring, concentrating on speed and conditioning. For the speed drills we did a bunch of resistance running and countless sprints. For example, we would put a harness on our upper bodies with a long flexible band attached to a weighted cart and pulled it like a sled dog would.

The philosophy behind that was that if you could pull the sled as you raced down the field with added weight lugging behind you, then it would help you feel more weightless when you ran without it, which should increase your speed.

We also worked on our footwork with what were called ladder drills, which was a rope that looked like a ladder on the ground and we would do specific drills with it: high knee runs, lateral drills going side to side through each squared space as you moved up the ladder, things like that. For conditioning runs, we had to perform 200 and 400 yard sprints.

These longer runs helped develop endurance, but they pretty much sucked as our legs would blow up with lactic acid after the first couple of tries. Guys, including myself, definitely preferred the shorter sprint workouts to the endurance runs. All in all, our training was comparable to the kind of workout a sprinter would do. These were done throughout the week.
Weightlifting was also a part of our conditioning, and we concentrated mostly on the power lifts, which were squats, the bench press, and power

cleans. Those always reminded me of Geno's old routine but with much more weight. Weight training was equally as important as the running, and both were done at every workout. After a while, it got pretty demanding and all in all lasted about three hours per workout.

Those early workouts of the Jacksonville Jaguars were held in various locations because their facilities were not yet finished in early spring of 1995. Those facilities would eventually be inside the renovated stadium which was referred to as the old Gator Bowl.

All of the team's facilities would be inside and underneath the stadium: locker room, meeting rooms, trainer's room, the weight room, even the cafeteria. When it finally did get done, it was all very plush, but in the meantime we held our running in the outfield of a baseball field where the local minor league Double-A team, the Jacksonville Suns, played their games, and our weightlifting was done at a nearby Gold's Gym.

In the past, the old Gator Bowl was used for the annual Florida-Georgia college football game, which is still held annually in Jacksonville, and the old USFL Jacksonville Bulls also used the stadium. They used to call the Gator Bowl their home field.

Jacksonville was definitely a football town. It had always been a "quasi-college town", having a population who were predominantly supporters and fans of the universities of Florida, Florida State, and Georgia. Nevertheless, they showed a great deal of support for the Bulls team during their short time of existence.

The town went crazy, I was told, when it was announced that Jacksonville would be the 30th franchise in the NFL. You could say they were football crazy when we arrived. I mean, the Jaguars were the only professional team in the city, not like in Chicago or Boston where there are three to five pro teams in different sports.

People were excited to finally have a team that they could call their own. It was really cool in that respect. We all were all very well received when we would venture out on the town, usually on our off days or on nights before we had a day off. I always felt a little taken aback by the attention because I knew that I was just trying out for the team and that my outcome was still far away.

Maybe it was because I had been burned before, I don't know. It just didn't seem right, I guess. Some 'clowns' would act as if they were already on the team when in reality they were just hoping to be.

They would wear their Jaguar-issued shirts out at night and announce that they were a member of the Jaguars to anyone who would listen. Of course that always got them some extra attention. But, to each his own I guess. Hey, if they needed that to pick up babes or to make themselves feel good, then so be it. I just thought it was pretty ridiculous, really.

For the record, some of those guys never made it anyway. The group I ran with was pretty cool. We always had a good time and worked hard when we had to. They were mostly in the same situation as I was. We were a bunch of vagabonds and retreads who had failed to make it in our initial attempts to join the NFL and were hoping to catch on.

The Jaguars did have some big name guys who were signed as high priced free agents, such as Steve Buerlein, who was out of Notre Dame and had been a starting quarterback in the league, and Jeff Lageman, the first big free agent acquisition of the Jaguars who came down from the NY Jets, where he had been a first round draft pick.

Other guys like Kelvin Pritchett and Joel Smeenge who had made good names for themselves in their respective careers came in too. Then in the draft came the likes of Tony Boselli who would eventually have a huge presence on the team. But, those guys were shoo-ins to make the squad. It's funny too, they could have gone out all the time and been recognized and received all the attention they could handle, but they usually didn't.

They didn't have to flaunt anything for people in Jacksonville already knew who they were. It was kind of like the guy in the bar that talks a lot looking for attention compared to the guy who stands in the corner minding his own business. One is confident and secure, and the other one isn't. One you better worry about, and the other is all smoke and mirrors. That was the difference between some of the guys during that first spring. Me? I loved going out and having a good time, but I was focused on what I was really there for.

As the spring wore on, we graduated into real football practices and mini-camps, held at Bishop Kenny High School, the school where I had my "workout" back in December. Although these practices were done in helmets and shorts, they were regimented in typical Coughlin fashion, fast paced and physically challenging. He worked us hard during the actual practices, and the conditioning afterwards was at times excruciating. It was something I was used to though, thanks to my previous tenure with Coach Coughlin and the workouts with my dad.

I did have one advantage going into these practices. I knew what to expect. Some of the older veterans who had played for different coaches in the league were bitching and moaning at times about how tough he ran things, but just like when he arrived at BC, I felt as though he was testing players to see what they had deep down. Little did they know what was ahead of them, when we would actually be in full training camp.

The NFL players union would only allow a coach to do so much. They had guidelines to follow, such as: you could only have on-the-field practices for so many days in a week and for so many hours during the off-season. Coach Coughlin pushed those guidelines to the maximum limit, so much so, that a couple of guys complained to the union, anonymously. I didn't mind it, but shit, who was I to complain? I was happy just to be there.

I made every effort to try to stand out as much as possible, for the mere fact that I kept reminding myself that nothing was a given. After all, I was still at the bottom looking up. Word also got around that I was one of Coughlin's players from college, which wasn't necessarily a bad thing, but I didn't want anyone to think that I was getting any kind of special treatment.

If they knew Coach Coughlin like I knew him, they would have known that would have never been the case. Nonetheless, I didn't want anyone, the staff or the players, to think for one second that I was only there because Coughlin was doing me some kind of favor.

I made sure that at every opportunity I would jump in line to get another repetition at whatever we were doing. For example, when we had a punt coverage drill, you had to show that you could beat the defender off the line of scrimmage, then race down to wherever the punt returner would catch the ball and pretend you were in position to make a tackle (we weren't in pads so there wasn't any actually tackling at this point). The faster you got down there, the more you stood out in the minds of the coaches watching that specific play.

I felt good doing that but I took it a step farther. Most guys were getting one or two "reps" during that drill. When a call was made to execute another, some of them wouldn't readily jump out there when the special teams coach called for someone, anyone, to come out and take another rep. I always tried to jump out there and get three to four more reps. The more reps you got in, the more coaches would have a look at your ability.

I was in good condition and I knew that I couldn't rest on my laurels, so I was always jumping at the chance for another opportunity and another chance to impress someone. A couple of guys would joke around with me about it but I didn't really give a crap. I kept the mentality that this was it, come hell or high water.

The practices were pretty exhausting, especially for guys who had not worked under Coach Coughlin's regimen. He ran a tight ship and didn't let up on his intensity. Some guys just didn't care for it. I really didn't know any better, to be honest.

I had never played for another coach in the NFL, so his style wasn't a problem for me, but it was for other guys who came from different coaching styles in their past. I had a conversation with a veteran running back who had been in the league for about three years before arriving in Jacksonville that told the story.

After one of Coughlin's particularly grueling practice sessions, the whole team was dripping in sweat and pretty damn tired. The running back sat down next to me at my locker and asked "You chose to come here?"

"Shit yeah, this was the only choice I had. This is my last shot to make it, so it doesn't matter to me what he makes us do," was my honest response. I was thinking the whole time that this was nothing compared to the winter conditioning that Coughlin headed up back at Boston College. At least I wasn't puking my guts out. He just shook his head and wiped his face with a towel and said, "Damn!"

I called my mom and dad pretty much every few days during the week and went down on the weekends to stay with them when I could. They were doing great, enjoying their retirement in their own fashion as usual: golf, beach, and drinks with friends, etc. It was always great to see them and my dad loved it when his son, the "professional football player" came home.

I felt good about my performance throughout the off-season, but there was still a ton of uncertainty as to where I stood on the team. I mean, we were always in shorts and helmets, so no hitting ever took place. Although I had increased my speed and agility, and my stamina was second to none, I often wondered if I was fast enough or even impressive enough to make the team. It's a commonly known thing that some players look great in shorts, but could they really stand out when the pads came on?

There were guys who were way better athletes than I was, even at the linebacker position. I knew that and it gnawed at me every night when I flopped into bed. Some were faster, some were stronger, but I knew the equalizer in this whole epiphany was going to be Training Camp, for it wasn't just about how fast and athletic you were, but more to the tune of, can you play the game of football? Were you mentally and emotionally strong enough? Were you a smart and instinctive player?

A common joke within the ranks of the league was towards a guy who "looked like Tarzan but played like Jane", meaning that there were guys that could lift a ton of weight in the gym or could run a blistering 40 time, but could they, or better put, would they meet the running back in the hole, tackle him in the face, and knock his ass down right then and there? Could you take on a three hundred plus pound offensive guard and stymie him enough to plug the hole, so the running back had nowhere to go? Were you instinctive enough to figure out if the offense was running a pass play or a run play, in a second's notice?

Here's a little hint for all you non-football players. Offensive linemen come out low and hard pretty much straight at the defense without hesitation, when it's a running play. On a passing play they stand up immediately, for they can't cross the line of scrimmage or go down the field until the pass is thrown or it will be a penalty.

If the offense was going to run a draw play, a paused running play, if you will, the offensive lineman would stand up for a brief second and then come out at you. I was always taught to read the running back, back from my days at Boston College. I had a Graduate Assistant, Pat McCormick, who played college linebacker at Brown University, and he taught me how to read an offense either out on the field or in the film room. He would show me how to study film for hours. We used these 8mm roles of film that were always breaking. I had to learn how to splice the tape when it broke, which was common, so I could keep it from screwing up and continue my film study without disruption. It was invaluable training and instruction and truly helped my game. Those mental sessions made me even more instinctive for I knew what to look for in an offensive play.

The good thing in all of my uncertainty with the Jaguars was the fact that I knew I wasn't going to be let go before training camp, which is when the pads came on. That's when I knew I would have the best chance to impress the staff and my teammates. My best attribute as a linebacker was reading plays before they unfolded. I knew that Coach Coughlin and Coach Szabo knew that, but I would have to prove myself all over again. However, nothing was a given. That was the business.

The offseason ended in mid-June, which gave all of us about five weeks off. Most, if not all, headed out of Jacksonville to either go see their families, girlfriends and/or return to their respective hometowns. I spent my days at my parents' home, pretty much like I had done before I left for Jacksonville. I got up early to the sounds of Geno's weights clinking and clanking on the living room floor. I got my workouts in every day, running at the field, where dad still accompanied me, and getting my weight training in at the local gym. It was good to have a little break from the monotony of the mini-camps and off-season conditioning program. In my downtime, I played a bunch of golf, sometimes with mom and dad, but mostly with just Geno.

The time away from my parents didn't change much in my relationship with Geno. I was in even better shape than when I last left him and yet he still always wanted to mess around and challenge his youngest son. I again accompanied him to his doctor's appointments, which he enjoyed as did I. Any opportunity to hang out him and my mother, Joanie, was always a great time.

I'll never forget during that time away from the Jaguars, when he had to have some outpatient surgery to remove another sun-damaged spot. This time it looked so painful. They cut out this lesion in between his thumb and pointer finger, the spot where it looks like webbing in our hands. He never complained, though, and he was back to playing golf within a few days. He looked good, still the same old Geno, working out and telling stories about how he used to run through guys like me while playing football. We had so many laughs together. It was always great to be home.

He and Joanie were still so much in love. He really worshipped her. He was always hugging and kissing her. I loved seeing it. They had a very special bond. I am sure they had ups and downs in their 30 plus years of marriage like most relationships do, but she was his "Joanie", and he loved her so much.

That was another thing Geno and my mom taught me: how to love and how to treat someone that you love so much. He always held open the car door for her and never let her carry anything too heavy. He never missed an anniversary, a birthday, Valentine's Day, or anything. The way he treated my mother always stood out to me. It was like the old Stevie Ray Vaughn tune, "Pride and Joy", with the lyrics, "I love my lady, heart and soul, love like ours will never grow old. She's my sweet little thing, she's my pride and joy."

All of that reinforced the fact that a man can be tough and stand up for what he believes in, but at the same time he can be a gentleman and truly love his mate and children with words and affection.

Geno and I grew especially close during those five weeks after those arduous workouts. We would sit up late at night talking about life, family, opportunity and the good grace of God. He was a believer in the Good Lord, and so was I. God came first, then family, something that I have never forgotten. He was also happy that "his" bartender was home, so when that clock hit five in the afternoon, I could serve up a few cocktails. It was like two old buddies reminiscing about the past and looking forward to the future.

We talked about his football and boxing days and what life was like back when he was growing up, reminding me over and over again, that back in his day they didn't need all of the pads that football players wear today. He told tales of knocking down bigger guys in the ring, how he would set them up with some punches to the side of the body and then faking it when the time was right and coming up with a left hook that would send them down to the canvas. "The bigger they were, the harder they would fall," he would always say.

He would tell me how he used to step on the necks of the defenders as he would run over them on the football field. He always said those things with this big grin on his face but his steely eyes told the real story. You know how you can look into someone's eyes and see what they're all about or if they're even telling the truth? I never looked into his and questioned any of it.

After all the years of our discussions though, there was a strange anomaly that I had always thought about and pondered over. We never talked about the war. All this time together he never told me one story about his time during World War II, his flying, his training, his experiences, anything. It was a blank in my mind. Why? It was like taboo to even bring it up, at least that was my understanding, or maybe it was because he never brought it up in our conversations.

However, all of that changed late one night. It was just me and him sitting at the kitchen table having another one of our talks after Joanie and Bob had gone to bed, and he dropped a few bombshells on me. He had a good amount of Canadian Club whiskey in him and he started to tell me a story that I never knew about him, but it was one that would never leave me, especially as my date with destiny fast approached.

JUNE 9TH, 1944

I jogged towards the house after having spent an hour working on my wind sprints and agility on the street outside my folks' house, a few weeks away from my biggest challenge yet. I immediately went inside and walked into the kitchen to grab a bottle of Gatorade. Dad was sitting at the kitchen table by himself so I plopped down across from him, exhausted. He was dressed in his usual daily attire, Bermuda shorts and a golf shirt with the sleeves pushed up. I was in my sweaty workout outfit from that evening's round of training.

It was past midnight and Geno was on a roll. I knew he had a slight buzz on, but so what, he deserved his "drinks" and who was I to think otherwise. I can't remember how many times I filled up his glass that night, but he always seemed to remind me how to let the faucet run and only make one pass through it with his glass full of whiskey. That was what he called a 'splash'. To me it was more like gasoline, which is pretty ironic for it seemed to fuel his fire.

He started performing his usual skit, telling the great stories that I had heard my entire adult life. The Orange Trojans, "Two Ton" Tony Galento, and what life was like way back when "in his day." He had me laughing and shaking my head at the amazing tales that he always told. Those stories never got too old for me. He had my utmost respect and if my father wanted to regurgitate his stories again and again then so be it. He earned that right. But then, out of nowhere, something incredible happened.

For a brief moment after one of his many stories, there was a slight pause, and I made my move. Not that I had planned it, it just seemed to come out naturally, like it was the right time to ask. In an instant, I got up the nerve to ask him about the seemingly secret part of his past that I never really knew about: the war. I got up out of the chair and walked to the fridge for more Gatorade when I turned around and asked, "Dad, how come you never talked to me about your time during the war?"

His mood changed almost instantaneously, like those words touched a nerve. His jolly and energetic personality quickly turned. He gave me that look, the same look I saw when I was eight years old as he defended my brothers and me against our menacing neighbor all those years ago. He leaned back in his wooden chair, folded his arms and deliberately responded, "Well, what do you want to know?"

I walked back to the table, pulled up a chair across from him and replied, "Well, I know you were a bomber pilot over in Germany during World War II. But, I really don't know much else other than that. What was your life like during and after the war? I mean, what went on?" I asked with great anticipation as I had harbored those inquiries for most of my life.

I can remember the ensuing hours of conversation like it was yesterday. There we were, just the two of us, like we had done so many times before, on the golf course, out on the field or just walking on the beach, sitting and reminiscing. Geno was holding court once again telling tales like his life was some sort of fable from a historical novel.

But, the stories weren't made up, like fiction, but rather the true accounts of a man who had lived through so much. I didn't know it at the time, but this conversation would carry much more weight in my eyes, much more than the stories past as Geno was about to embark on another very important life lesson for his youngest child.

The expression on his face had changed the second my words rolled off my tongue. His massive and hairy forearms clenched. His eyes were somewhat bloodshot and his demeanor became extremely serious. He started off on his story and I can remember staring directly into his eyes. I was fixated on him as he began his response to my questions.

As his story unfolded, I felt like I was having an out of body experience, like I had left that kitchen and found myself on board his B-24 bomber, the Naughty Angel, some fifty years ago. I found myself visualizing every detail as he described them. Slowly and deliberately he began:

"Back in the war, we would send radio signals to the Germans, enticing them to a fight. We felt we were superior pilots and we wanted them to challenge us in the air. We also knew that our own fighter pilots would soon be arriving to escort us to our destination that day. We were confident, almost cocky even, and we were always ready for a battle.

"Our fighter planes, the P-47 Thunderbolts, had an eerie similar look to the enemy fighters. The German fighters were the Focke-Wulf's, or FW 190's as they were called by the men. We had studied them so much so that we could see them in our sleep. Both fighter planes had a snub nose in the front of the plane and from a distance it was tough to tell which was which.

"We had encountered them in most of our bombing raids, sometimes in big numbers. We were somewhere near the border of Italy and Austria on our way to bomb Munich, Germany, when we thought we saw our escort of P-47's approaching, but we were wrong and in an instant we were fighting for our lives!"

I was transformed while listening to his every word. My mind was beginning to paint pictures of everything he was telling me. He had become a narrator, as he told the story in third person, like it was some kind of movie he was describing:

As the large contingent of the 24's were approaching the Tyrolean Alps, the Naughty Angel was situated in the D-7 position in the formation box, which was in the back and lower than the aircraft in the front. The Naughty Angel was once again having engine trouble and it seemed like it was singled out. That was very common, like a lioness going after the weakest animal in a herd. All hell broke loose as the German fighters, FW 190's and Messerschmitt 109's, descended upon the B-24's flying in tight formation. Machine guns were manned at every position in the "Naughty Angel".

The enemy fighters came out of the sun and before anyone knew what was going on, the German pilots had made their first pass without anyone in the formation firing one shot. It soon transformed into a spectacle almost like the 4th of July with tracers going every which way, whizzing by or rapping into the fuselage with an indescribable crash.

The cacophony was deafening. The machine guns on the Naughty Angel erupted. The smell of cordite was everywhere. Adrenaline was pumping through everyone's veins. After two or three passes, the enemy fighters had done quite a lot of damage to the Naughty Angel. Over the intercom, numerous voices could be heard shouting:

"FW at eleven o'clock. Two ME's on our tail. Take him, Vinnie. Bobbie, ya drilled him. Look out two more comin' to you! Oh shit, Taylor's going down." Hendrix was suddenly hit by shrapnel from an exploding 20mm shell that slammed into the fuselage and he fell back against the bulkhead, "Bobbie's hit."

Gene pointed to his copilot: "Glenn get back there and see what you can do," but before he could move another engine started to trail smoke. The shouting continued: "Number three's on fire, Feather number two, Glenn! Geno, it's a runaway! Holy shit, they're everywhere! Two more FW's, twelve o'clock high! Take 'em, Johnny! There goes number one, feather it, Glenn! Done! Oh shit, we've only got number four, we're in real trouble now, watch it, Glenn! Done! I got one! Me, too! Gene, we got one good one and one runaway, we're in big trouble. Cap, we're losing fuel. We gotta get outta here!"

All around them a handful of 24's were in flames, smoking or spinning to the ground out of control. Gene commanded with urgency: "Three more guys are going down, we've had it too, bail out you guys, bail out!"

At that moment the intercom cut out. Bleech crawled out of the tail gun and made his way towards Marimpietri, Hendrix, Guthrie, and Moses. Moses had come down from the top turret with a pencil sized gash on his cheek from a 50 caliber round that had grazed him within a fraction of an inch of his life. He struggled to make his way towards the others. He motioned to the ground. Everyone was shouting over the din.

"It looks real bad. We gotta get the hell out of here! The intercom's gone and my hydraulics are dead." screamed Julius Moses.

Val Bleech chimed in, "Shit, we're never gonna make it! We got only one engine and we're leaking fuel bad!"

Gene struggled to keep the plane flying. The aircraft was almost uncontrollable by then and it took every ounce of Gene's strength to keep the plane level. Engine #3 was on fire, engine #1 was already shot out and #2 had a runaway prop. He had only one engine working at full capacity. The bomb bay slowly opened as Gene released the bomb load to lighten the weight of the plane to help keep the aircraft flying level. It also gave them all a place to bail out as was standard practice. Glenn grabbed his parachute and placed Gene's chute beside him.

Hendrix scrambled up to his feet and grabbed a waist gun on the starboard side of the aircraft when he was hit in the shoulder by a round from a Folke-Wulf racing straight for him. Guthrie had just come out of his ball turret position in the belly of the plane when Hendrix was hit. He tended to his crew member and quickly gave Hendrix a shot of morphine.

Their years' of training were starting to become reflex action. Moses and Guthrie held on for dear life as they each tried to grab onto Hendrix so he wouldn't fall out of the smoldering aircraft through the open bomb bay door. Suddenly everything went dead, the communications and the hydraulics. Consequently they never heard the alarm bell, the buzzer, signaling that it was time to bail out, but they all knew instinctively that it was time to go. They all cinched up their chutes and started taking turns shooting, while others struggled to hold Hendrix up.

Marimpietri strapped on his silk chute. He always felt that a silk chute was the best and he always commandeered one for himself, but this time it had apparently been damaged by a burning tracer round and was smoldering. Bleech noticed it and started patting it down to try to dampen the burning cloth.

By now the Naughty Angel was severely shaking, and nearly stalling in its efforts to remain flying on only one good engine. Bleech knew that he had to bail out, but hesitated. Pete stood up and feet first dropped through the bomb bay door. (Vincent "Pete" Marimpietri, the youngest member of the crew, never made it as his silk chute failed to open properly. It had become engulfed in flames and he fell helplessly to the earth.)

Moses, Lindberg, Spargo, and Guthrie all jumped out of the bomb bay. Bleech tied off Hendrix's chute's rip cord to a heater cord and pushed him out after the others had bailed. He then immediately followed behind. Folcik came out of his nose turret position and saw Gene fighting with the controls. Gene took one hand off the wheel and starting motioning his hand up and down to signal Folcik to abandon the plane. Folcik pulled the nose wheel release and it fell out with a thump as there were no hydraulics. Feet first he slipped out of the port in the nose of the Liberator and deployed his chute.

Gene then gave the order to Glenn to abandon ship and Glenn reluctantly departed while his friend held the plane as steady as he could. Chaos was continuing to go on all around them. Gene gave one last effort to keep the plane level to make sure that everyone had gotten out. He then got out of his seat, checked the flight deck, and then disappeared out of the bomb bay. The Naughty Angel immediately went into a side slip, rolled and then dove and within moments crashed into the mountain side, bursting into flames upon impact.

As the men floated in air, they had a vivid, front row seat of the plane that they had loved so much go down in flames. They instantly entered a surrealistic world as they watched the formation slowly draw away from them while they were continually being swooped upon by German fighters.

The roar of the bomber's engines and the scream of the German fighters with their guns blazing slowly gave way to the whoosh of the wind created by their rapid decent. John Spargo, the bombardier, was later quoted as saying, "The loneliest feeling in the world is knowing you are going down and you are watching the rest of the formation fly away, knowing full well that they couldn't do a thing to help you."

For a brief moment they were all transported in their minds to their parachute training but quickly snapped back into reality as they saw the Naughty Angel burning on the mountainside and the ground beneath them quickly approaching. The men all hit the ground hard. Gene's parachute oscillated only one and a half times before he crashed into a grove of fruit trees and was left dangling helplessly in the branches of a tree, semiconscious.

As they scrambled to rescue Gene from the tree and gather their chutes in order to bury them, they wondered what was in store for them next. Too bad for them, that the terrifying hell they had just encountered was only the beginning of their horrific and unbelievably challenging 11-month saga in captivity in this, the greatest World War.

LIFE AS A POW

Gene and his crew landed all throughout the countryside after their plane crashed. They had all made it safely to the ground except Marimpietri. There was a sudden sadness as the crew witnessed his death. Gene and Glenn landed near one another as did a couple of the others. Glenn immediately unbuckled his chute, quickly hid it under some bushes and then he ran to Gene's aid and tried to wrestle him out of his tangled chute.

They knew that the Krauts must have seen their parachutes as they descended from the sky and were most likely on their way to capture them. In the distance they could see a farm house and watched as a woman came out and walked towards them with a sandwich and a glass of milk in her hands.

She called out to them in German, something which neither of them could understand, but they could tell that she was friendly and welcoming, which seemed strange considering the circumstances. Before they could even take her up on her offer, a rag tag group of armed old men and young teenage boys ran up to them as Gene and Glenn were immediately surrounded. The old men carried worn-out hunting rifles while some of the boys had pistols, while others held nothing more than pitchforks. They were what was appropriately called the Home Guard.

Almost immediately, one of the old men waved his rifle at Gene and Glenn and motioned for them to walk towards the farm house. The German woman had already scurried back to her home still clutching her supposed gift for the captured airmen.

The Home Guard then directed Gene and Glenn to stand up against two separate trees that were about twenty yards apart while they surrounded

Gene and Glenn in a semicircle set back about ten yards. They each pointed their weapons at the two captured pilots. As one of the old men directed the group to "fire" at the American soldiers, Gene and Glenn could hear the distinct "click" sound that resulted from the empty chambers in each weapon. They didn't know whether they had any ammunition in those damn things or not.

The Home Guard took much joy in taunting the downed airmen. Gene and Glenn were both certain that they would indeed be shot. They stared at the ragtag group of homeland "protectors" and cringed after each directed command was given to shoot, hoping that there weren't any forgotten bullets left in those chambers. It was a very scary situation that lasted for almost fifteen minutes. Gene and Glenn said nothing as they both thought their lives were over.

Suddenly, from behind the barn, a squad of German soldiers came running towards the group led by an officer holding a pistol. The soldiers were all carrying machine guns. The officer shouted something to the Home Guard group and they all lowered their weapons and backed off. These uniformed German military personnel took over and as Gene and Glenn gazed over at one another in a pure look of shock, they quickly recognized the fact that they had officially become Prisoners of War.

They were loaded into a troop truck and found members of their crew except for Moses, and of course the "baby" of the crew, Marimpietri. They drove in stunned silence as they tried to calm themselves after such a horrific sequence of events. They were dropped off in a town called Lienz, Austria, at a local jail and were ushered in with guns being stabbed in their backs.

The German guards had to kick out all of the local drunks from the cells to make room for the crew. While Gene and his remaining crew members were separated into two adjoining cells, Gene put his fingers to his lips to signal that none of the crew were to speak.

It was a cold night and the men had to huddle together and literally cover themselves with just two thin blankets among them to stay warm. Hendrix was in considerable pain and Gene kept shouting at the prison guards to get him some help, but was ignored. They did everything they could to comfort him. They hardly got a wink's sleep on the cold, hard cement floor.

The next day, all except Hendrix and Moses were put on a train to Frankfurt. Hendrix was taken to a local military hospital to take care of his serious shoulder wound. Moses was immediately placed into the custody of an SS officer and taken away into solitary confinement by the Gestapo, the secret police of the Nazi's. They had immediately separated him from the crew on suspicion of being a Jew because of his last name.

Frankfurt was the home of Dulag Luft, which was the Luftwaffe Aircrew Interrogation Center. All United States and Allied airmen who had been shot down and captured were taken there to be interrogated and harassed in the hope of giving the Nazis important military intelligence.

Upon arrival in Frankfurt, the men were ordered off the train. As they waited to be taken to the interrogation center, a very dangerous mob scene was starting to form. Frankfurt as a whole looked like a desolate place littered with bombed out buildings.

The British air forces (RAF) had heavily bombed Frankfurt in retaliation for the Nazis bombing their beloved old city, Coventry. Many people used the main railway· station, locally called the "Hauptbahnhof", as a meeting and gathering place. The German guards had left the airmen outside the railway station as they went inside to grab a smoke and a hot drink. Only one guard remained to keep an eye on the newly captured crew.

A group of German civilians started to form a big circle around Gene and his men. The angry mob had grabbed whatever they could get their hands on: pieces of wood, pipe and most alarming, long strands of rope. One civilian started to form the rope into an improvised noose. They started shouting at the crew in German, "American murderers", "American shitheads", and "Kill the bastards!"

"I think those bastards are going to lynch us, Mac!" Lindberg shouted out above the crowd noise.

"Don't move. If we run, the guards will shoot us for sure," Gene commanded back.

"What the hell are we supposed to do?" a frightened Glenn Strong questioned.

"Just sit tight and don't look scared. That guard just went in to let the other guards know what's going on. Keep your wits about you." Gene countered back.

Just then the rest of the guards came out of the railway station with their weapons at the ready and pointed them towards the mob.

(In German) "Stop right there or we will shoot!" the officer shouted as he fired his pistol in the air. The other guards all pointed their machine guns at the approaching mob.

Immediately realizing that the guards meant serious business, the mob froze and backed off, still spitting their insults at the vulnerable airmen. Slowly they dispersed.

"Whew, that was damn close!" Gene said as he shook his head.

Spargo softly whispered, "I was sure we were goners."

Gene tried to ease the anxiety of his crew. "Look, we are protected by the Geneva Convention. They have to protect us. They sure as hell can't let us be murdered. We are going to some prison where we'll all be interrogated. Remember, you give only your name, rank and serial number. Got it?" They all nodded.

The German guards then pointed in the direction of a small, waiting German truck. The Americans were forced into the back of the vehicle and taken to the center where they would spend their first seven to ten days in captivity.

All Allied airmen were sent to the center as soon as possible after their capture. They were immediately separated and each new prisoner was kept in solitary confinement as they were skillfully interrogated for military information of value to the Germans.

The Germans didn't resort to torture, although they did try to break their captives' mental spirit in order to get them to give up pertinent information. The pilots of each crew were interrogated the most intently because the Germans knew that they had all of the important data: bomb targets, tactics, plans, etc. Gene was determined to not get broken down and to definitely not give anything up. He muttered to himself over and over again, "Name, rank and serial number."

He was sent to solitary confinement time and time again in between interrogation encounters. He would only be fed once per day by the Germans
with a small ration of potato soup being the delightful entrée bestowed
upon their honored guest. The Germans figured that malnourishment was
just one of the ways to break the airmen down.

Inside his solitary cell, Gene performed countless pushups and sit-ups to
keep his strength up. He would also perform his "shadow boxing" as best
he could when the slim ray of light illuminated his cell just perfectly. He
wanted to keep in as good a physical shape as possible, for he always felt
that was the best way to stay mentally sharp.

He figured out really quickly what the Germans were up to. They would
first have a German officer come in and berate him. The German officer
was dressed in the uniform of the notorious SS and his manner was very
threatening and verbally abusive.

He would try to tear Gene down mentally and emotionally, even at times
getting a bit physical. He would grab Gene by the collar and shake him and
tell him how bad a pilot he was and that the United States and its allies
"could never win this war!" He tried to beat him down with the hope that
eventually he would just give up and deliver information. Too bad he didn't
know the background of 1st Lieutenant Gene McManus.

After an intensely grueling interrogation by that officer, he would leave and
then a second officer would come in, but he acted very differently from the
first. This "other" officer looked American and even sounded American.
He pretended to be some sort of ally, like a good, friendly guy who was
sympathetic to the plight of downed pilots. This guy tried to befriend Gene
and offered him cigarettes. He acted like he wanted to just "to get to know
Gene better." He asked him about where he grew up and brought up things
like American football and such.

He enticed him with better food and accommodations or more cigarettes if
he gave the first supposed SS officer something to "hang his hat on". He
sneaked in questions like: Had all of his crew made it out of the plane, or
where they were headed to before they were shot down, things like that.

The second officer's approach to garner information was done in a more
subtle manner than the first's. However, after a few days of these little
games, Gene figured out that this was an old-fashioned game of "good cop,
bad cop".

There were many pilots that were fooled by this "duet" style of finding out information. The Germans constantly claimed to have gathered continuous "new" information from the new "enrollees" by telling them that they had already obtained names of unit commanders, information on new tactics, new weapons, new targets, new strategy and even orders of battle.

Naïve and/or careless U.S. airmen would cave in from time to time to the clever ruse. In their defense, these captured airmen had just overcome very traumatic catastrophes in the air, so it was a lot easier said than done to be strong enough not to give in. Gene relied on his mental and emotional toughness to get him through these demanding times. He was constantly encouraging himself to "stay strong".

When Gene was finally let out of solitary, he found himself with the masses of other American and Allied aircrews as they waited to see where they would be headed for more of a permanent POW camp. As Gene spent his time out in the exercise yard with other captured airmen, he tried to continue his physical fitness as best he could by running laps around the compound and performing his usual pushup and sit-up routine. He would encourage his crew to do the same, and most did. In fact there were other groups of fellow POWs who joined in or had their own regimen going on although they were feeling weaker by the day from the lack of enough food.

Gene soon found out that he, Glenn Strong, and Lindberg would be sent to the South Compound of Stalag Luft III where all of the captured officers were sent. Second Lieutenant Spargo was sent to SL III as well, but he would be placed in the West Compound. All of the other enlisted non-coms, such as Folcik, Guthrie and Bleech were sent to Stalag Luft IV, which was located directly north of SL III and near the Baltic Sea.

Hendrix was eventually released from the hospital and sent there as well. Moses, after he took several beatings, eventually convinced the Gestapo that he in fact wasn't a Jew. He finally just pulled down his pants during one of his umpteenth interrogations and whipped out his uncircumcised penis. They immediately recognized the fact that he wasn't Jewish and sent him to join the other non-coms at Stalag Luft IV. It would serve as a running joke within the crew of non-coms during the remainder of the war. They often laughed at the thought of Moses waggling his "Johnson" at some SS officer.

Gene's new "home", Stalag Luft III in a town called Sagan, was located 100 miles southeast of Berlin in what is now Poland. It was one of six POW camps operated by the Luftwaffe for downed British, Polish and American airmen.

The Geneva Convention of 1929 was created to dictate the ethical treatment of prisoners of war. Many, but not all camps adhered to the treaty. The prisoners weren't treated terribly badly but they were certainly not given any comforts. The overall outlook and attitude was pretty grim, for after all, these men were prisoners, victims of war, and considered the enemy.

When Gene, Lindberg, and Glenn arrived, they stuck out like a sore thumb. Their uniforms were reasonably clean and they were wearing boots in good condition. As they entered through the gates with dozens of other newly captured POW's, they noticed how barren everything was. Men were seen mulling around, unshaven and unkempt. Most were pretty emaciated from lack of nourishment and were wearing ill-fitting clothes and worn out shoes.

Gene and Glenn were directed to a block building where they were stripped naked, given a two minute raw, cold shower, and were handed a new set of clothing along with an overcoat and shoes. The guards didn't quite ask what size they were, they just handed them whatever they had. All of the men at Stalag Luft III wore the same attire except the Nazi guards and officers who were outfitted in their military uniforms. All of the Nazi personnel were armed.

The three officers were escorted to the barracks housing the base commander. They were introduced to Colonel Delmar T. Spivey, the SAO (Senior American Officer) who warmly greeted them and introduced them to the other officers standing in the room. Col. Spivey told them a little of the recent history of the camp including the story of how fellow POWs had finally escaped in March after crawling down a three hundred foot long tunnel dug underground, affectionately called in code-speak as "Harry".

He told them that although security had greatly tightened, everyone was still expected to assist in any efforts to help fellow POWs escape. He shook their hands, they saluted and were then escorted towards the barrack they would be staying in. Gene gathered Glenn and Lindberg together and gave them a pep talk.

"Listen up fellas, looks like this is going to be our home for a while, so let's make the best of it. We have got to stick together and get through this goddamn mess!" Gene demanded. "I'm going to do my best and keep in shape. Just taking a jog or two around the camp, making sure I keep myself upright. You should do the same, but let's try and not overdo it for we must think about conserving our energy. If we cave in to this bullshit we'll end up like many of these sappy looking men we see around here. I won't have it, so keep your chin up and most importantly let's try and stay out of trouble."

"Yeah Mac, but man this place looks like we just walked into hell!" chimed in Lieutenant Strong.

"It could be a lot worse. I heard some guys talking about what is happening over in Japan. They say this is nothing like it is over there," added Lindberg.

"Don't get caught up in what other men are doing unless it's something positive! I see a few baseball and football games going on. I am sure we can get involved in some of those! Keep your morale up, dammit! We are going to need all of our strength to get through this!" Gene concluded.

Although Col. Spivey had not filled them in on all the details, Gene and the two members of his crew eventually found out about the numerous escape attempts that had taken place prior to their arrival at Stalag Luft III. Escapes were much harder to accomplish, though, after what had happened earlier that year in March. It was historically called, "The Great Escape", where over 76 men got away through that long tunnel, "Harry".

However, all of them were recaptured. It came to Hitler's personal attention for it caused a major diversion from Germany's desperately depleted troop levels in the struggling and apparently losing war effort. So much so that Hitler ordered 50 of those escaped POWs to be shot. To send a message, he also ordered to have their ashes placed in urns and taken back to the camp. Escapes became even more dangerous, but the attempts nevertheless continued.

Guards were distracted by the different athletic games that took place. They often placed bets on the different events, even with the American and Allied airmen. Cigarettes were the most popular currency for the Germans while food was the most treasured booty for the Americans.

Gene was a big favorite during the football games although he was already losing a bunch of weight because of the very limited diet he had been subjected to. Eventually he would lose half the size he was back at Rutgers, but he still stood out. When not playing ball, he would play golf with made up clubs, balls and creatively manufactured "greens" and holes - anything to offer a distraction, not only to the guards but also to keep the prisoners' minds off the ongoing malaise of a POW camp.

Gene and the entire POW camp would spend the next six to seven months eking out a living and just struggling to survive. Over time food became more and more scarce. The Germans had enough trouble feeding themselves, much less the POW's they were charged to guard, who were well down on the list of their priorities.

The rations given out to the prisoners were insufficient to sustain health and failed to meet even the minimum requirements of the Geneva Convention. If it were not for the International Red Cross who shipped food, serious malnutrition would have been very common.

However, the delivery of these much needed supplies also depended on the uncertainties of the wartime rail service in Germany. The Americans and Allies were destroying rail yards and shooting up freight trains carrying supplies and packages to the POW camps. Also, there was the fact that the Germans would withhold the delivery of Red Cross packages as a sort of group punishment if needed, especially after an escape attempt or a serious disturbance.

The German guards consisted of non-flying Luftwaffe officers and/or enlisted personnel who were generally not qualified for frontline duty. Many of them were old and also uneducated, and some had been wounded from earlier battles. There were prisoners who tried to get along with the guards and there were others that despised them, but overall there was a general respect for all involved, guards and prisoners. Both of the groups didn't truly want to be there. All wanted the war to be over.

The situation turned worse nearing the end of the month of January 1945. Germany was experiencing their coldest winter in recorded history with blizzard conditions and temperatures well below freezing. The American and Allied troops were pushing into western Germany as the Soviet Union's Red Army was rolling into the eastern part of Poland. Hitler's regime was experiencing tremendous pressure from both sides but he most feared that the members of the Stalag Luft III camp would be overrun and liberated by the Russians.

Hitler wanted to keep the Allied airmen as hostages. The Luftwaffe guards were terrified of being captured themselves by the Communist forces. There was a sense of tense pandemonium starting to set in, for the Russians had penetrated to within 20 kilometers of the camp. All day and all night long the thunder of distant artillery could be heard. The Nazi guards grew very nervous and were clearly full of fear.

Conditions in the Stalag III had become untenable. Keeping warm had surpassed the need to eat. The Red Cross had shipped briquettes to be used for heating, but the Nazis had commandeered much of the supplies. Each barracks had fashioned makeshift stoves from large tin cans that had contained food. They would be filled with the meager store of briquettes and lit.

To supplement the limited heat produced by these "stoves", many floor boards were ripped up and broken into pieces. Throughout the day and night, airmen would take turns standing by these totally inadequate heating devices. They would rotate back and forth so that no one froze to death or got frostbite. Sleep was measured in minutes, not hours, and it was only possible while huddled together in a mass of bodies. Gene tried his best to keep the spirits up in his barracks by encouraging his fellow POWs to do limited exercises, such as simple jumping jacks, to build up their body temperature.

As a soldier would die of disease, malnutrition, or the cold, he would be stripped to his underwear while his socks, clothing, overcoat and blanket would be distributed to someone in greater need. Then he would be buried. The conditions had become horrific and deadly.

Then, around 10 o'clock on the night of January 29th, the Luftwaffe captors stormed into the barracks and ordered every man out into the marshaling grounds where they were told that they had to pack everything up and get ready to leave for they were immediately to move to another POW camp.

There was a dramatic frenzy to make improvised packsacks loaded with essentials of stashed food and layers upon layers of clothing and blankets in order to survive the severe conditions. That night there were already over six inches of snow on the ground and more was continuously falling, along with icy winds blowing at unbelievable velocity. Over 11,000 Allied airmen prepared to march in the subzero temperatures towards the southwest, their next destination.

As Gene, Glenn, and Lindberg got as much stuff together as they could, Gene reinforced the idea of sticking together to the other two men, "Stay close, we'll get through this!" Teams within barracks cleverly fashioned sleds using floor boards and clothes line. They were piled high with supplies they were certain would be needed as they had learned they were not going to be transported by truck, but by foot.

Every available sock was put in layers over shoes. Those who had shoes with flapping soles fashioned metal soles out of tin cans and wrapped them with socks to secure them to their shoes. Others made makeshift hats out of cut-up blankets tied to their heads with rope. Every piece of available material was gathered to use as some sort of clothing or equipment anticipated to give aid and warmth during the impending march to where, they had no idea. They could begin to feel the earth shake with the concussion of the Russian artillery now closing in on the camp.

If they thought that living in Stalag Luft III was bad, they had no idea what was coming next. 2,000 men from the South Camp were ordered to clear the way for the rest of the 8,000-9,000 other airmen. They traveled through the rugged terrain, hour after hour, battling the blackness of night with blizzard winds whipping them in their faces at below zero degree temperatures.

When they did stop for a little rest or sleep, it was every man for himself. They would find little refuge in barns, on the floor of an abandoned old tile factory, or whatever shelter they could find. The German guards did allow men to build fires if they could get them going. Men would also bundle together using the heat from one and other to try to keep warm as best they could.

They marched for three to four days in that treacherous weather. After a couple of hellish days and nights, some men would give up or would just lose their minds. The men who couldn't go any farther would just lie down and freeze to death. It was a dreadful scene. It was the utmost battle of survival any had ever encountered. The men who died were stripped of their jackets, gloves, socks, and boots.

It was some of the most primal situations that these men or anyone had ever witnessed. It was sad but very necessary for those who tried to continue on. As the half-mile line of men each passed another dead body of a fallen comrade, who lay barely clothed in the snow, no one could bring himself to look at him as they trudged by in the nighttime blizzard.

Not only the POWs suffered, but so did the Nazi guards. All were exhausted and near collapse. When they came upon a small hamlet of farms, they were all directed into the barn and huddled together to keep warm and catch a few hours of much needed sleep. Escape attempts were still encouraged and some 32 men, who felt in good enough condition did try to flee, although most, if not all, were recaptured and felt their fatigue even further from the energy wasted.

Men were encouraged to keep changing their socks to keep their feet as warm as possible. They learned that they could keep a pair of wet socks tucked inside their shirts so that their body heat would eventually dry them enough to be put back on and reused. That's why socks were stripped off of fallen soldiers to keep the supply of warm socks going.

They never received enough rest, even having only four hours of sleep in the first 27 hours of marching. Unless a soldier passed out, it was too cold to actually get any sound sleep anyway. Everyone became increasingly exhausted and hungry. C-rations, normally designed for one man, were available but they didn't amount to much nutrition as they were being shared between two or three men.

Men started to hallucinate over time and dreamt that they were somewhere else. It was very common during that death march to hear a soldier babble about something that made no sense at all and wander off into the night never to be seen again.

On the third day of their forced march, Gene started to lose it. He found himself doubting if they were all going to make it. He envisioned his life before all of this living hell, when he shelved his dreams of playing college football and put his education on hold. It meant nothing compared to what he and members of his crew were going through now. He could have given up. Hell, it would have been easier. He could have just lain down and let the Good Lord take him right there in a town that he couldn't even pronounce.

That day, as he walked through the first steep terrain of the Frankenwald Mountains, he had had enough. Another solider had just fallen down face first and wasn't getting back up. Tears started to well in Gene's eyes. He was desperate as were all the rest of the remaining men trudging along with him. He continued to forge on knowing that he had a life to get back to, a life that he had worked so hard to attain.

During this historical "death march", men often reminisced amongst each other about what their life had been like before all of the horrors that were happening in front of them. It was a way to keep their sanity. Gene tried to keep his banter going. However, as he walked along with Glenn, he finally snapped:

"All my life, all my dad ever talked about was having enough money. He didn't want me to do nothin' but get a goddamn job and make money. He didn't want me to play football, didn't want me to box, nothing! Just get a job and make some goddamn money so I could help out the family! Well, I'm coming home to ya, Pop! I'm comin' home. This fucking war ain't gonna stop me. I ain't gonna let this war stop me from comin' home to you and ma. I gotta a little girl I have got to get back to. She needs her Daddy! Screw Hitler, screw the Nazis, screw 'em all.

"I worked too damn hard to die in this fucking hell. I'll fight, Ma. I'll fight. You want me to get in that ring and box? Well hell that's what I'll do, so help me, God! I'm gonna show up on your doorstep one day after all of this bullshit! You wait and see. I'm gonna make it back home, I am! I promise you that!

"These bastards ain't gonna break me. No way in hell!" He cried as tears streamed down his face and froze on his cheeks. He had never let go like that, especially in front of members of his crew! Ever! He had lost all control, but as men did back in those desperate moments, Glenn stepped in and offered a "shoulder to cry on". Sadly for them, they didn't see that there was more hell to come.

They made their way into a town called Spremberg and were loaded into what were called "forties and eights", which were boxcars designed to carry forty men or eight horses. These modes of transportation had originally been used for moving livestock. Now they carried men.

Their true capacity was for no more than forty men, but each car had to make room for nearly sixty men. They were packed in those damn things like sardines and were forced to sit in single file lines like you would if you were riding in a toboggan, or half would stand while others would sit. They would trade positions when deemed necessary.

The boxcars headed south towards Stalag Luft VIIA, just outside the town of Moosburg in southeastern Germany, roughly 40 miles north of Munich. Ironically it was the same city that Gene and his crew were to bomb on their last mission before they were shot down.

Even over the rumbling of the freight cars, they could hear the bombers passing overhead dropping their bombs in the distance. They hadn't bathed in months. They were emaciated, starved and covered with lice. The food on board was very scarce, if any at all. Water was hardly offered. As the boxcars lumbered through the frozen countryside and bombed out cities, many of the men had dysentery, a disease characterized by diarrhea with passage of mucus and blood caused by some sort of infection.

Men were throwing up all over the place and it felt like they were in a moving cell that became increasingly rotten with the stench of vomit and human shit. Plus, they had to deal with the smell of dead men who didn't make it. The only true ventilation in the cars came from two small windows near the ceiling located on the opposite ends of each other. This slow methodical journey lasted a full four or five days! It was punctuated by many stops and backtracking to avoid bombed out rail lines.

They made it to their final destination and the boxcar doors were finally opened. Stalag Luft VIIA at Moosburg was a disaster. The camp had been originally built to hold 14,000 French prisoners. In the end, over 130,000 POW's of all nationalities were confined into that small, compact area.

Some of the barracks were nothing more than empty shells with dirt floors. 500 men were crammed into these buildings, if you want to call them that, which were originally suited for only 200. These facilities were all infested with vermin: rats, mice, cockroaches, etc. At least when springtime came to the area of Moosburg, Bavaria, some of the more creative POWs managed to be housed outside in makeshift tents. The camp resembled a giant hobo village as members from different Stalags continuously arrived. Miraculously, there was just enough food to keep everyone alive, but many died of pneumonia and dysentery.

All of Gene's crew were eventually evacuated to Moosburg, although the only members that Gene saw were the ones he had traveled with from his former camp. As winter slowly gave way to the warmth and colors of spring, everyone's spirits began to rise. They spent the following two and a half months at Moosburg waiting for the end of the war.

They all knew it was imminent for they figured they wouldn't have been forced on their death march and boxcar ride from hell without the looming threat to the Germans from the Soviet Union from the east and the American and Allied forces from the west. They had been told that the Allies were already in Germany and the Russians were moving in on Berlin. The end of the war was near and they all hoped that they would be freed soon if they could survive the almost unlivable conditions.

On the morning of April 29, 1945, one day before Hitler committed suicide in Berlin, the prisoners heard the rumblings from elements of the 14th Armored Division of General Patton's 3rd Army. They scrambled for safety under the barracks or hugged the ground as bullets cracked over their heads. Chaos was everywhere. P-47s and P-51s roared at treetop level over the camp with their guns blazing. They took out fleeing Nazis.

High up in the sky, prisoners could see the contrails of bombers as they headed towards their targets in Germany. They could tell by the shape of some of the contrails that fighters were engaged in dogfights with the last remnants of the Luftwaffe. The SS had long since vanished from the camp and the last remaining guards were packing up and leaving. Some of the more hard-nosed guards remained in the towers and tried to secure the perimeter of the camp. POWs shouted and cheered every plane that buzzed the camp.

Finally, the American task force broke through and the first tank crashed the barbed wired fence as it rumbled into the camp. The prisoners went wild. They were finally free! Some of the guards were rounded up, beheaded or shot, while General Patton himself pulled up in his jeep with his shiny chrome helmet glinting in the sun, white silk scarf wrapped around his neck and his matching ivory-handled six shooters belted on each side of his body. There was no mistaking the famous general, and they were thrilled to see him.

"Bet you sons of bitches are happy to see me!" he loudly proclaimed to the men who could barely hear him over the thundering engines of the tanks that now surrounded the camp.

That was the understatement of all proclamations in history. Through all of the chaos, Gene and Glenn looked at each other, smiled and cheered with the only ounce of energy they had left. Without saying a word, they knew they had survived, together!

Eventually, Gene and all of his fellow POWs were assisted onto troop transport trucks that streamed out of the camp to take their joyous passengers on the journey to France. As the sun settled over the horizon, they arrived at a makeshift staging camp affectionately called Camp Lucky Strike. They all had more food in one night than they had had in a month. Fattened up and full of piss 'n vinegar, they were ready to go home.

God Bless America!

COMING BACK A WAR HERO

The war was over, and like many others, Gene was loaded onto a ship and sent home. He had gained back a good amount of the weight that he had lost as a POW. He looked forward to getting back to the life he had left and was eager to rejoin the Rutgers University football team. As he stood on the rolling deck of the troop ship, he envisioned the moment when he would see his parents and his daughter and get back to the life he had left behind.

No one could have ever imagined what he and all of his fellow POWs had gone through. It had been, to say the least, the worst of all nightmares. But like many others, the experiences that Gene had faced throughout those try-ing times left him with a renewed sense of values, a strengthened love of country, even further improved leadership skills, and an improved ability to live in harmony with others under difficult circumstances. I guess living through that hell would do that to a man, and it did so for many, including Gene.

On a bright, sunny, New Jersey afternoon, there was a knock on the front door of Edward and Claire McManus's home in East Orange. Claire and Edward were in their backyard doing some gardening. When they heard the rap on the door, they hurried together to see who it was.

They both opened the door and there standing on their front stoop, in full uniform, was their beloved Geno. Claire instantly burst into tears of joy and Edward beamed with pride. Gene's daughter, Susan, now two years old, stood in front of him for the very first time. He picked her up and hugged her so tightly. His wife came in close as well. They all hugged Geno so hard he thought they would break him in half.

Their Geno was safe and back home. Upon his arrival back in the States, one of the first orders of business for Gene was to receive his honorary discharge as a 1st Lieutenant from the Army Air Corps. The ceremony took place on September 20th, 1945. He ended up being a highly decorated war hero when he returned home. Among his highest honors were as follows: winning the Air Medal with three clusters for his work that went above and beyond the call of duty while with the Army Air Corps.

His citation included glowing reports of his many exploits as a pilot: like getting his plane back to base after successfully dropping his bomb loads on intended targets, especially Ploesti, even when his plane was having all kinds of engine trouble and taking on flak and enemy fighter planes. Those acts were seen as valiant as many pilots would have turned back to base without finishing their mission if they were experiencing engine trouble alone.

He also received two Oak Leaves, which symbolized bravery in service under enemy fire, a Theatre Ribbon with three battle stars, honoring his exemplary service in the European theater, as well as the Presidential Unit Citation which recognized the extraordinary efforts and leadership within the 459th Bomb Group. He was extremely flattered by the recognition, but held in his heart a sad feeling that so many others who perhaps deserved more would never come home, especially Vincent "Pete" Marimpietri.

Yes, Gene came home a war hero, not that he ever bragged about it. Like many others, Gene never thought his call of duty was anything extraordinary, nor did he really want to talk about his experiences. He looked at his wartime duty as something that he was supposed to do, to perform his duty for his country to the very best of his abilities.

Like many men, Geno came home from the war and stood out among the masses for his remarkable accomplishments. He had showcased his leadership, courage, and bravery during his horrific time spent during the greatest World War. He had helped America maintain her freedom. He had beaten the odds of learning how to fly, having never flown before, and survived the arduous learning process of mastering the "truck," the B-24 Liberator. He took care of his men the best he could, and most importantly he came home safe and sound, although at times it didn't look like the latter was going to happen.

After his honorary discharge, Gene enrolled back at Rutgers University in Business Administration with the hopes of getting into real estate when he received his degree. The offer from Prudential still stood, as did his place on the Rutgers football team. He was very eager to get back onto the grid-iron, compete with his teammates and to be a different kind of leader than he had been throughout the past four and a half years.

He was named an honorary captain of the 1945 Rutgers football squad under the direction of legendary coach Harvey Harman, who was also a veteran of WW II and was eventually inducted, posthumously, into the College Football Hall of Fame in 1981 after compiling a 74-44-2 record over a 14 year span.

Gene helped lead Rutgers towards winning the Middle Three Conference Championship during that first year back from his days as a POW. The uniform and equipment had changed very little, still small shoulder pads, no thigh pads, limited knee pads and no facemasks were standard fare. The leather helmets had a little more cushion from what he remembered, but still provided very little protection.

The next year, 1946, Gene was 26 years old as the Rutgers squad was lit-tered with war veterans who eagerly looked forward to finally getting their "football legs" back underneath them. Other than a handful of games the previous year, most of the veterans hadn't played organized football for some time.

Gene gained some valuable experience in 1945 and looked forward to the following year in 1946 to once again establish himself as the number one fullback in the backfield of Rutgers' Wing T-formation. He also played both ways, as most of his teammates did, playing linebacker on defense. He wore his traditional number 31 on the back of his jersey. He was a punish-ing runner and lead blocker when called upon. He also threw a couple of touchdown passes in some big wins for the team.

The Rutgers team finished that season once again the Middle Three Con-ference Champions as they compiled a 7-2 record. They lost a heartbreaker on their opening weekend, 13-7, against Columbia University, who was looked upon as one of the powerhouses in the East in 1946.

Rutgers then went on to lose only one game after that and finished with a five game winning streak. Their biggest win during that stretch was on the road against the famous Harvard Crimson, who happened to be undefeated at the time. The Scarlet of Rutgers upset Harvard that day 13-0 in front of a huge crowd. Gene had a big game and one of his standout plays was seen as a series of photos on the cover of The Boston Sunday Globe the next morning.

It had been a perfectly timed screen pass from the quarterback that he took down the left sideline after some nifty moves, to set up a big score. He was also pictured inside the sports page as he deflected a forward pass to thwart a Harvard score in the first period, which turned out to be the closest Harvard would come to scoring the entire day.

Gene's last game as a collegiate football player was a huge honor. He was selected to the Eastern College All Stars team that would take on the professional league New York Giants at the Polo Grounds in September of 1947. He headlined that game with the 1945 Heisman trophy winner, "Mr. Inside", Doc Blanchard of Army, as they both were recognized as two of the top fullbacks in the country that year.

As he stood on the sidelines right before kickoff, Gene scanned the field to soak up the atmosphere. He then started to pan his gaze across the stands to witness all of the spectators who came out to watch that charitable game, his last game as a football player. The glory he felt was indescribable.

He drifted into a collage of many other thoughts, thoughts about all that he had been through up until that point: putting his dreams on hold for his family, flying his crew aboard the Naughty Angel, surviving the harrowing shooting down of his B-24, losing the young Marimpietri, facing death in the bitter cold in Germany, and coming back home a highly decorated war hero.

He had beaten the odds during his lifetime in so many different ways, ways that many could and would never truly understand. But he knew deep in his heart that he had truly accomplished everything he had set out to do.

He snapped out of his thoughts as he heard the coach of the All-Stars team call his name, "McManus. You're in!" He grabbed his helmet one last time and with a big smile on his face thrust it on top of his head for his final moments as a football player.

As he finished telling me his tremendous story, it felt like it was some sort of tale. But it wasn't. It was real, and I was floored. I soon realized that I had been viewing a surrealistic movie in my consciousness as my father had been telling me his story. I had been so mesmerized by his narration that I had lost all sense of where I was.

Time had been replaced by attention to every detail he told of his extraordinary experiences. Slowly the reality of my surroundings started to come back into focus. I found myself still sitting at the kitchen table. He was staring at me with a slight smile on his face. In a slow, but deliberate manner, he said, "You know, Tommy, I've never told anyone that whole story. Now, you know."

Within a few moments we both realized that we had been sitting there most of the night as we saw the moon beaming in the western sky through the front kitchen window which signaled to us that it was getting close to a brand new day.

He continued his story as he filled in the blanks of his life. "When I came home life wasn't the same as I had left it. Hell, I wasn't the same. Although we had another daughter together, your sister Linda, my first wife and I drifted slowly apart. Her name was Ruth. I grew very close to Linda but never really clicked with Susan. We just never saw eye to eye I guess. They are your sisters, though. Don't you ever forget that Tom. They're your family!"

"I had joined the Air National Guard while at Rutgers and became a Lieutenant Colonel. I met your mother shortly after I divorced my first wife. Your mother just blew me away. I knew from the moment I laid eyes on her that she was the one. I never had that true loving feeling until I met my Joanie. She was a Captain in the Air Guard and a flight nurse on board. And a very cute one at that! We would fly all over the world together. I even showed her where the railway station in Frankfurt was, where they wanted to hang me and my crew."

"I went back with the Prudential after graduating from Rutgers and after I married your mother, they transferred me to Chicago, where all you kids were born. And the rest, as they say, is history."

As he had put the final stamp on his most profound story, I found myself sitting there quietly without even being able to string a mere sentence together. I was so absorbed in all that he had just told me that my mouth couldn't even move. I just sat there, in stunned silence, and admired the man more than ever, for he was indeed my father, but now he was so much more than that. He was my hero!

A LIFE'S WORTH OF LESSONS

I leaned back in my chair across from him with my hands resting on top of my head and was totally mesmerized by the story I had just heard. I still couldn't speak. I just stared at him in awe with even more tremendous pride. He had always been the one man whom I had aspired to be like my entire life without even knowing all that he went through.

Now it was so much more. It all came to me in an instant. Up until that point, I had just accepted my dad for who he was, a tough loving disciplinarian, who loved his wife and his family. Now I knew why he was who he was. I finally understood him, which meant everything to me. It was like our relationship came full circle, at that precise moment, and I loved him even more.

But, the lesson wasn't finished. As I sat there in awe of my dad, I began to see that all I had aspired to achieve in the upcoming weeks paled in significance in the context of what he and so many others had gone through in that war. I finally managed to utter a few words and a question that I desperately needed to know: "My God, Dad, that's unreal. It's unbelievable. I can't even fathom going through that. How old were you?"

"I was 24!" he responded without hesitation as he looked deep into my eyes.

"Holy shit", I thought to myself. He was the same age as I was at that time. I immediately questioned in my mind if I would have had the courage and bravery to live through what he went through. Words could not describe how right then and there I held my father in even higher regard. He was my age and had gone through hell. How could I ever have a complaint about anything or take for granted what I had?

In the serene silence of those moments, he softly spoke: "War is terrible, Tom. I would never want you boys to ever have to go to war. It's all about killing. Many men went overseas to fight for our country's freedom and many didn't come back. And those who did make it back were never the same again. It's something that you never get over."

I reflected on that and said, "After all these years, with all of our talks, you never mentioned the war. I was always afraid to even bring it up to you, until now."

"I could sit here and tell you all about the war, everything I saw, everything that me and my crew went through, until I was blue in the face. Yet, you still wouldn't quite understand what it was like. It was absolutely horrible. Unless you lived it, you wouldn't be able to totally comprehend what I was telling you," he soberly responded.

"I was responsible for my crew. I had the responsibility of making sure that they came back home safely to their loved ones. One of my guys didn't make it. He was the youngest member of my team and above all the rest he was the one I wanted to look out for the most.

"When his chute didn't open, it was the most gut-wrenching moment I had ever had up until that point. People like me fought for this great country, so that we all could have our freedom. Those Nazi bastards wanted to take over the world and I was going to do all that I could to never let that happen."

He sat in silence for a few moments, obviously consumed by his thoughts, and then in a very deliberate motion he picked up his glass full of melted ice and the last drippings of Canadian Club in his left hand and slowly raised it to the sky. With his right hand he followed with a slow, gentle salute. I couldn't think of anything that would have been an appropriate response. I could only say: "Dad, I never knew that about you. You guys were incredible!"

Not wanting to bask in his glory, he immediately changed the subject to the uphill battle that I faced in front of me. "You have worked real hard, Tom, and you look real good. I am so damn proud of you for the way you have busted your butt and the way you have kept your dream alive. A lot of guys your age would have packed it in a long time ago. You stuck it out. You are a few weeks away from training camp and you face a tremendous opportunity. You are more than ready. Keep working your tail off and when you get up to training camp you have to maintain the mindset that you can do it. You must outwork everyone and make sure that you stand out in the coaches' eyes. I know you can do it!" His face lit up with a big, broad grin.

"Thanks, Dad. You and I worked together. I'll never forget the way you have helped me. When I make it this time, it will be for the both of us!" I replied as we both got up from our chairs and gave each other a big, sincere hug.

Then, as he had done a million times before, he grabbed my arm with one of his vice-grip like hands and with his other arm started giving me playful rabbit punches to my side. "And by the way, you're lucky it's not me your going against cause I'd run right through ya!" he quipped. "You wouldn't stand a chance!" I mused back.

"Maybe we should do more running tomorrow, don't ya think?" he asked as we were face to face, or I should say, face to neck.

"What's this we stuff again? You've got a mouse in your pocket?" I responded to him jokingly as I had many times before.

We then gave each other another bear hug and grappled in our standard dance, laughing the whole time. He then said the words that I always cherished and can still hear ringing in my ears: "I love you, Tom."

"I love you too, Dad. You're the best." I responded with all the sincerity I had in my body. "You better get some rest and we'll catch up in the morning. By the way, try not to get the peanut butter all over the front of your shirt in the morning, all right?" I finished as we parted ways. It was about 4:30 in the AM.

He staggered towards his bedroom as I told him I would lock up the house. After locking the front door, I went very quietly out the back patio door. The remaining moon lit up the entire golf course. I stood there in silence trying to take in what had just happened. I couldn't stop thinking that the man I always looked up to was now so much more than that.

It was like he was suddenly some kind of superhero in my eyes. I could have run through a brick wall for him right then and there. If he could withstand all that he had to face when he was my age, then, dammit, I could handle anything that was going to be thrown my way trying to make the Jaguars football team.

My mind raced as I thought of all that he and his crew had gone through. Those guys were the real men. I learned that night and concluded that toughness didn't come from winning some bullshit fistfight or crushing some running back at the goal line. No, toughness is what those men and so many others did in that generation. They all came together as a team, as a unit, as one. They dropped everything in their lives to go into battle and save the United States of America.

It was a night of historical learning. I suddenly came to grips with what is really important in life. His generation gave so much more of themselves so that I could enjoy the fruits of a much simpler life in America.

And they did it because it had to be done. They didn't need to talk about it after it was over. It wasn't a victory to celebrate, only a cause to be won and to help live life as free men and women and move on. Any memories would be too painful to recall. Men died but were never forgotten. Others lived to build America. My dad was an integral part of that history and I didn't know the magnitude of it all until then.

When I went back inside, I lay down on the couch. As I had done my whole life, I said my prayers before I went to sleep, but this time I added the most sincere prayer ending that I could assemble together. I closed my eyes tightly and said to the Good Lord, "God Bless those men and God Bless my Geno!"

Crew in Italy
(Dad, standing far right)

Eastern College All Star Football Team: These are the boys who will play the New York Giants in the Polo Grounds Wednesday night. Front row (left to right): Art Young, Dartmouth; Al Patrella, Canisius; Paul Walker, Yale; Johnny Martin, assistant manager and mascot; Bill Sullivan, Villanova; Jim Enos, Army; Joe Ososki, Fordham; Arnold Tucker, Army; Paul McKee, Syracuse; Fred Grace, St. Bonaventure. Second row: Eddie Zanfrini, *trainer; Lou Daukas, Cornell; Don Kasprzak, Columbia; Bob Orlando, Colgate; Andy Gustafson, backfield coach; Tass McLaughry, head coach; John Dell Isola, line coach; Steve Cipot, St. Bonaventure; Tony Stellani, Delaware; Joe Bartos, Navy; Jim Andrejco, Fordham; Bernie Check, Niagara. Third row: Dr. Ernest A. Weymuller, team surgeon; Tom Hayes, Army; Jack Medd, Wesleyan; Merrill Frost, Dartmouth; Sam? ...* *Western Maryland; Harold Tarzel, Army; Bill Schuler, ? Gene McManus, Rutgers; Jim Hefti, St. Lawrence; Doc Blanch? Army; Glenn Davis, Army; Shelton Biles, Army; Hank Majli? N. Y. U.; John Vaina, manager. Back row: Joe Watt, Syra? Red Moore, Penn State; Burt Vander Clute, Wesleyan; Ed St? Colgate; Bill West, Army; Eddie Allen, Penn; Jim Carring? ...*

Eastern College All-Stars Team Photo
Dad in-between #74 and #22
Doc Blanchard #35; Glenn Davis #41

Gene & Joanie at dinner

Family Photo
(cool plaid shorts, huh?)

THE LONGSHOT

I arrived in Stevens Point, Wisconsin for the first ever Jacksonville Jaguars training camp in the middle of July in 1995. I knew going in that I was a long shot to even make the team, but I was very determined to show the coaching staff that I did belong.

I still felt that there were a few coaches on staff who thought that I was only there because Coach Coughlin was doing me a favor. They never said it, but I could feel it. In my mind, I knew that I had to work extra hard and show that I was fighting for a spot on that team much more than anyone else.

When I went to our first few meetings, the first being a special teams meeting, where we went over every special team drill: punt coverage, punt return, and kickoff and kickoff return, I saw something that confirmed my place on the team and in the coaches' eyes. When the special teams' coach put up the depth charts for the very first time for each one of those teams, the name McManus was on the last row of each team, meaning that I was about on the fifth string, looking up.

I knew that only the first couple of rows, up to the second string, or the backups as they were known, had the best chance to make the team. Fifth string meant that I would barely get enough opportunities to even show that I could make a difference during each one of the next few weeks.

The days to follow were to be special teams' drills. That meant that if I got one opportunity, or repetition as it was called, during a specific drill, then I better make sure that I did my job absolutely correctly, whether it was blocking someone successfully on any of the return teams or getting down the field in a timely fashion to make a tackle on one of the coverage units. I was going to be tested to my limits and I knew it. I had to grab the attention of the coaches or I was toast.

I also knew going in how making a team works because I had been through it before with New Orleans. There are the starters, who were pretty much locked in to make the squad. A lot of the starters were predetermined by the amount of money that the team had already invested in them, whether as a high-priced free agent or a highly drafted rookie.

To be honest, most of the starters who were at the top of the depth charts were very good players. I mean, management wasn't going to pay incredible amounts of money to some player who was a dog. Management was sometimes wrong in their assessment of their accumulated talent, but they were right much more often than not.

Then there were the backups, listed right behind the starters. It was common knowledge that if you were a backup, you better make an impact on special teams or they would find someone who would, and you would quickly be out of a job.

When I got to my first defensive team and position meetings, I was down on the depth chart there as well. I was on the bottom of the list. A little bit of self-doubt crept in, but I knew I had worked too hard to get to this point and fail. Plus, I always reminded myself of the trials and tribulations that my father had gone through at the same age as I was at the time.

Training camp was your typical camp run by Tom Coughlin. It was very physically demanding, whether it was practicing in pads multiple times per day or the conditioning that we were put through each day. Practicing in pads meant that there was a lot of contact, a lot of hitting.

We did have to be careful not to get anyone hurt, so there wasn't a lot of tackling to the ground during camp, but as a linebacker, I still had to take on much bigger offensive linemen and try to defeat their block or run into them hard enough that I could plug up the hole that the running back was trying to get through.

Then came hitting the backs. They were pretty big guys, too, not built like a linebacker per se, who as an example, I weighed about 245 pounds or more. But the typical back was around 225 pounds. However, with their advanced speed it brought extra power to their frame. That was, if they weren't afraid to use it and get wracked by one of us linebackers.

So whether I was taking on a 300+ pound lineman or hitting a running back at full speed, it took a huge toll on the body. This went on day after day after day, for many weeks. I started off a little rusty practicing in pads, for I hadn't worn them in almost two years, but I did settle down after a few days and got back to the style of football I was used to playing back at BC.

Conditioning drills consisted of numerous sprints. We would have twelve to fifteen 120 yard sprints for time, meaning you had to cover that ground in a specific amount of time based on the position you played. Lineman had a couple of extra seconds to cross the finish line after each sprint, and defensive backs and wide receivers had less time to achieve the expected sprint times.

We also ran gassers, which consisted of running from one sideline to the next and then touching that line and turning back to the sideline where we had started. Sometimes we just had to run there and back but sometimes we had to run double that for each sprint. We would do anywhere from 4 to 6 of these reps which covered anywhere from 100 to 200 yards. It was grueling exercise, especially after a full padded practice.

I knew what Coach Coughlin was doing. It was just like he had done at Boston College. He wasn't necessarily "weeding out the weak" like he did at BC, but he did want to see who would go the extra mile when they were worn out and beat down.

Some of the veteran players didn't actually appreciate what Coughlin was doing. They felt that he was being too excessive with his practice schedules and conditioning drills. They had no problem working hard, for most of the players knew what it took to make it to the elite level, but they also knew that Coughlin was treading a fine line as to what was allowable at practice per the players union's agreement with the owners of the league and what was deemed to be excessive. Sometimes he cut the line so thin that a couple of the veterans, in an anonymous fashion, contacted the union to complain again.

For me, I didn't care what he was doing. It was brutally hard but I knew this was my last shot and I wasn't, by any means, in a position to complain. I had it emblazoned in my mind that I would push myself to the upper limits and never let anyone outwork me.

I believe to this day that it made me stand out as someone who could handle that type of adversity. Hell, with what my dad went through during his days as a POW, especially on the death march with soldiers dying left and right, there was no way I was going to cave in to running excessive wind sprints.

Wisconsin was supposed to give us a little reprieve from the Florida heat, but, unfortunately for us, a heat wave ran through the Midwest that summer and guys began dropping like flies.

Coughlin would state in every team meeting that was held that, "No player would make his team in the tub," meaning that if you weren't on the practice field and in the training room you wouldn't make the squad. Now we all knew that didn't ring true for everyone, especially guys who had signed big contracts, but for me and many other guys trying to make it, it absolutely rang true.

I did have a bout with fatigue during camp. I tried to hide it by not telling anyone, but one of the veteran defensive leaders and a guy who turned into a good friend of mine, Jeff Lageman, noticed my appearance. He approached me in the training room after practice one afternoon. I had dropped 15 pounds in 4 days and I must have lost some color to my face because he asked what I was weighing. When I told him, he brought the head trainer, Mike Ryan, to my attention and told him the news. They both suggested that I take a couple of days off.

"No way. I can't afford to do that. This is my last shot. Just give me some supplements and I'll be fine," I quickly responded, knowing that if there was one guy who couldn't afford to miss any time, it was me. At least that was my thinking. I ended up drinking cans and cans of pure protein drinks. They actually tasted pretty good and little by little I gained most of my weight back.

After a couple of weeks, a couple of guys who were ahead of me on the depth chart at the linebacker position started missing practice time, which meant that I would get more opportunities. That helped me out a bunch, especially when we ran full speed goal-line drills. They consisted of the offense and defense lining up against one and other with the offense trying to score a touchdown and the defense trying to stop them.

The offense ran mostly running plays, much to my liking. I never looked forward to the pass drill exercises, for I felt they could expose my weaknesses. During those specific drills, we would have to cover a running back in open space, one-on-one, meaning there were no other players around to impede his route. They would run a pass pattern and I would have to try to cover him. They were so fast and it really wasn't my forte, so I never felt good, or even looked good during those drills.

But, the goal line drills were right up my alley. One thing that I could always do was hit. I loved the contact aspect of my position, especially in smaller confined spaces, like the goal line stand situation. I would come up and slam into the running back with a crushing blow, as his or my helmet usually came popping off from the force of the impact.

I don't care what any coach says, they love it when their linebackers are physical. You can run and cover the pass and that was important, but they thrived when a linebacker came up and smashed the runner, or as we would call it, "laid the wood" to the running back. Damn, I loved that part of the game.

We broke training camp in Wisconsin after about three and a half weeks and headed back down south. Training camp was far from over, but we would soon trim down practices to one per day for we were in the middle of the preseason. We would play five preseason games that year, and as we approached the last couple of games, the pressure of making the team mounted higher and higher. I played okay in the first couple of preseason games, making a couple of tackles, including one or two on special teams, but I was still listed down at the bottom of the depth charts.

My mind was consumed daily with wanting to know where I stood on the team. It seemed that every play that I was out on the field was my own personal "Super Bowl", meaning that I had to stand out every chance I got even if it was for about five plays during a game, which was the case for the first few preseason games.

I talked with my mom and dad by phone a few times a week, not really being able to offer them much on where I stood because I didn't really know myself. My dad would always finish the conversation with: "Just keep working hard and lay it all out there. All you can do is to try your best." We would always say our "I love you's" prior to hanging up the phone as we had done so many times before.

Then a little luck came my way. During the week of the fourth preseason game, both starters at inside linebacker (our defense called for two inside linebackers) had gone down with injuries and would not be suiting up for that week's game. One of the backups also went down, so that meant that I moved up the depth charts. My confidence grew as I knew during the week that I was going to be given more opportunities to be in the game. My 5 plays per game as in the weeks prior jumped up to over 25 plays per game, and I made the most of it.

The fourth preseason game that year was the first ever home game in Jacksonville, in front of the home town crowd. Over 70,000 screaming fans showed up to see us play the St. Louis Rams, and my mom and dad were in attendance. Jacksonville had tried for over a decade to get an NFL franchise so the fans were pumped up to see their team for the very first time in live game action.

I had a bunch of tackles, a sack, and was a pretty active linebacker, which meant I was around the ball quite often. I was getting off blocks and I was making tackles on the opposing team's running back near or at the line of scrimmage, meaning that he wasn't gaining many yards against me. I ended up being the leading tackler at my position for that fourth game, which brought me even more playing time for the final week and game of the preseason.

I would see my parents after the game but couldn't really spend that much time with them for I was expected back at the hotel. We would go get a bite to eat and my dad would critique my play as he had done so often in the past. I enjoyed it, for I knew he knew what he was talking about and it was always great to see them.

Whether I made the team or not, I knew in their hearts that they were proud of me. I was just hoping that I had done enough to survive the next day. That was the day the team would be cutting down their roster. I made the first round of cuts, which took the team from around roughly 85 players down to the low 60s. The final cuts would come after the last preseason game.

Cuts came on a specific day after the fourth game. It was usually done on a Tuesday and the staff member who let the specific player know that he had been cut was called the "Turk". He would enter the locker room or pay a visit to your hotel room and tell you that "The coach wants to see you and bring your playbook." If those words came out of the "Turk's" mouth directed at a player, that player knew that his dream was over.

It fucking sucked, getting cut. I'm not going to lie. I still had vivid memories when the New Orleans Saints cut me and the "Turk" called my hotel room to give me the news. It's the worst feeling in the world for a football player. Although they don't come right out and say you don't have the skills to make their ball club, they're not that classless, at least from my experience.

They usually say "We've got to let you go", or "We aren't keeping enough guys at your position to keep you on the team." But regardless of what the say, they're basically telling you that you're not good enough. It's the hardest thing a football player has to take. Even the guys who make the team feel bad for the guys who get cut for they know you've worked your ass off during camp and they know that your dream of playing in the NFL is probably over. As Coach Coughlin would often say: "If it was easy, then everyone would be doing it!" He was right on the money.

The last preseason game was against the Denver Broncos, again in front of the home crowd. I was told before the game by my linebacker coach, Steve Szabo, the importance of the game for me. He was the one who first called me out of the blue to see if I wanted to work out for Coach Coughlin.

"You need to have your best game tonight, Tommy," he started off. "Only your best will earn you a chance to make this team. You need to know that going in," he continued. He finished with a pat on the backside and said, "Good luck and go get 'em!"

I knew he was right. I had one more chance. It was solely up to me to determine whether I was in or out.

I entered the stadium with the team in front of another momentous, raucous home crowd. This was a huge game for me, and it was so very appropriate that my mom and dad were in the stands once again as they had been so many times before. The stage was set and the setting was incredible, at least to me.

The veterans, who had already earned their spot on the team, and the starters, who also had already made their mark, wanted nothing more than to get this game over with so that the regular season would start. For me, this was it. This was my start, or my finish.

A good game that night and I had a good chance to make it. A poor outing and my dream was over. The pressure mounted. I said my prayers before the game at my locker asking the Good Lord to keep me healthy and to please allow me to be at my best.

I had a good, solid performance. It wasn't great but I was very active. I made a handful of good solid tackles. I made all the right calls for the defense, as every middle linebacker needs to do, getting them in the right alignment and making sure the pass coverage was right. I was always my hardest critic, but I felt good about what I did out there.

I didn't make any spectacular plays like a sack or an interception but I was more than decent. My task was to be a leader and direct traffic, get a play in when I could, show I could hit, but make sure my defense didn't make any mistakes.

As the final whistle blew, I knew now it was up to the coaches to decide if my effort was good enough. They knew that I wasn't their starting middle linebacker, but now the question was whether they could use me as a backup who could play special teams and who had a specific role on their defense: to help stop the running game of the opposing team when needed, like on the goal line.

I met my parents in the parking lot and was greeted by our normal round of hugs. My mom of course said, "You played great," just like the great mother she was. My dad reached out and pulled me close and said, "Good game".

Neither one of us felt confident that I was a locked in to make the team. I think we were both jaded from my past experience with the Saints. Back then we both felt that I was a shoe-in after my performance in the last pre-season game to make that squad back in 1993, so we approached this time with more of a conservative look. We both knew that it could go either way. We again went out to eat, and enjoyed each other's company.

At the restaurant we ran into one of the quarterbacks, Steve Buerlein, and some of his family. He impressed my dad so much by offering to pay for our drinks that night. My dad always brought up Steve's name when talking about the team and saying how "Great a guy he is." A little kind gesture went a long way with my father and after knowing his life story I can understand why.

The final cuts were to take place the following day, so this time I didn't stay up too late. I learned my lesson from my last go-round. I said my goodbyes to my mom and dad, not knowing my fate, and let them know that I would call them immediately when I heard something, good or bad. They dropped me off and headed back down to their home in New Smyrna Beach.

THE MOMENT OF TRUTH

The next morning I awoke to a ton of anxiety and nervousness. I quickly showered and headed to the stadium. I went straight to the locker room, keeping my head down, hoping not to run into the "Turk" in the hallway. I went to my locker and sat there and waited. A bunch of the veterans were getting their weightlifting workout in while waiting to go out on the field as a team for some conditioning, a ritual held the day after every NFL game. The thinking was to get the blood flowing and, hopefully, to drain out any bumps and bruises from the previous day's game.

As I sat there wondering what was going to happen, I saw the "Turk" enter the locker room out of the corner of my eye. He had a sheet of paper in his hand and was looking out over the room, obviously trying to spot one of his targets. Fuck, I thought to myself as I leaned over, resting my forearms on my thighs with my fingers crossed in each hand.

I kept my head down, praying silently that he wasn't going to be standing in front of me if I looked up. Needless to say, I was scared shitless. Would he call my name or pass me by? I swear I could hear the second hand clicking on the clock on the wall, even though there were players all over the place. Other guys were saying their "goodbyes and good lucks" to the players who already had been paid a visit by the "Turk". The waiting to see if the "Turk" was going to call my name seemed to last a lifetime.

The tension was more that I could bear so I finally got dressed in my official Jaguar workout gear and headed out to the practice field, not knowing if the "Turk" was going to pluck me from the hallway or not. I kept looking over my shoulder as I walked towards the light of the outside of the stadium and the practice fields. No one said a word to me, so I really didn't know what to think, and quite frankly I didn't trust my instincts as to where I fell in the lineup on the team.

When I reached the practice field, I lined up in the stretching formation as I had always done during training camp. We stretched and then the conditioning coach blew the whistle, which meant that it was time for our 100 yard sprints. These weren't full speed sprints but just enough to get the blood flowing and the muscles stretched.

As I made my way down the sideline, (I always liked running next to it for some reason), I was in a little bit of shock. The reality of what was happening, or what wasn't happening, hadn't really sunk in. A veteran defensive back named Vinnie Clark came up to me after one of his runs as I waited my turn for the next run back, "Congratulations T-Mac. You've been ballin' man." He relaxed me but I was still in a fog. I just couldn't get my brain to work as I ran back down the field.

When the conditioning drill was over, Tom Coughlin blew his whistle to announce that it was time to huddle up before we broke from that day's session. All of the players gathered around Coach. Some of the guys had an arm draped over the shoulder of a buddy. Coach Coughlin started to address what he referred to as "My first ever Jacksonville Jaguar team." I didn't even hear a word he said from that instant on as I kept hearing myself shouting in my head, "Holy shit! Holy Shit! I made it! I fucking made it!" I could barely contain myself.

We broke the huddle and Steve Szabo came over and put his hand out and offered me a congratulatory handshake. "Congratulations Tom. You made it. Now, you've got to keep busting your ass to confirm every day that you belong."

"Yes, Coach. Thanks so much. Without your phone call, I wouldn't even be here. I can't thank you enough for helping me get this opportunity." I was a little choked up but trying to stay cool in my sincerity.

"Hey, you did it all. I'm real happy for you!" He countered, sensing my emotion.

As I headed inside the facility, I had only one thing on my mind. I had to tell my best friend the great news. I ran to a pay phone and called my parents' house, collect. Once I got through, I was greeted by my dad: "Tommy, how'd it go?" he quickly asked. I could hear the anxiety in his voice.

"We did it, Dad. We did it! Looks like you can now tell all your friends that your son is a member of the Jacksonville Jaguars!" I could barely contain my excitement and pride.

His voice erupted in joy: "That's great Tom! You did it! I am so damn proud of you! You set a goal and saw it through!"

"No! We did it, Dad. You and me together. I could have never done it without you or Mom. I'll never forget what you did for me, Dad. I love you guys so much!" I countered back.

"Hold on, your mom's right here", he said and I could hear him tell her as he cupped the phone: "He made it!" When my mom got on the other end, she said with her warm loving voice, "Tommy, congratulations. I am so happy for you."

All I could say was: "Thanks, Mom. Thanks for everything. I love you! I'll see you guys up here for opening weekend next week." I finished and hung up the phone but not before I could hear Geno in the background yelling, "He did it!" I could visualize him dancing around the room in celebration.

I hung up the phone with a tremendous feeling of accomplishment. I had finally made it to the NFL. But I knew it was only the beginning for I would always have to show my teammates and the staff that they could count on me. I learned that from the greatest teacher I had ever had.

THE BEST OF TIMES AND
THE WORST OF TIMES

The 1995 inaugural season of the Jacksonville Jaguars was a tough one. The city had invested years of negotiations, incentive deals, promised supportive revenues and prayers to get their NFL franchise. Coach Coughlin had assembled the best team that he could muster given his budget and the available talent. Thank the Good Lord, I was one of them. Although our record didn't show it, we weren't a terrible team. Our record on paper sucked, but for a first year franchise team, we started to emerge.

Mark Brunell was proving himself as an up and coming starting quarterback with some unique and talked-about skills, often compared to a Steve Young type. Tony Boselli, the Jaguar's first ever first round pick in the draft, was already being touted as a potential Hall of Fame prospect.

Jeff Lageman, Kelvin Pritchett, and Don Davey, veteran defensive linemen, made their presence known on an unknown defense. James "Little Man" Stewart was a young tough running back, who was also a good friend. There were several more that no one had heard of, but they made significant contributions to the genesis of the Jaguars' later successes, such as Jimmy Smith, who before he broke out as a dominant receiver, was a great special teams player.

I played mostly on special teams and on short yardage and goal line packages, which were normally used when the opposing team's offense was going to go for a first down when the yardage was short. In a short yardage situation, it had to be 3rd & 3 or less for me to be called onto the field. On the goal line, the opposing offense usually was at or inside the 5 yard line and going in for a score. My job on both of those types of situations was to help stop that team from converting a first down or to stop them from scoring. I was good in that role for most of the time.

During those specific situations, the opposing offense's play call was typically a run, usually between the offensive tackles. My job was either to make the tackle or at the very least plug the hole that the running back was trying to get through that was created by a center, guard, or tackle. Basically, it was to stop the run. It was my "specialty," so to speak. It wasn't that I couldn't cover the pass, but I was much better known as a "run stopper".

In my first year with the Jaguars, I looked forward to playing on any play, no matter the circumstance. However, I was considered a role player, which can be crucial at times, depending on the situation and at what point that situation comes up during a game. Most teams are made up of starters and backups, some of whom had specific roles on the team.

As a backup, my role was to perform and make tackles on special teams and when called upon to stop the run. Different players had different roles. For instance, there is a specific role on every team called the "gunner". His job is to line up out wide during a punt formation on fourth down and get down the field faster than anyone else and either make a tackle or to down the football. Although his role wasn't a huge one, it was still very important.

During that first year, I actually got the chance to start two games at middle linebacker due to injuries to the starter ahead of me. Once that happened, I got to taste what it was like to start in the NFL. My goals instantly changed after that. Making the NFL wasn't enough for me any more. My new goal and target was to be a fulltime starter, although I knew I had a good player in front of me who was a high round draft pick. He had a big paycheck and would be given every chance to be "the guy", so I faced quite a challenge in that regard. When called upon, I had to impress enough so that when the starter did go down again, the coaching staff had confidence in me to fill the void left by that injured starter.

It was terrific good fortune and pretty coincidental that my parents lived somewhat close to Jacksonville. New Smyrna Beach was so close that they could drive up and make all of the home games, something they couldn't always do while I was at BC.

It all seemed so perfect. I was realizing a dream I had held since I was a little boy, battled through my own adversities as a player and, in my quest, was playing in front of the man who helped pave the way for me my entire life.

It was so amazing to be so close to my mom and dad, not only geographically but personally as well, and share this great experience with them.

After every home game I would race to the locker room, quickly shower up, get dressed and head out to the players-only parking lot. There were always some friends and family at the games and we always had a little tailgating action going on after each contest, as did most of my teammates and their respective families. As I approached each small gathering in the lot, and said hello to various people, my mom and dad's car was my only actual stop.

Geno would have his chair set up with a beer in hand, just like he always had done. He was usually holding court with anyone who would listen. My friends who came into town always loved to hear his tales, his insights, his advice, his analysis of the game, whatever he wanted to talk about. He was given the utmost respect by all of those who were there. They all knew that he knew a great deal about football and what it took for someone to succeed.

I would sit down next to him and he would start to critique my play like he had since I was a very young kid and we would discuss all aspects of the game that had just been played. A couple of teammates would occasionally drop by to have a beer and just say hello.

He would often engage in a discussion about some aspect of the game that was just played. They could tell he knew what he was talking about so they obliged, but it was more just out of respect I guess. I always thought it was very considerate, and I would return the favor when the situation called for it.

The party would resume back at an oceanfront condo that I was renting with my friend and teammate, Pete Mitchell, another BC alum. He and his family, including at least one of his three brothers, would attend most of the home games. He was the youngest as well in his family so they always wanted to be close with him. Our families got along great. Pete and I had a close bond and our respective brothers and other family and friends became close friends too.

We had a third bedroom in our apartment which was used as a spare room, so I always let my parents sleep in my room and we would crash wherever we could find a spot. Our parties would last well into the night, even after all of us boys went out and hit the town at the beach. They were great times, and even though it's as cliché as it sounds, I was living the dream: friends, family, condo on the beach, pro football and, yes, the local nightlife.

During the games I did start, they were played in front of the home Jacksonville crowd. The highlight of those games for me was against my "home team" that I rooted for when I was growing up, the Chicago Bears. Coach Coughlin actually named me an honorary captain for that game, something he did throughout the year with different players for different games. I was thrilled and flattered especially since my mom and dad were again in attendance.

That game was extra special as a bunch of family and friends from back home joined my mom and dad in the stands. Included were my brothers and sister, Mike Flood and Murph, Geno's old coaching buddies, and a couple of my close friends. We lost that game by only three points. It was a tight game and, as always, a tough loss, but I ended up having had a pretty good game and led the defense in tackles.

During my brief stretch as a starter that year, I was mostly used on first and second down. Most teams back in the mid 1990's would run the ball on those early downs, with the hopes of gaining positive yardage, which usually equated to about 3 to 4 yards per carry, unless the running back broke a long one. If they accomplished that goal, then when it was third down, they wouldn't have that far to go, typically another three to four yards, or less. Statistics have always shown that most teams convert on third and short, gaining another set of downs.

My job was critically important to our defense's success. If a defense stops the opposing offense for little or no gain on first and second down then it is a lot harder for that offense to convert a first down from third and long, which would be considered seven yards or more.

You may often have heard the defensive jargon, "three and out". That means to stop the offense on three downs and force them to punt, which gave your offense the ball back. Some teams would throw the ball on those early downs and I usually had to cover a Tight End, which I could do decently. I had to show that I could get it done on passing downs so that the staff didn't feel that I was a liability in that department. It's a funny thing, though, once you are labeled a specific "type" of player that label sticks with you until you prove otherwise. All right, that's enough of the X's and O's bullshit.

I was having the time of my life, on and off the field, and my dad was so much in his element. He couldn't stop himself from bragging that his son was a linebacker in the National Football League! He was so damn proud and happy, and quite frankly, I was happy for him, and for my mother too. She loved the game as much as we did.

Maybe Geno felt as though he was living vicariously through my NFL career. After all, he had been a hell of a football player himself who had chosen to decline the opportunity to enter the fledgling professional football league in the late 40's. But now his son was there and he knew the long road it had taken me to get there. I always played for him. I truly did.

Sure, I played for my team and for myself, but my greatest motivator was to play for Geno's approval. He was my father, my mentor and my best friend. Life was so damn good! Unless you've ever made it to the highest level in a sport, you cannot completely understand the euphoria and gratitude you hold for all who helped you achieve your life's ambition. I had made it to the "big leagues" and my dad was there to see me play. How great was that? Trust me, words can't even begin to describe it.

During the middle of the season, we had a stretch of games that were played on the road. The injured starter, whom I had replaced, came back healthy, which meant I was relegated to a backup spot and a special teams player. It was somewhat tough to take, although I saw it coming.

I thought I was better than the starter, given the opportunity, but sometimes you just have to deal with the cards you are dealt, so I went about my business and contributed as much as I could when I was called upon to do so. I yearned for more, but I also felt very fortunate to be where I was.

I talked with my parents every week, more than once usually, and filled them in as to what was going on, on and off the field. During this time, I can remember my dad was starting to complain about some back pain when we would talk on the phone, but it never stopped him from continuing his daily morning workouts, or walking 18 holes of golf.

I didn't get the chance to see them that often during the weeks that spanned out during our away games, but I did get the chance to drive down there on one of my off days, always on Tuesdays, which was mandated by the NFL. I looked forward to every break I had when I could go home and see my mom and dad. On one such day off, I drove down and did just that.

I looked out the back patio when I arrived and saw my dad walking home from the golf course, tugging his walking cart holding his golf bag behind him. He always chose to pull his clubs on his old hand-pulled cart rather than drive a motorized golf cart which he characterized was for "Old Farts."

Real men, he proclaimed, pulled their own weight. However, he didn't look his normal self. He looked tired and was slumped over as he seemed to be dragging his cart behind him with a lot of effort. There didn't seem to be his usual sprightly cadence to his step. When he approached me, he told me that his back was hurting, but he just did get finished playing a full round so I thought that was to be expected of a man in his mid-70s, even if he was somewhat fit.

It was always great to see my folks and it was like we never left each other. We had a few beers after Dad cleaned up and talked about things, same as usual. I spent the night and most of the next day before I headed back up to Jacksonville. I organized plans for them to come up for Thanksgiving and spend it at the condo. We had a home game that weekend, so it was much easier for them to come up and stay the weekend than for me to go down to them for half a day.

Geno's 75th birthday was on the following Monday after the holiday, so we planned to celebrate all of it in one big long weekend party - Thanksgiving, his birthday, and of course, some NFL football!

I went out to the local mall on the Friday before the Thanksgiving holiday and bought my dad his birthday present. I knew exactly what I wanted to buy for him as I had thought about it for weeks. It was awesome knowing that I could afford to buy something cool for him.

It was a new TV and stereo system that would be delivered to his home in a couple of weeks. It was the least I could do for him. He deserved it, as did my mom. They deserved anything and everything that I could give them. I knew Geno would be totally pumped to watch his son play football on a brand new 36-inch television.

He and his Joanie also loved to listen to their favorite music. They could play all that big band music from the 30's and 40's as loud as they wanted. I asked the salesperson to scan and print me out a picture and description of his new kickass system so I could at least have something to give to him on his special day.

After the November 26th game against the Cincinnati Bengals, which we lost 17-13, our weekend was pretty much wrapped up. We all ended up back at the condo as usual. As we were finishing up the festivities that evening, Dad had gone to bed somewhat early. He wasn't feeling very well. He had a slight fever and had complained of being very tired. It was only about 8:30 so it wasn't like he went out that early, but he retired to my room much sooner than normal for him, especially after a game.

Everyone pretty much filtered out of the condo after that and the Mitchell brothers, with me and my brother Mike, readied to head out for the night. We were always full speed when it came to drinking and chasing girls, so this night was really no different.

Before I left, though, I told my mom that I would head down to the local pharmacy and pick up Dad some flu and cold medicine. I didn't really keep any at the house. I never really needed it. If I was sick, I would just see the team doctor and he would give me medicine as needed right there at the facility. I never had to see an outside doctor or buy any household medicines, which was just one of the perks of being a professional football player.

So before I would meet up with everyone, I went out to a pharmacy and came back with a bunch of stuff. I figured I would get one of almost everything because I didn't really know what ailed him except that he was running fever, and no one feels good when they have a fever. The faster you can get some relief from it, the better you feel. That's about all I knew about medicine. I think I came home with two bags full. I dropped it all off gave it to my mom, kissed her goodnight, and headed out.

When Mike and I returned home a little early, he went directly to the bathroom and I headed for the kitchen to raid the fridge. To my surprise I found our mom standing in the kitchen. She was just standing there, staring off into space, apparently waiting for our return. She asked if Mike and I were the only ones who came back, which I assured her that we were. She then looked at me in a way that I had never seen before. She very calmly, but very deliberately said in a soft voice, "Tommy, your dad is sick."

"Yeah, I know. He's not feeling well, huh? What's he have, the flu or something? Did the medicine not work?" I responded.

"Tommy, listen to me. Your father is really ill. He didn't want me to tell you boys this yet, but he's been diagnosed with cancer!" she said to me.

I immediately pulled her close and hugged her. Mike also came into the kitchen as he overheard her upon his return form the bathroom. All three of us just stood in the middle of the kitchen in a family embrace.

Cancer! The scariest word I had ever heard in my life. My father had cancer! I immediately went into defense mode and told my mom that I would set up a second opinion through the Jaguars' team doctor and we'd make sure that their doctor knew what the hell he was talking about. Geno was tough as nails, I kept telling myself. If anyone could beat cancer, it sure as hell was my father.

After all he had been through in his life, all of the life and death experiences he had faced, all the adversity he had overcome, surely he could beat any illness, even something as serious as cancer, which up until this point I didn't know anyone who had suffered from it, at least not a loved one.

The next morning when we all got up, Geno was in a good mood. I was still in some serious denial about his diagnosis. Nothing had really registered with me and I really didn't even want to bring it up, nor did Mike. We didn't share the news with the Mitchell family either.

It was all a minor setback in my eyes and when he didn't mention it, I felt as though that he was thinking the same thing. My folks were supposed to hang around that day, to at least celebrate Geno's official 75th birthday, and until Mike had to catch his flight back to Chicago, but they decided to leave and go home. Mom said Dad was just not feeling good and wanted to be in his own bed at home. I was disappointed, but understood. I mean, who doesn't want to be at their home in their own bed when you don't feel good?

Mom and Dad packed up their belongings and were set to head back down to New Smyrna Beach when Gene asked Joanie if she would drive. That was very unusual because he always drove wherever they went together, but I didn't really give it much thought. I thought to myself that maybe he was still tired from his fever.

I had the next day off so I told them that I would drive down to New Smyrna that afternoon after practice and meet them at a restaurant we often went to, around seven o'clock that night. We could celebrate his birthday there.

We all said our goodbyes and then they drove off. Mike and I didn't really talk about the news too much during our short drive to the airport and although we were both concerned for our father we didn't feel like it was life-threatening or anything to that extent. I didn't mention anything to any of my friends either, but I did get the chance to talk with our head trainer who promised he would in turn get the second opinion set up for me. I was extremely grateful. I was also confident that these doctors would take care of him. That was something I was really sure about.

I was eager to get down to New Smyrna Beach that night to celebrate Geno's 75th birthday. As soon as I could get cleaned up and dressed, I hauled ass down to the restaurant where we had planned to meet. I couldn't wait to get there to show my dad his birthday present. My parents were waiting for me at a booth and both looked like they were already having a good time. Dad said he was feeling better and he actually did look better.

After our initial hellos, I plopped down next to my mother and sat directly across from Geno. I was extremely excited to tell him what I had gotten for his birthday. After we ordered our food, I asked him if he was ready to see his present. His eyes opened wide in curious anticipation, wondering what I was going to give him. I told him to close his eyes tight. He did so, almost like a child would. I pulled the picture out of my pocket, opened it up and slid it across the table so it was right in front of him.

I told him that he could open his eyes. When he opened them up and looked down at the picture, it took a second or two for him to get through reading the description of his new gift. He paused for another moment as he stared at the picture. When he looked up, our eyes met and his were filled with tears. I was taken aback for I had never, ever seen my dad cry before. I had never seen that emotional side of him, not that he wasn't capable of it, I had just never seen it. He wiped away a tear and said, "This is the nicest thing anyone has ever done for me."

We both got up and shared an emotional embrace. There was no joking around, no rabbit punches, just a good old fashioned love-filled bear hug. My mom was smiling from ear to ear. We sat back down and he immediately turned into an excited birthday boy, talking about the TV and asking me when it was coming and asking me to tell him all about the stereo and such.

I was thrilled that he was so happy with my gift. I was especially touched by his genuine emotion. We finished our dinner and I left the restaurant and headed back up to Jacksonville. All the way I had a tremendously happy feeling that I had touched him in that way. I loved that man so much and he meant everything to me.

A couple of weeks passed before I could see my parents again. We were on the road playing games in early December, so I was always busy practicing and going on some charity talks to local schools. Our contract called for us to do that and, honestly, most of us really enjoyed doing it.

In the meantime, my folks and I talked pretty much daily and Geno would always say that he felt okay, but started to complain that his back was still hurting him pretty bad. When I would get my mom on the phone, she would pretty much say that he was just abnormally tired.

Then the day came when my mom and dad were due to come up to Jacksonville to see the specialist for his second opinion at the local hospital. I raced over there after practice to meet them. Pete Mitchell, whom I now had told what was going on, came with me. We always rode together from the beach to work anyway so he obliged my request to stop off at the hospital with me before we drove back to the beach. He also wanted to see my dad.

As we pulled up to the hospital, they were just coming out. My dad looked really tired and was moving relatively slowly. His appearance looked pretty much the same as before but I could tell that his energy level had noticeably fallen way off. He obviously wasn't feeling too good and just wanted to get back in the car and head home to New Smyrna. He gave me an "it's going to be okay" line and slumped into the front seat of the car on the passenger side. He immediately put his head against a pillow that he had brought for the trip and closed his eyes.

I gave my mom a big hug before she got in and she told me that she would call me later. I didn't say much on the way back to the beach condo, not knowing really what to think until I talked with my mother, except that he looked nothing like himself for the first time since I had been told the news. Pete and I rode back to our condo in silence, respecting the fact that I was deeply consumed with my thoughts about my father.

Later that evening, I went out onto the patio of our condo and dialed their number. When my mom answered the phone, she, too, wasn't herself.

"Hey, Mom it's, Tom. How did it go today?"

"Not good, Tommy. Not good at all. The doctors told us that the cancer has spread all throughout his body. The back pain that he has been having the past couple of months is because some of his organs are swollen," she said to me with a fear and trembling in her voice that I had never heard before in my entire life.

"Well, what did the doctors say they can do? Will they give him chemo treatments or will he need surgery?" I asked with the hope that there was going to be a positive answer. Unfortunately, for my dad, my mom, and our family, there wasn't.

"There's nothing they can do, Tommy. It's too far spread. Your father doesn't want to go through any treatments just so he can be kept around, feeling sick all the time!" she responded almost in a defensive way for her Geno.

I asked as my heart began to race, "Mom, what does that mean? What are they saying? Is he going to die?"

She answered with a quiver in her voice, "They've given him two months to live, Tommy!"

The phone must have been silent for I don't know how long. It seemed an eternity. I couldn't believe my ears. She continued, "I'm sorry, Tommy. I'm really sorry! He loves you so much, you know that! There's nothing they can do. Try and get down here to see him when you can."

Tears started sliding down my cheeks. I didn't know what to say. I didn't know what to do. My father was dying. He was going to die. I never thought that it would have come to that, at least not so soon.

"I'll be down there tomorrow, Mom. I've got to see the trainer in the morning, but I will leave as soon as I can." I deliberately responded trying to sound reassuring and strong.

"Please tell the doctors that we thank them for everything. They were really great. Please tell them how appreciative we are for all of their help," she concluded, showcasing the classiness that she and Geno always had.

"I will, Mom. I will. Mom, I love you. I'll be there soon," I said as I slowly hung up the phone. I sat down in stunned silence thinking about what I had just been told. Two months. Two fucking months! I couldn't believe it. My dad was on his way out.

I started bawling as the ocean wind blew across the patio. Pete came out, touched my shoulder and sat down beside me. He tried to console me, telling me how sorry he was. It was sometime later that he told me that his dad, Scott Mitchell, was sort of a confidant to my dad. They only had known each other for a short time, but he had confided in him in confidence about his sickness. I don't think I slept that entire night.

The next morning I got up early and headed to the stadium. Once again it was a Tuesday, our day off, so only the injured players would be there. When I walked into the trainer's room, I saw that one of our team doctors was there. He had heard the news and wanted to tell me how sorry he was. I thanked him for all of his help and asked if he would keep the matter as private as possible. He agreed.

I hurried up with what I had to do at the stadium and in the locker room and headed back down to my parents' home. When I arrived in the mid-morning hours, my dad was still asleep. I gave my mom a big hug and she informed me where he was. I walked out onto their patio overlooking the golf course so I wouldn't make any noise and wake him. He soon woke up and met me out there.

After our initial greeting, I got up and offered to make him some pancakes for breakfast. I told him to stay seated at the patio table until I came back. Joanie would have normally done it, but since I was home I insisted, which I had done numerous times before. He always liked my pancakes so I obliged him again.

As all three of us sat there on the patio and ate, it was all so unusual and so unbelievably painful knowing what I had heard the night before, although I didn't want to show it.

At the same time Geno looked pretty much the same as he always had, just his actions were noticeably slower. His face might have been drawn a bit and he definitely looked tired, but he didn't look like he was on his deathbed or anything like that. He still looked like the same old Geno. After a few moments, I got up the nerve to ask him, "Dad, why don't you want to get any treatment and try to beat this thing?"

He didn't answer me straight away. Instead he took another small forkful of the pancakes. Then he looked up at me and, in a tone I was unaccustomed to hearing, said softly and deliberately, "Tommy, there's nothing they can do. It's too far along. I don't want to be around here taking hundreds of pills every week and have you kids seeing me walking around like I am half-dead. That's not me."

He paused a moment and then continued, "Hey, you know what, sometimes you win some and sometimes you lose some." His response penetrated deep into my heart. It was all I could do to control my emotions. I knew at that instant that I had to be the one who was strong, not for me, but for him, and especially my mom.

To be honest, though, I respected his decision. It was definitely very sad, but he felt he had lived his life and when you are 75 years old and lived the life that he had lived, I believe you have every right to make that kind of call. I understood to an extent what he had meant. He wanted to be remembered for what he was, not some laid up, weak and sick father. Still I was devastated inside.

Later that evening, as I was regrettably getting ready to leave, I kissed and hugged him goodbye, certain that I would be seeing him again. My mom walked me out to the car and we talked for a few moments.

"Mom, is he okay right now? He doesn't even look that bad!" I inquisitively asked, still not totally believing the inevitability of the situation.

Without hesitation she responded in a very direct and strong tone, "He's going to be around for a while, Tom. He's not going to die tomorrow or anything like that. You go and take care of your business and he'll be here when you are finished with the season. That's what he would want you to do."

In that brief moment in time, I saw in my mom the strength and a stoic attitude that I had seen throughout my life. I always talk about how tough my father was, but my mom was always the "rock" of our family, always standing by her husband and kids no matter the circumstance. It was a powerful moment.

I hugged my mom so tightly during that goodbye that I can still feel her touch. Tears were streaming down my face. At that moment, she once again had become a pillar of strength when, out of my dad's sight, I was in such a state of almost uncontrollable emotion. The ride back to Jacksonville was a sad and lonely trip.

Our next two games were on the road and then the final game for 1995 at home in Jacksonville was on Christmas Eve. I couldn't wait for the season to be over. I mean, I stayed focused as possible but all I could think about was how was Geno doing. I called home every day, more like two or three times a day to get a report from my mother. She always said that he was just really tired but nothing new was happening.

One Saturday night, before our last away game of the year, I went to my meetings and then to Catholic Mass, as I had always done the night before a game. It was always held in one of the meeting rooms at the hotel which was used as a makeshift chapel. Coach Coughlin was at the Mass each and every week, as well. I always sat in the front row near the wall and farthest away from the aisle. It was never a packed house, only about a dozen or so players and coaches were ever in there.

After that evening's Mass, as our priest, Father Tom Willis, was clearing his "altar", I took a moment to say a few extra prayers to reflect and just to feel at peace. Mass was always a very tranquil and spiritual place for me, and now more than ever before. To my surprise, as I sat there in silence with my head down, I was greeted by a fellow worshipper. He gently put his hand on my shoulder and sat down beside me. It was Tom Coughlin.

He put his arm around me and whispered to me in the most sincere and heartfelt tone that I had ever heard from him, "I heard about your dad and that the doctors gave him two months to live. I'm real sorry to hear that, Tom. You get down there and see him as much as you can and spend some real good time with him. We'll be here for you if you need us."

I responded with a "Thanks, Coach that really means a lot." I immediately thought to myself how incredibly nice and sincere that was coming from him. People can say what they want about Tom Coughlin, the coach, the Super Bowl winning coach of the 2007 NY Giants. Players, past and present, can bitch and moan and cry about how tough he was and still is to this day, but I'll never forget that moment we shared for as long as I live.

Tom Coughlin, the man, is a wonderful human being, and when he said those heartfelt words to me that night, it showed that there is a difference between Tom Coughlin, the coach, and Tom Coughlin, the man. He got up and walked out of the chapel. I sat there again for maybe fifteen minutes just thinking about my Geno and Coach's unexpected visit and words of comfort.

I went down to my folks' home on the next Tuesday and spent some great time with my dad, even though he was always tired and was beginning to look frail. He didn't look like he was really ill, but he was starting to show some signs that the cancer was affecting him.

I guess part of that feeling was that I never could get to grips with the thought that he was going to die. I mean, I knew what I had been told was true, but when we were together, we didn't miss a beat and we didn't really talk about it. He wanted to know how things were going. He said he would try and watch us on TV as much as he could, but what he had missed, I filled him in on.

Those moments we spent together, we talked about football and about life, not really about his illness, although he would always make sure to say, "You've got to promise me that you'll always take care of your mother." He really knew, of course, that I would. I loved her equally as much and I always let her know that. But, that request has always been with me. My best buddy asks me for that kind of favor, then it's a favor that I take to my grave. God only knows he would have done the same for me.

The last game of the year was at home against the Cleveland Browns. We were 3-12 heading into that final game. It had been a tough year on all of us, the team, the players, the coaches and the fans. Let's face it, that kind of season blows, no matter what the circumstances. Although I took pride in my performance and played to win, I have to admit my mind was else-where. I couldn't wait for the clock to read zero so I could get the hell out of there.

My sister, two brothers and one of my very good friends, Willy, all sat in the stands that day. The plan was to leave immediately after the game and head down to Geno and Joanie's home and celebrate Christmas. I hadn't seen my dad for about a week and a half, so I was very eager to race home with everyone and see him. It would prove to be a Christmas holiday season that I would never forget.

OUR GENO

The late afternoon sun was glinting on the windshield as we drove down to New Smyrna Beach from the stadium. By the time we got home the sun was setting in a brilliant display of warm colors, but my mind was not on sunsets, beach or golf. I was focused on my dad.

I can't remember what the conversation was about during that trip. I can only remember that when we first got into the car I asked my sister, Moira, who lived near Mom and Dad, how our dad was doing. She gave me the old safe cliché, "He's had his good days and he's had his bad days." I was waiting to see for myself and I couldn't wait to get there.

As soon as we walked through the front door, my mom greeted us, but put her finger up to her lips to signal us to be as quiet as possible. I gave my mom a big hug and immediately asked where Geno was. She let me know that he was sleeping in his bedroom and that we should be very quiet. "He's expecting you, though," she whispered.

I softly tiptoed into his room and could hear him breathing in the dark bedroom. He was lying on his back with the blankets pulled up high under his chin. When I walked up to be near his head, I was totally shocked by his appearance. All of his girth in his neck and shoulders, barely showing through the sheets, was practically gone.

The cancer had taken away the thickness in his body that he had worked so hard on throughout all of his years. He looked like half the man that I was used to seeing. I kept my composure as he slowly opened his eyes. I instinctively leaned over closer to his head. His voice was very low and hard to hear as he spoke in a very groggy voice, "Tommy, how are you? How did the game go?" I wasn't sure how I should answer because I did just wake him from his sleep and could see he needed nothing but rest.

"It was good, Dad. We won the game." I responded, not really wanting to go into detail.

"That's good. That's real good. I'm so proud of you, Tommy," he responded in a very soft, weak voice. He was dropping in and out of sleep during our very brief conversation.

"I know, Dad, I know. Get some rest, Okay? I'll come back and see you in a bit," I said to him, trying to hold back tears. For the first time since the announcement of his dreaded illness, I was really scared. I knew the way he now looked that he was feeling the terrible effects of his horrible disease. All I could do is just stand there, looking at my dad as he succumbed to sleep, totally devastated by the realization that he had so radically changed and declined in his health since I had last seen him.

I walked out of his room and hurried straight back out to the front of the house. I didn't want anyone to see me. I knew without question that he was dying. I lost it. I started bawling and swinging my fists through the night air. I began to hyperventilate and damn near lost all control. I didn't know what to do. I was just walking around in circles in a stupor.

I felt completely lost with nowhere to go. After a couple of minutes, Moira came out the front door to join me. I immediately grabbed her and hugged her tight. I couldn't stop crying. She just kept saying that it was going to be okay, comforting her baby brother. I eventually regained my cool and headed back inside. Christmas dinner was about to be served and I knew that I couldn't be seated at the table without being able to control my emotions. That would not have been good for anyone. I frankly didn't even feel I could eat anything. I had no appetite, but I also knew that Mom had worked very hard to present a Christmas dinner for the family.

We all sat at the kitchen table with the head of the table's chair strangely empty. The man of the house, our leader, was not sitting there. No one even attempted to fill that spot or remove the chair. Before Joanie sat down though, she went into the bedroom. A few minutes later, to my utter surprise, Dad came out supported by his Joanie. Mom slowly and deliberately guided him to his seat. He was wearing pajama bottoms, but he also had on a bright red Christmas sweater. He did his best to put a smile on his face as he sat down at his place at the table. The old soldier was once again with his family.

We said our family prayer and began to eat. I kept looking at him and smiling. It was so good to see him up and sitting with us. He didn't last very long, though. He probably only took a couple of bites of the great spread that Joanie and Moira had put together, as they had always done so many years past.

My mom got up to help him up and I immediately jumped up to grab his other side and together we assisted him out of his chair. We walked him into his room and gently laid him down on his bed. He fell right to sleep and we walked back to the table. His presence at the table gave everyone a great shot in the arm, just like a leader's presence should do.

The whole family stayed together for that next week. About a month and a half prior to Christmas, my brother Mike and I, plus our friend Willy, had made plans to spend New Year's up in Chicago at Mike's apartment. I was very reluctant to go for I didn't really want to leave.

My mom did a good job of convincing me to go and have a good time. She tried to reassure me that "he'll be here when you get back." So our plans remained intact and I also told Bob that I would pay to fly him up there as well, so he could see some of his old friends. We wouldn't be leaving until a couple of days before the start of the New Year so I got the chance to hang out with the family and spend some quality time with all of them.

On December 28th, the day of my parents' anniversary, my mother told Mike and me that Geno wanted to see us for a moment. We went into the room as he lay in bed. He was coherent and, although he didn't spend every waking moment in bed, he was always very tired. He asked us if we would go out and get some flowers for his Joanie, but to not let her know what we were doing.

He was the classic gentleman, never forgetting his anniversary with his beloved Joanie, the love of his life. We went out and did what was asked of us and brought a little card that went with the bouquet and took them into the bedroom for Geno to see. That was another one of his special requests. He signed the card and put it into the small envelope. He then asked if we would deliver his gift to Mom so that she would have something from him on their big day.

We left the flowers on the kitchen table with the note attached so that when Joanie came back from an errand they would be waiting for her. Mike and

I sat in the living room where the old football star and boxer would do his daily workout routine. The weights were still parked in the corner.

We watched Joanie open the card. She hesitated for a moment after reading it and immediately went into the bedroom to be with her man. I walked into the kitchen to read the card and see how he had signed it, being the nosy son I was. It was pretty hard to make out what he wrote because it was scribbled. It simply read, "Love, Geno." I remember thinking how great their love truly was. Here was my father facing his imminent death and he had remembered that day was their 32nd anniversary. What a romantic!

Later on in the day, after a few hours had passed and Geno was still in bed sleeping, I walked into his bedroom to check on him as I had done numerous times during that week. I found him sitting up on the edge of the bed, just staring off into space. I kneeled down in front of him and tried to place myself so that my head was below his head and I could look up into his eyes. He barely had the strength to raise his head. We then shared a moment that has lasted with me forever.

As I knelt there in silence, time stopped. I didn't know what to say. If I spoke I would have broken down anyway. All kinds of emotions filled my body. Geno then slowly placed his hand on my broad left shoulder and in a tender moment softly stated, "You know, Tom, we'll always be pals."

I managed to respond, choked with sorrow, "I know, Dad, I know". I rose up, leaned over to within an inch of his left ear and whispered, "I love you so much, Dad. I always will." I gave him a long hug letting his last words soak in. He had been my father, my mentor, my teacher, my inspiration, my friend, my trainer, my golf partner, my strength, and my deeply loving patron. And now, he called me his "pal." He had never called me his pal before, but that little word meant more to me then, as it does today, than any word I would ever hear from him again.

"We'll always be pals," are the last words my father ever said to me. He was right. He hit the nail right on the head. We were pals, forever. I have never forgotten our final moment together and I never will as long as I am on this earth.

Eugene E. McManus died on the last day of 1995 with his loving wife and daughter by his side. I got the call early that morning after a long night out on the town in Chicago. When my mom told me the news I slammed my arm across Mike's kitchen counter in his one bedroom apartment and I think it shook the whole building. I was so very upset, not for just the fact that my father had passed, but also because I wasn't there.

I was so convinced that I would see him again and now it wasn't going to happen. I felt tremendous guilt for a long time after that. But after it was all said and done, it ended the way it should have.

I really don't think my dad would have wanted me there, or any of his boys for that matter, to see him die. He just wanted to be with his Joanie until the end. He would have preferred for us to always remember him as the vibrant, generous, vocal, and lovingly humorous, upbeat man that he had always been, not the frail old man dying in his bed. When I look back on that fateful day, I am indeed glad that God led me to the decision to be in Chicago with my brothers and friends rather than watching Geno slowly slip away.

We held the funeral service back up in Chicago at our old parish, St. Mary's of Buffalo Grove. We planned not to have any kind of wake, so we kind of put the two together. The family stood by the entrance of the church and greeted every person in attendance as they came through the door before we started the service. I was amazed at how many people showed up. One after another came through those doors to pay their last respects to the old coach and friend.

There were people there whose names I couldn't even remember, people whom my parents hadn't seen or heard from in over ten years. And they were sobbing! I can remember many telling me how sorry they were and how great a man my father was. I kept thinking about how many lives that my dad had touched. That is what says it all. When it's my time to go, I hope that I will have had as great an impact on people's lives as he had. I was once again in awe of my father.

After the ceremony, we gathered together a select group to give Geno a final goodbye. My mom had his body cremated and we had a special plan for where we wanted to bury his ashes. About thirty of the immediate family and dear friends of Geno walked up the sideline of the football field at St. Mary's, located just outside the fence to the cemetery that had been there for a hundred years.

My brothers and I dug a deep hole right next to the fence, placed a young tree in the ground and spread his ashes all throughout the bulb of the tree.

We covered the hole with the remaining dirt and packed it tight. We then placed a plaque in front of it and secured it into the ground as the tree overlooked the football field. It read:

"In Loving Memory of Eugene E. McManus, "Geno", Father, Friend and Coach"

How fitting it was. It was the perfect place to rest his ashes and for me it was everything. It was the first football field that I ever played on and the field on which Geno had coached so many young boys. I swear I could hear him say, "It's a war out there. You gotta fight till the end!"

As everyone headed back to their cars, I took a few minutes and stood next to the tree. I gave it a couple of soft and slow rabbit punches, then hugged it tight and whispered, "You're the greatest dad. You'll always be the greatest!"

I didn't ever want to let go of that tree. I could have stayed there forever. I could envision Geno standing on that field like he did so many years before waiting for practice to end so he could take us boys home in his Cutlass Supreme. Mike came up from behind and put his arm around my neck saying, "He was something else, wasn't he?" Indeed, he was.

My parents' good friends and part of the coaching trio with Geno, the Murphy's, held a get together afterwards and we did what all good Irish Americans do when one of their fallen brethren has passed. We drank and gave many toasts to our friend, patriarch and inspiration, Geno. All of our tears turned to happy smiles and laughs as we celebrated his memory for many hours reminiscing about the old war hero, the football star, the boxer and coach, and most of all, our dear friend.

LIFE WITHOUT GENO

After the storm had passed and the festivities were over, Mom, Moira, Bob and I all headed back down to Florida. Mike had his life in Chicago working, so he stayed up there. We all settled in for our next chapters in life without our fallen hero, or at least so I had thought.

The first night back, after everyone had gone to bed, I laid on the living room floor trying to fall asleep. The memories of Geno, clanging those damn weights to playfully wrestling around with me, hung deep in the air and started to consume my every thought. After the dust had settled and I had gotten back to reality, the sadness crept in and paid me a visit, again.

I sat up in the quiet of the dark of the room and just started bawling. It was a deep and sorrowful cry. I missed him so much already. I hadn't let it all out since I answered that phone call on the morning of his death. It all felt so tragic. He wasn't going to be there in the morning. He was gone.

All at once, it hit me too hard. The memories of my father covered me like a blanket there that night. It was a good cry though, you know what I mean? Sometimes you just have to get it out. I tried to lie down and catch my breath.

I quickly figured out that I wasn't going to be able to fall asleep, so I got up and went outside through the back patio door. I started walking down the first fairway of the golf course, when suddenly a peaceful calm came over me. The tears stopped flowing and the smiles came to the forefront of my troubled mind. It was a surreal yet beautiful moment in my life. A huge comforting emotion came over me and told me that everything was going to be all right. My body suddenly became warm.

I began to visualize my dad in a better place for I believed he had a higher calling from the Man upstairs. I could see him in Heaven. He was the ole Geno too, with his big arms and shoulders, laughing and telling his stories.

In a sudden rush it gave me an incredible sense of calm. And then, in the blink of an eye, I got the urge to run, to just flat out run as long and as hard as I could go. No 40 yard dashes, no stopwatch-sprints, just me hauling ass in the middle of the night, with thoughts of Geno hitting me during every stride. I was in jeans and nothing else; no shoes, no shirt, no anything, just me and the moon and stars lighting up the midnight sky.

I took off down the middle of the fairway and didn't want to stop. I kept running and running and running, fairway after fairway. I ran for I don't know how long, pushing myself to the utmost level. It all became so refreshing. I felt fast too, which was kind of cool, to be honest. It felt like I could have run forever. I finally came to a halt as I panted heavily in the cold night air, creating a cloud of fog around me.

I was covered in sweat and my emotions immediately changed from doubtful, negative thoughts of loss to very positive ones of future and potential. It all came together to me in an instant. Yes, my father was gone. He was the one who had taught me how to compete and how to play the game, how to win, how to be, all of it.

Most importantly, though, he taught me, over everything else, was how to be a man, and being a man in this world who is true to that label means that sometimes you have to deal with adversity. You have to face it, overcome it and move on.

I had faced it before in my football career, but now it was personal. I came to the realization out there that night, right then and there, that my father wouldn't want me to be sad anymore. He would want me to be inspired by him from all of the experiences he had lived himself and all the advice he had given me throughout my life. He would want me to hold him close to my heart and continue on in the kind of fashion that he would have, given the same circumstances.

"Don't you dare use my death as a crutch!" I could hear him say, "That is for the weak-minded. Be strong and go on with your life and be the man that I taught you to be!"

Yeah, it was all coming together in an instant. My first season in the NFL was over, and now nothing was guaranteed. "What have you done for me lately?" was instilled in me by my father for as long as I could remember and he wasn't just referring to the NFL. My new challenge was now right in front of me. Last year was last year and that doesn't guarantee you shit in this world. I knew I had to work even harder to continue to fulfill my dream and to take care of my mother the best I could.

If I was to maintain my position on the Jaguars, then I had to beat out the new crop of talent that would be assembled for year number two. It was a very deep and shaping moment in my life for I believed Geno would be watching my every move. There was only one thing I had to do and that was to work my ass off and prove myself all over again. That's what we would have done if he was around anyway.

I was signed to another one year contract with only one guarantee: That I would be a part of the off season conditioning program and be brought back to training camp for another tryout. There were no guarantees that I would play for the Jaguars again.

Before we reported for the offseason program, I found myself shuffling between Jacksonville Beach and New Smyrna Beach, visiting my mother as much as possible. When home, I would often visit the same football field where Geno and I had spent many a day. I would set up my screwdrivers and run sprint after sprint just like we had so many times before. I worked harder than ever, knowing that I had to prove my worth once again to Coach Coughlin and to his staff.

When up in Jacksonville, I ran on the beach, typically during the hottest part of the day, although January through March in Jacksonville can be quite cool especially east of the intercoastal waterway, which separated the mainland from the beaches area. Locals called it the "ditch", and if you lived at the beach, you only crossed the ditch if you really had to.

I loved running at the beach with the waves crashing on the shore. The beaches in Jacksonville were perfect for a workout, especially when the tide was low because it was always hard-packed sand throughout the vast majority of it. I would perform sprints, agility drills, pass coverage and technique drills, etc.

Plus, it was perfect for it acted as a form of resistance running. The sand always offered a little "give" to it, which made me have to dig out of my cuts that much harder. It felt like how a tennis player on a clay court must feel when trying to change directions. It's much harder than on a hard court or grass for that matter. That type of training made it a little easier when I would wear my football cleats on grass and perform the same drills.

The beach was always a spiritual place for me. I could look over the horizon or up in the sky and just feel Geno's presence. At the football field it was eerily similar. It was like he was there with me the whole time, watching over me, goading me on to work harder.

When a parent dies, it's an indescribable moment in one's life, especially when that parent was such an incredible influence, like my dad was to me. I found myself talking to Geno time and time again and becoming closer and closer to his spirit. It gave me a great spring in my step. I felt like I could go harder and longer than I ever had before. I would envision Geno telling me "Let's do one more," which always brought a smile to my face.

I talked with my mom constantly and enjoyed seeing her as often as I could. She kept herself busy, too. She had a tremendous support group of friends that she not only met with Dad in New Smyrna Beach but also friends from back home in Chicago who would take trips down to visit her. Bob was still living with her while going to college and Moira was close by in the next town. I kept her up to speed with what was going on with me.

When I would visit, we would play a little golf, hang out at the beach and visit some of the local flair of taverns and restaurants. Of course, we always brought up our Geno in conversation. The somber feelings always turned to happiness as we would reminisce about Dad and all of the funny things he used to do, like get up early for his morning "snack" and leaving peanut butter stains on the front of his shirt, or when he would put on garden gloves for his weightlifting workouts with his sleeves pulled up high just like his sons wore them and of course, remembering his deep belly laugh.

I fortunately was able to purchase a house for my mom in New Smyrna in the same golf community that she and Geno had been living in. It was a nice little duplex that backed up to the green of the seventh hole. She loved it when I was home. I loved being there, too. I hugged her as much as I could, always telling her that I loved her so very much.

Bob and I grew extremely close. He would accompany me to the football field and read me my sprint times when he could. We would head out for a night of fun on occasion, too. I always made sure that I got my workouts in while down there whether back at the same local gym or out on the field. That was always a priority. We always made sure that we would have a good time after my work was done, whether it was just Joanie or with Moira too. We all held up really well and turned a tragic circumstance into a positive experience by being with one another as much as possible, just the way Geno would have wanted it.

When the offseason program began at the end of March, I was determined to improve my standing on the Jaguars team. The offseason was pretty easy compared to the year before. We still busted our ass but most of us knew what to expect. We worked out Monday through Friday, but again had Wednesdays and the weekends off. I was maturing physically, holding a higher weight while gaining some much needed speed. I felt that I was even more in my athletic prime, meaning that even though I was getting bigger, I wasn't slowing down. In fact, moving around was becoming easier and seemed more natural, even with the added weight.

The guys on the team grew close and, even though we had different cliques in the locker room, we all respected one and other and had a general caring for each other. My "clique" was basically the single guys, and we would go out a few times a week as a group. Why not? I mean, we had a lot of free time on our hands, so what the hell. What else are young, single, NFL players in their athletic primes supposed to be doing with their free time, right?

Whatever the case, we always got our workouts in. Workouts were generally finished by noon and we had all day to do whatever we wanted. I loved living at the beach. People were just so laid back and friendly. I was always very open and welcoming if someone wanted to say hello or stop and get an autograph for their kid, nephew, or whomever. I always obliged that request, when it came.

Pete Mitchell and I rented another apartment together. This time it was in a high-rise right on the water. It was a great time and a great experience. We traveled when we could, anywhere we wanted to, within reason. I had saved a good amount of my salary during the past season, so I had a nice cushion that offseason.

I wasn't really thinking about the future, financially, so I have to be honest, I spent a good amount of cash during that time. I would head to Chicago and stay with Mike, usually for a long weekend. We would party a bunch, hang out with old friends and just really enjoy being with each other. We, of course, spent a lot of time talking about Geno and our upbringing. I just know in my heart that Dad loved the fact that his family was really close.

In 1996 the Jaguars made some really strong moves during the offseason, bringing in more seasoned talent, most notably guys like Keenan McCardell, a hugely reliable receiver, John Jurkovic, who was a very talented defensive tackle, and Eddie Robinson, a great outside linebacker who came from the Houston Oilers.

The 1996 draft that year for the Jags was equally remarkable. They took Kevin Hardy, an outside linebacker from Illinois, as their first pick. In the second round, they took Tony Brackens, a stud defensive end from Texas, and Michael Cheever, the highest rated center coming out of college that year from Georgia Tech. In the third round came Aaron Beasley, a big strong cornerback from West Virginia.

Those four guys would go down as one of the best draft classes in the history of the Jaguars. I became good friends with all of them. They were all hard workers, great players, and cut from the same cloth as me. They also loved to have a good time, so we meshed well, to say the least. Michael Cheever and I became best of friends and made sure the times were always good, and man, we had some really good times!

I had a poignant impromptu meeting with Coughlin one day during the offseason in the weight room. It was towards the end of the offseason after we had had a couple of mini-camps and a bunch of on-the-field practices. I ended up the offseason in the same place as I had at the end of the 1995 season, penciled in as the second string middle linebacker. However, Coach Coughlin made it known to me directly that I had to be a standout on special teams in order to keep my place on the team. It was a very sobering but motivating conversation.

We split up at the end of June for a welcome break and had about a 5-week layoff until the start of the run-up to the preseason games. Training camp was going to be held in Jacksonville. Thank goodness we didn't have to go back up to Wisconsin. Traveling to Wisconsin, walking back and forth to different classrooms for meetings and then just being away from home was just a pain in the rump and I wasn't even one of the married guys with kids. That had to be especially tough for the guys who did.

Jacksonville would prove to be no walk in the park either, although our facilities were plush, especially compared to training camp in Wisconsin the previous year. Having training camp right outside the stadium was very convenient, too. However, summer time in Jacksonville can be flat out brutal. The heat and humidity was totally debilitating, draining and seemingly impossible to deal with. I can remember waking up to the local news channel and seeing a pet advisory during the really hot days, which were abundant.

I always thought how screwed up that sounded. Yeah, save your pets, so they don't get heat exhaustion and die, and here we were running around in pads and black helmets! It was so hot that I used to just piss in my pants, literally, if had to take a leak. I was too tired to walk or to jog to the Porta Potty. It was even hotter in there anyway.

I was drinking a ton of fluids to stay hydrated, so if I had to go, I went, right down my leg. It was just water anyway, at least that was what I would tell myself. Conserving energy was crucial in making it through training camp practices in the Florida heat. Eating lunch in bed was too. After the morning session and a shower, I would race to the hotel, grab a couple of sandwiches, eat them in bed, and then take a two-hour nap. Those days were long, about 12-16 hours, with practices, weight room workouts, and three-hour meetings at night. Grabbing that little nap was crucial.

Coughlin's thinking was that we had to practice in what we were going to play in during our first half the season - sun-baked and humid as hell temperatures. He was right. If we could handle the heat, then it would give us even more of a home field advantage when opposing teams came into town, especially the teams that came from up North.

The visiting team always had to wear their dark colors and they stood on the sideline that had direct sun on it the entire game. We wore our white jerseys and had shade on our sideline during the second half. It was just a little bit of a secret weapon. Teams would be gassed by the second half and, although we were tired too, we had grown used to it.

I took Coughlin's advice to heart, even though I was disappointed that I wouldn't be given any realistic shot at the starting job. I still knew that I had to impress anyway I could. I approached the 5-week layoff with one goal in mind. If my role was going to be just as a special teams player and as a goal line and short yardage linebacker, then I had to cut some weight and become even quicker and faster, since I wouldn't have to be taking on a bunch of 300+ pound, overweight offensive linemen down after down.

I had 'ballooned' up to the mid-to-upper 250 pound range during the off-season program and going into our mini-vacation, so I made the decisive and declared decision to get down to the 245 pound range. Believe it or not, ten pounds made a big difference.

I spent the next five weeks running as much as possible in the heat and visited my mom as often as I could, spending a couple of weeks with her during one stretch. I cut out all of the bad foods and kept my drinking to a minimum.

I also worked every day to my limits trying to achieve my goals. I arrived for the start of training camp in incredible shape and tipped the scales at an astounding 246 pounds. I even garnered the attention of the special teams' coach, Larry Pasquale, who said that I looked as good as he had ever seen me look, which was nice.

I was so very determined to not only to make the team that year but to also be looked upon as an important asset to the franchise. Throughout that whole period, I kept my dad's memory and legacy close to my heart, and believed that he was watching over me. That always gave me that extra incentive to succeed.

Little did I know at the beginning of training camp just how important my role was going to be that season and how even more special my second year on the Jaguars was about to become.

A YEAR TO REMEMBER

I made the team once again as the preseason ended. I felt pretty confident and secure with my position on the team, but you never know what is going to happen until the "Turk" passes you by.

Coach Coughlin told me that I had to have an impact on special teams to make the club so I knew going in that I had to do just that. I ended up as the leading tackler on special teams during the preseason, and along with all of my teammates I looked forward to the start of the regular season.

The roster had a ton of turnover on it from year one to year two. A good number of veterans and first year players from year one were still there, but there were many from the previous season that didn't make it.

An exceptional rookie class was added along with new veterans who upgraded some key positions. Guys like Jimmy Smith started to emerge, showcasing his skills into what was a potential Hall of Fame career. Pete Mitchell was making a name for himself as a go-to guy for Brunell, along with Keenan McCardell, who was a standout receiver and a great leader.

Leon Searcy was added and joined Tony Boselli to create an outstanding pair of bookends at offensive tackle. Joel Smeenge was a great, seasoned player, and a fan favorite, at defensive end. Lageman, Jurkovic, Kelvin Pritchett, Dana Hall, Derek Brown, Dave Thomas, Willie Jackson, Don Davey, Natrone Means, Paul Frase, Dave Widell, Travis Davis, Chris Hudson, Rich Tylski, Mickey Washington, Brian DeMarco, Bryan Schwartz, Ben Coleman, all held vital positions. Special team standouts Bryan Barker, Reggie Barlow, Randy Jordan, Mike Hollis, Brant Boyer, Jeff Kopp, Ty Hallock, and I all had very important roles on the team.

On paper our team had a bunch of talent. However, we knew we had to prove it on the field of play. We all busted our ass and believed that we could be a good, solid team, maybe not a contender yet, but definitely one with enormous promise. To top it off, the great Clyde Simmons joined us at the end of the preseason and had a huge impact on the team right away. He was a great player and a huge leader. We were right there and ready to make a name for the Jacksonville Jaguars. Our second season had not even begun, yet we all could see its potential and we were brimming with confidence.

We started off strong by beating the Pittsburgh Steelers in the opening game in front of the home crowd. They had just come off of a Super Bowl appearance representing the AFC. It was a huge win for us and showed that we really could fulfill the promise we had before that game.

But then things started to change. We dropped the next three games, all on the road. They were games that we were in the whole time but couldn't pull out the victory. Guys were pissed off but there was never any finger pointing that went on. Credit must be given to Coach Coughlin and the organization for bringing together guys with great character and confident leadership.

I was relegated to backup duty, content, but not totally happy with my situation. But, I was playing professional football and I genuinely liked the guys on the team. I played on all of the coverage units on special teams and was called upon in short yardage and goal line situations like I had been the year before. Sure I wanted to be the starter, but I knew the deal and no matter how hard it was to handle sometimes, I tried my best to embrace my standing on the team.

My mom and brother Bob would often come to the games. We had parties after the games as usual, although they weren't quite the same without our Geno there. Mike and some of my BC college buddies and hometown Chicago friends would come to visit. Life was great. I was "living the dream". I had no real complaints. I could take my mom out to dinner and buy drinks for all of my friends and family whenever it was called for.

Then something happened that I didn't see coming but was always ready for. As a backup in the NFL you have to prepare yourself to be the starter in case something happens to a starter in practice or during a game. If the starter goes down or misses any time at all you've got to be ready. Heck, his shoe could fall off and they need you to go in for a play or two. Like all of my backup brethren, I was prepared in case anything like that happened at the middle linebacker position.

Bryan Schwartz was the starter and was a decent player. He was athletic as hell and big for a middle backer. Yes, bigger and more athletic than I was, although he could have used a little more toughness, in my opinion, but he was "their guy", and he did have tremendous potential.

I can't say that I really liked it all that much but, he was a high round draft pick and I knew the deal. I couldn't do much about it anyway, except to keep working hard in practice and play well in my role. I didn't sit there and cry in my milk. I did my job to the best of my ability and felt lucky that I was playing in the National Football League.

To be honest, coaches want their backups to be ticked off that they're not the starter at their position. If they weren't, then they could be seen as complacent, which means you're not striving to get any better, you're just content with being the backup. No coach wants that on his team.

We were up in New England playing the Patriots during the fourth week of the season. We were getting our ass handed to us, quite frankly. We were down all too quickly 22-0. The defense was on the field and all of a sudden Schwartz went down with a knee injury in the second quarter. In a flash, I was thrust into the starting defense. I would have to call all the defensive plays, as most middle linebackers do, and make sure that I didn't screw it up.

Knowing the calls and learning the defense came easily to me. The "smarts" of the game of football were never a problem. I played a couple of series right before halftime, made a couple of tackles and was so overblown with emotion that I didn't know what to think.

When we got inside the locker room after the end of the first half, we all learned that the knee injury to Schwartz was pretty damn serious, most likely season-ending. Now, that sucks. No one wants to see one of his teammates go down with that kind of injury, no matter the circumstance.

There are no really adequate words to describe how you feel for a fellow teammate who goes down with a serious injury like that. The words "That's unfortunate, disappointing and just terrible" just don't quite cut it. I made sure that I told him how sorry I was and I sincerely meant it, but he was pretty despondent and should have been. It's a tough thing to go through for anyone.

My linebacker coach, Steve Szabo, approached me in the locker room and told me the deal. "Schwartz is out and now you're in. Do your job, nothing more, and nothing less." My feeling of feeling sorry for the starter immediately turned to optimism for now I knew that I had gotten my shot, not for a play or two, but a real shot. If I fucked it up they'd find someone else to replace me, but there was no way I was going to let that opportunity slip by me.

Then something happened that I'll never forget for as long as I live. After my quick meeting with Szabo, I headed to the bathroom to go take a piss. As I approached the room, Clyde Simmons passed me coming the other way.

Now, keep in mind, the NFL has different terminology when describing different positions. For example, wide receivers are named the X and Z position and the Tight End is the Y. Well, the middle linebacker is referred to as the "Mike". With that being said, as I headed to the john, Clyde stopped me.

You have to picture the significance of this brief encounter. Clyde was a big name in the NFL, had the respect of all of his teammates, as well as the opposing team and all of the media. There is sort of a special aura and respect a player like Clyde had, especially for a backup player like I was. So when he asked with a serious tone, "So, you're going to be the Mike now, huh?" that was a powerful and very meaningful question.

"Yeah, Clyde. That's right. I'm going to be the Mike!" I replied back to him.

He looked me square in the eyes and tapped his fist on my shoulder pads and said, "Well then, go and be the Mike!"

I was taken aback a bit, but at the same time, it got me even more pumped up. He had immediately given me his vote of confidence and for it to have come from him was pretty damn cool. Clyde Simmons of the great defensive line of the Philadelphia Eagles along with the late Reggie White and Jerome Brown, and Mike Golic, had told me in that one quick line to be confident and get the job done. That's what true veteran leaders do. Well, I never lacked confidence in that department, but it was awesome to hear that from him anyway.

The outside linebacker coach, Lucious Selmon, the older brother of the great Lee Roy Selmon, was a good friend of mine. We had a great relationship and he always believed that I could be a starter someday in this league. He was a very likable guy on Coughlin's staff and was also somewhat of a confidant to me, always telling me to "Hang in there. You'll get your chance one day."

He was always on the sideline during the games and always made sure that the right personnel were on the field for each particular play for our defense. After the kickoff to start the second half, our defense was ready to take the field and just before I was about to run out, he grabbed me and put both of his massive hands on my shoulder pads. He looked me straight into my eyes with a penetrating directness and said, "This is your defense now. Go out there and prove it to them!" Man, I loved hearing that from him.

We ended up losing that game 28-25, but made a terrific comeback. Our defense held them to six points in the second half and I ended up making ten tackles in one half, playing only first and second down.

That year was such a huge emotional year for me. My dad had died the year before in a quick and tragic way. I was three years removed from tending bar in downtown Chicago and now I was the starting middle linebacker for the Jacksonville Jaguars in the National Football League. I'd thought I had died and gone to heaven!

There was a very emotional scenario that took place before every game for me that I have never really shared with anyone before. I used to stare at this picture of my dad, Mike and me that was taken at a wedding of a couple who were friends of mine and Mike and our family. We had known them for a long time and while we were at one of that weekend's festivities, someone had taken our picture.

Mike and I weren't looking at the camera but Geno was staring right at it. He looked like the typical Geno: big shoulders, huge forearms, and that steely look on his face. I kept that picture in my locker and always took it with me when we traveled for road games. Before each game when I was about to take the field, I would sit there fully dressed in my uniform and pads, with a towel draped over my head with that picture cupped in my hand.

I would just stare at him and I swear I could hear him telling me once again that, "There are no friends on that damn field! Run right through 'em Tommy. And remember I'll always love ya!" It would bring a tear to my eye every time, but it also got me even more determined to succeed.

When we played on the road, I would pick out a spot on the top row of the opponent's stadium and pretend that he was standing up there, with his arms crossed, and studying every single play, like he did back when I was in high school. Deep inside, I would play as though he was going to critique my performance after each game, although by then I was always my own hardest critic. Sure, I had coaches and teammates to answer to, but he was still my classic inspiration. It was an unbelievable time in my life, not only for me but for my mom, my brothers, my sister and my friends who knew and loved Geno.

I played the rest of that entire regular season as the starting middle linebacker. My mindset changed immediately as I took on my new role and prospered in it. I felt like I had paid my dues getting to that point and that I was showing the NFL that they had made an initial mistake about me: that I could in fact thrive in their league and be a significant contributor.

I would always get choked up talking about it with family and friends. It was a coming of age for me, so to speak, and although I had wished with all my heart that Geno would have been there, through my faith in the Good Lord and deep in my heart, I knew he was watching every bit of it.

One day, I received a letter from Mr. Flood. He knew all about what was going on with me in Jacksonville and always tried to watch my games at a pub near his home. He would ask his local bartender to turn on the Jaguar game every Sunday, which always got a curious look back at him like, "What do you want to watch that game for?" A lot of friends and family had very similar experiences in their respective hometowns.

I opened the letter and it read, "Your father took care of Schwartz, now the rest is up to you!" I loved that letter for no other reason than, yes, Geno was in heaven looking down on his youngest son as he was living his dream that he worked so hard for. It was just another small vignette of emotion that went on all throughout that year.

But wait, it gets better. Our record after eleven weeks of the regular season was 4-7 with five games to play. There were a couple that we let get away.

But, as the saying goes, you're only as good as your record shows. Ours showed that we couldn't close the deal. We played teams tough, but, in the end, we couldn't get it done.

Then we got hot, winning four in a row, including a Sunday Night nationally televised game against the Seattle Seahawks, in which the defining moment came when we stopped them on a tremendous goal line stand where they had four tries from inside the 5 yard line and we stuffed 'em.

My friend and cohort and other short yardage and goal line linebacker, Brant Boyer, and I made three big plays in a row. It was huge and it played a big part in the victory. Man, did we party that night! How sweet it was after a victory like that, especially when we learned after the game that we now controlled our own destiny for the playoffs.

Heading into the final week of regular season play, our record stood at 8-7. Our upcoming game was against the Atlanta Falcons in front of our hometown crowd. If we won the game, we made the playoffs. If we lost, we all went home for Christmas. We were favored to win the game, but it was a nail biter that came down to the wire in the fourth quarter. In the final minute of the game, the Falcons drove the ball down the field. Thank goodness Tony Brackens was hustling on a specific play because he made a touchdown saving tackle. The Falcons were in scoring range! We were up by two points and all they needed was a field goal to win it.

Their kicker, Morten Anderson, who will go down as one of the best place kickers of all time, lined up to kick a seventeen yarder for the win. All that was needed was a simple chip shot to win the game and help the Falcons play the role of the spoiler. I was on the field goal block team and was lined up third from the outside. With all my might I crashed through my blocker, as other guys on the other side of the formation did the same. Tony Brackens, Don Davey, and Clyde Simmons (who was also known as a great kick blocker) all rose up high in the air.

It was the easiest kick in the world for Morten Anderson. He had made hundreds like it for years before. But, he missed it. He shanked it left. He missed the kick! Are you kidding me? There was immediate pandemonium inside Alltel Stadium. The fans went nuts, the players jumped up and down and Coughlin shook his head with a look of disbelief that quickly turned into a huge smile.

The Jacksonville Jaguars, in only their second year of their existence, were going to the playoffs. And to top it off, their unknown starting middle linebacker had been tending bar in downtown Chicago three years prior.

I finished the regular season as the team's third leading tackler with 119, and that was only playing primarily on first and second down. I also showed that I could in fact cover the pass having knocked down passes throughout the year, although I should have picked a couple of those throws off. But that's why I played defense, I guess.

I had proven that the Jaguars could count on me as their starting middle linebacker in all facets of the game. Like I said before, labels are hard to break sometimes, especially in the NFL, but when the opportunity knocks, you've got to be ready, and ready I was. Hell, it took me over three years to get to that point. Perseverance and belief won out. I proved that fact to myself and many others during that year.

Coughlin huddled us in together once we all got inside the locker room and made a very poignant statement, "We're in this thing to win it! Let's not forget that!" It was a statement that rang so true. We were a confident bunch, no doubt about it, but we knew exactly what he was saying. We were not cocky by any means but there was definitely no "deer in the headlights" type of feel to the impending playoffs.

Actually, we should have finished the season 11-5, but we dropped two games during the middle of the year to the St. Louis Rams and the New Orleans Saints whom we had beaten up and down the field, but in the end, lost the games. As we approached our first ever playoff game, we felt we could compete with anyone.

That wasn't the feeling throughout the NFL nor certainly with the Buffalo Bills, who had never lost a home playoff game in their entire playoff history; 9-0 all time at home in the playoffs! No one gave us chance, not the media, not the NFL and especially the Bills' star players with the likes of Bruce Smith, Jim Kelly, Thurman, Thomas, and so on.

"Jacksonville who? They're gonna get their ass knocked out of the playoffs as quick as they got in!" chirped Thurman Thomas, the great running back.

Our feeling was that we had nothing to lose. Let them talk. We got in on a lucky break, no doubt, but we started to pull it all together with that winning stretch. Our defense was playing decently. We would hit you in the mouth. We had some really good players on that team, a nice mix of veterans and rookies who made huge contributions. Our roster was full with football vagabonds, drifters, and castoffs from other teams, who had their careers resurrected with the Jags, including my own.

Our offense kept plugging along. Our offensive line was big and could push people around. Natrone Means and James Stewart were a strong one-two punch in the backfield. Brunell had shown that he was a top flight quarterback while Jimmy and Keenan had established themselves as two of the best receivers in the league. My personal attitude was the same as it had always been. They put their game pants on the same as we do and you play the game between the white lines, not in the newspaper, so fuck 'em, I would say to myself.

The playoff atmosphere is like no other. The media, the fans, just the whole experience is dynamite. The Bills' stadium was rocking, chanting at enormous decibels, "Let's go Buff-a-lo!" over and over again. I liked playing on the road. It was our team and staff, which totaled about 80 people, versus their 70,000+. The togetherness that we had on that team was a powerful force. The Bills may have had the history but we were ready to go into battle and make some history of our own.

The first quarter was terrible for us. Maybe Thurman was right. The Bills went up 12-0 early and we knew we had to claw our way back. And, that's what we did. Boselli started to handle the Hall of Famer Bruce Smith. Natrone Means ran like a steam engine, while Mitchell, McCardell and Smith all had big plays. The D regrouped after that first quarter and went toe to toe with the high powered "K-Gun" offense headed by another future Hall of Famer, Jim Kelly.

Clyde Simmons picked off a shovel pass and returned it for a touchdown. We held their running game in check and we ended up knocking Kelly out of the game with a concussion, which turned out to be his last game ever. In the end, Mike Hollis made a long range field goal that bounced off the goal post and miraculously tipped in for the score. That fourth quarter kick added to our own playoff lore. Yes, the Jacksonville Jaguars beat the Bills 30-27 in the AFC Wildcard game for their first ever playoff victory!

Now, we were rolling. At least I thought so. That victory gave us a huge shot in the arm and we looked forward to next week's challenge. If we thought that no one gave us a chance against Buffalo, well, multiply that by a thousand times for we had to travel to Denver to take on the league leading Broncos in the AFC Divisional playoff round.

John Elway, Terrell Davis, Shannon Sharpe, a stout offensive line, and playmakers at the receiver position all made up their awesome offense. Their defense had a bunch of great players on it as well: Michael Dean Perry, Alfred Williams, Bill Romanowski and the great Steve Atwater, to name a few. They had the best record of the entire NFL that year at 13-3. They were the number one seed in the AFC playoffs and to top it all off, they were a 16-point favorite heading into the game.

Everyone had written us off. This was Elway's and the Broncos' Super Bowl year, they all said. We thought otherwise. We knew we could hang, but I'd be lying if I said there wasn't a little self-doubt that we could actually pull it off. However, a little bit of fear of failure is good for an athlete and for a team; it keeps the fire burning inside.

I learned early in that week that I would be playing more than normal. On specific passing downs they would keep all three linebackers in the game (normally they would take one out, which would be me, and bring in another defensive back to help cover the speedy receivers), to help control Terrell Davis. As the game drew nearer, I was very eager to show the Broncos what we were made of and to the football world what number 55 was all about.

We awoke on the day of the game to find a columnist with the Denver Post, Woody Paige, ripping our team up and down. He wrote that we didn't belong on the same field as the almighty Broncos. He even referred to our team as the "Jagwads!" Typical local beat writer, not really knowing what the hell he's talking about! Should have done your homework a little better, Woody!

When we met for the pre-game meal, guys were visibly pissed off. It's one thing to not give us a chance, it's another to rip what we had accomplished and to show utter disrespect. We had beaten the odds and were now in the second round of the playoffs. I heard a lot of "Fuck Woody Paige!" that morning, which brought a big smile to my face.

Coughlin had members of his staff cut out that article and when we entered into the locker room it was plastered all over the place, just a little not-so-subtle reminder that no one gave us a chance. Again, the "us versus them" approach brewed very strong. We were all spitting nails and couldn't wait to get out on the field and go toe to toe. Then we would find Woody and shove a football down his mouth.

To top it off, NBC had already erected their studio set on the field for the next week, assuming that the Broncos would be hosting the AFC Championship. What? Even the TV network giant wasn't giving us a chance. That overconfident act by NBC added even more insult to injury. It was like they were pulling for the Broncos. I know ratings would have been huge having the Broncos advance, but that was bullshit!

After the pre-game warm up, we headed back into the locker room and guys were fired up. I sat at my locker with the towel as usual draped over my head and stared at the picture of Geno. I know what he would have said in this situation, "Knock them on their ass, Tommy!" I can't even describe the emotion I had right before we headed back out onto that field for kickoff. I could have jumped right out of my skin!

The first quarter was much like the week before against the Bills. The Broncos scored quickly and their defense stymied our offense. The score was 12-0 before we even knew it. Elway was sharp, Terrell Davis had a long run from scrimmage that took the ball down to the four yard line. We were in a run blitz call to the Tight End side and they ran the ball the other way which left us depleted to that side of the ball. But, hey, we lost that chess match for that particular play and with a great back like Davis, you couldn't afford to give him an inch, much less the weak side of the field.

Once the second quarter got going, our team settled down. The offense put a couple of scoring drives together. Our defense shut down the Broncos running game and didn't allow a score of any kind for the remainder of the first half, although Elway was still pretty powerful.

Natrone Means was playing his butt off, running through and around the Broncos defense. Brunell was in a zone and Mike Hollis made a couple of clutch field goals, one of which was right before half time. We went into the locker room at the break leading 13-12. We kept our composure and made it back. The locker room was buzzing, to say the least. We had taken their best shots and were still standing. There wasn't one guy in that place who didn't feel like we were going to win that game.

In the second half, we went up by ten points, on a beautiful throw and catch by Brunell to Keenan McCardell in the back of the end zone. Mark was flushed from the pocket, threw it on the run and put it in a great spot for his receiver to make a play. The Broncos kept coming back, putting a drive together in the fourth quarter to make it within 23-19.

I was having a great game. All of the linebackers were. The game plan called by Dick Jauron, our defensive coordinator, was brilliant. We shut down the Broncos rushing attack and made a bunch of plays against their passing game. I knocked down two balls thrown by Elway and also forced him to throw early twice by getting in his face as he was back in the pocket.

One of the balls he threw was a rocket over the middle. I reached up and jumped as high as I could, which was never really that high at all, and tipped it enough to thwart that play. My middle finger, which the ball hit directly, was swollen for about six months after that game. Man, Elway had a laser for an arm! To block one of his throws was like trying to catch a bullet.

Then Mark Brunell made his own history. On one particular play, he dropped back to pass and found no one open. He unexpectedly took off running up the middle of the Broncos defense, although the play called was not for a quarterback draw. Mike Cheever, who had replaced Dave Widell at center due to an early injury, led the way, making a key block. Brunell then used his speed and got to the outside. When it was all said and done he had run for about 40 yards to inside the Broncos 20 yard line, late in the fourth quarter. Our sideline went nuts!

Then something incredible happened and I had a front row seat for it. I remember kneeling as far down the sideline as I could, as close to the end zone as the officials allowed. They lined up for the next play and as Brunell scoured the field to check the defense's lineup, he noticed Jimmy Smith in a one-on-one matchup with the defensive back playing up close. That was like a gift from heaven for a savvy quarterback like Brunell.

Mark looked over at Jimmy and nodded. That was all that needed to be done. I remember kneeling there saying, "Holy shit, Jimmy's got one-on-one coverage!" Mark dropped back and lofted a beautiful pass into the corner of the end zone. Jimmy beat his guy off the line of scrimmage, got on his outside, and used his speed to get by him. Jimmy laid out for the ball and it landed into his "bread basket". Touchdown, Jaguars!

It was one of the most spectacular plays I had ever witnessed and it happened within a few yards of me. Our team went nuts and other than the 5,000 Jaguar fans who were sitting up in the nosebleed section of the stadium, you could hear a pin drop by the silence of the Broncos fans. They were in utter shock. We, on the other hand, could hardly contain our excitement.

We weren't totally out the weeds yet though, not with a quarterback like John Elway. After the ensuing kickoff, he immediately led his team down the field on a handful of passes and drove them in for a score. It was 30-27 with about a minute to go. The Broncos then attempted an onside kick. Had they recovered the kick, they would have had one more shot and with Elway at the helm we didn't want that to happen. But our fullback, Le'Shai Maston, recovered. Game over! Jags win! Jags win! Jags win!

It was a feeling of emotion I can't even begin to describe. The second-year Jacksonville Jaguars went into Mile High Stadium and shocked the football world! Some say it was the biggest upset in the history of the playoffs, at least during the 1990's. The Broncos hadn't lost a home game that entire year and hadn't lost a home playoff game since 1984.

We had done the unthinkable. We had believed in ourselves and played the game of our lives. I ended up with 11 tackles, two passes defended and two quarterback pressures. I played the best game of my life, in the biggest game of my life, and Coach Coughlin named me one of the defensive players of the game.

The locker room was in phenomenal pandemonium. All of the guys were hugging and yelling and giving high fives. I finally got to my locker through the melee, took off my shoulder pads and sat down in front of my locker. I grabbed my dad's photo and stared at it for what seemed like forever. I no longer heard the din in the locker room. My joy was being shared with Geno, one-on-one.

The plane ride home was a long one, and at first we were all so pumped up. Then after a while fatigue set in, guys started to settle down and most went to sleep. We were awakened by the airplane pilot over the intercom with the announcement that over 40,000 fans were at our stadium.

They had been there all day long and now they were waiting for their victorious hometown team to return. The pilot then did a "fly over" at 1,000 feet for the fans in the stadium. We were in a jumbo jet and this guy thought he was Tom Cruise buzzing the tower. I was sitting next to the window and looked down and saw all those fans. It was a pretty incredible sight!

We received a police escort from the airport down to the stadium. It was like a huge caravan, with players' and coaches' automobiles making their way to downtown Jacksonville. People were pulled over on the side of the Interstate highway, holding signs, honking horns and waving. It was crazy! When we arrived, we parked our cars and headed into the stadium through the tunnel.

I had this tremendous feeling of gratification, satisfaction and vindication for all that it had taken me to achieve and then be able to witness this momentous celebration. I was so absorbed with our tremendous victory and my performance. I had proved that I could play in this damn league and now no one could take that away! As I was walking through the masses of people inside the tunnel, there was a ton of noise and craziness going on all around me and all I could think about in the bedlam was my dad, my pal, Geno.

I kept telling myself over and over again, "We did it, Dad! We did it!" I could feel his spirit within me every step I took. Tears started to well up in my eyes. It was an epiphany, a surreal moment for me. I couldn't hear anything. I just felt my heart pounding and sensed the vision of my dad smiling and giving his big belly laugh in agreement.

As I walked towards the opening of the tunnel that led us out onto the field, I saw in the distance two people with teal colored #55 jerseys. There were so many people around that at first I couldn't see who they were. I looked at my watch and it read two o'clock in the morning. I was thinking, "Who in the heck would be here at this hour of the night, wearing my jersey?"

As I got closer I realized that I should have known better who it was. There they were, just the two of them waiting for me, my mother and my brother Bob. The love of Geno's life and the Matriarch of the McManus family had the biggest smile I had ever seen on her face. It was all so fitting. She was there the whole time, as was Geno, believing in me and cheering me on.

I walked up and gave her the biggest hug I could gather. A tear from my eye fell onto the back of my jersey she was wearing and I didn't ever want to let her go. Bob gave me a hug, too and said, "You little shit. You did it!" I picked him up and swung him around. I knew deep in my heart that this accomplishment, this vindication, all of this glory, wasn't just for me. It was for the entire McManus family, all in honor of our Geno.

After the embraces, I gathered myself and said, "How did you guys get in here?" knowing that the Jaguars didn't ever let anyone through the front door unless you were an employee of the organization. "I just told them that I was your mother!" Joanie said with a defiant and direct tone.

"You want to go out there with me?" I asked, pointing to the field surrounded by 40,000 screaming fans. They both gave me a look like a child in amazement.

"C'mon, let's go!" I said, as I put my arm around my mother and led her out into the January night in front of the screaming Jaguar fans. The color, lights and music blared so loud from the scoreboards at each end of the field, you would have thought we'd won the Super Bowl. It was a night we would never forget.

1996 AFC CHAMPIONSHIP GAME

The next week was something that most of us on the team weren't quite used to. The national media was all over the place; Sports Illustrated, CNN, ESPN, USA Today, to name a few. They all came down to Jacksonville to witness and talk with the Jaguars who were one game away from the biggest show on earth, the Super Bowl. They camped outside the stadium and watched our every move.

I was interviewed by the likes of the Boston Globe, the Boston Herald, all doing stories on the former Boston College linebacker who in a roundabout way, made it to the top of the elite. The Chicago Tribune did a fantastic story on me, the former bartender who realized a dream. They even titled it, "A Toast to Perseverance." In it they talked about the death of my father and the inspiration he was for me. It was great recognition for both of us and I loved it. If a professional football player says he doesn't care for the acknowledgment of his success, then he isn't really telling the truth.

I didn't need the limelight per se, but it was nice to be recognized for what I had overcome to realize a dream. I worked hard to get there but I always knew I was also lucky to be even given a shot at getting back to the NFL.

I knew more than anyone else that if Tom Coughlin didn't know me from BC, then I probably would have been a sales representative for some company out in "the real world". That way of thinking always kept me grounded and made me never take anything for granted. The whole "What have you done for me lately" message that my dad instilled in me was so deep and entrenched in me that it could have been inscribed across my chest.

It took all of my focus to not think ahead this time. We were one game away from the Super Bowl, but I knew, as did all of teammates, that we had to get through the New England Patriots, on the road once again, to get there. I was very focused, determined and confident, as were my teammates, to get to the Big Show. We were going back to the place where my role on the team changed dramatically. As a team, after going toe to toe with the Patriots in week 4, we were very familiar with the Patriots and pretty much knew what to expect from them.

The Patriots were led by Bill Parcells, the Hall of Fame coach. He had built them into a winner and quite frankly, a tough-assed team. Tom Coughlin was a part of Parcells' staff back in the early 90s when the New York Giants won the Super Bowl and both teams were built very similarly.

They had a tough, pound-it-out running game led by Curtis Martin, another future Hall of Famer, a passing attack with Drew Bledsoe at the helm, Ben Coates, a very athletic and tough Tight End who was Bledsoe's go-to guy, and a defense that had Willie McGinnest, Chris Slade, Ted Johnson and Teddy Bruschi to lead that tough, hard-nosed bunch. They also had very solid special team players who always came to play. It would be a game marked by physical abuse at the line of scrimmage, with the team that won those battles most likely winning the game and heading to New Orleans for Super Bowl XXXVI.

We had a great week of practice and traveled up north to the frigid temperatures of the northeast. I never bought into "a Florida or warm weather team can't survive in the cold." Hell, we all came from different parts of the country. The media always made it out like we all grew up on some Caribbean island, for crying out loud. I didn't mind the cold, especially for a football game. Hell, it's what I grew up in. Now living in the cold is much different, but to me football in January should be played in the cold anyway. We were ready for the biggest game of our lives.

We arrived at Boston's Logan Airport and headed out to Providence, Rhode Island, and stayed at some fancy hotel. We held our final walkthrough practice at Brown University with snow covering the whole field. We were a loose and confident team. Afterwards, we started throwing snowballs at one and other. I realized quickly to get out of the way of a Brunell thrown snowball. It was a freaking missile. I could have used him when I was a kid, battling my older brothers in numerous snowball fights up in Chicago.

The local and national media were all over the hotel, interviewing the stars of the team and Coach Coughlin. They made it out to be a mentor against student type of match up when they referred to the two head coaches. I never thought of it like that, but that wasn't much of a concern to me.

I was focused on knowing that I had to be at my best in order to help our team win. I was determined to even better my performance from the week before. I constantly visualized in my head time and time again about making a bunch of tackles and big plays and what the locker room would be when we pulled off a victory.

My brother Mike and some of our old Chicago friends made the trip out to New England for the big game. We made plans to meet at a restaurant located near our team hotel the night before the game. It was also Mike's birthday that night, so I looked forward to hanging with him.

After my responsibilities with the team, meetings and such, and doing a couple of interviews, I headed to greet my brother. We were extremely close and shared a common bond when it came to our father and to the game of football.

He was a great player in his own right and as his younger brother, growing up, I had always wanted to be tough like him.

He loved the fact that his "little" brother had made it to the top and he always believed that I did belong. I looked up to him still and he would give me great advice, not to mention his words of encouragement which he always let me know.

At the end of the meal, I had to say my goodbyes and head back to the hotel for more meetings and then eventually for some good solid sleep, that was if I could get to sleep, although a couple of Excedrin PM's always did the trick.

Before I left the table, Mike slid over an envelope with a letter in it. He asked that I not open in it until I got back to my hotel room. He escorted me out of the restaurant and we gave each other a big hug. It was an emotional time for us and I loved every minute of it. He left me with a boisterous "Go get 'em tomorrow, kid. Go and kick somebody's ass for me, will ya?"

"Absolutely, Mike. You got it!" It was so great to have him there for the biggest moment in both of our lives up until that point. When I got to my hotel room after my team duties, Pete Mitchell, my roommate each and every game, hadn't made it back to the room yet. I sat down to read the note that Mike had given me earlier. It read:

Dear Tom,

Tomorrow at this time you will know if you're going to have the chance to play in the biggest spectacle in all of sports. To play and be the starting middle linebacker in the Super Bowl is going to be the most incredible feeling of accomplishment and gratitude. You will have the opportunity to satisfy a tremendous goal that you and I would dream about in our years growing up together. THE STARTING MIDDLE LINEBACKER IN THE SUPER BOWL! I shake with such tremendous pride that it brings me to tears. What Dad would have given to watch you walk onto the field in New Orleans.

After the game in Denver, you have shown to be a leader of the defense for the Jaguars. Make no mistake about that Tom! You have earned your right to be there! Explode onto the field with enormous confidence and destroy New England!

I have to say that the love and pride I have for you cannot be matched with words. I am extremely grateful for your friendship and so proud to be your brother. Good luck and know that I am by your side always.

And also know this, you are one game away from the Super Bowl and our dad will have the best seat in the house watching you from Heaven!

Your friend always,

Mike

P.S. An interception and the game ball would be a hell of a birthday present!

I hadn't shed a tear all week long, but after reading that incredible letter, all of my emotions came flooding out. All of my tremendous emotions that I had throughout that incredible year came to the forefront right there in that Providence hotel room.

The life and death of my dad was the biggest inspiration I ever had when I played the game of football. How I wished he could have been there in person, although I truly believed that he was right there with me in that hotel room. I could have suited up for that game right then and there. I couldn't have thanked Mike enough for that letter. It meant everything!

The atmosphere at the AFC Championship Game was incredible. Hundreds of media credentials were handed out and a lot of those people aligned the sidelines. The buzz at Foxboro Stadium was deafening. The second year Jaguars were one game away from the Super Bowl and some former bartender was starting at middle linebacker! The hair rises on my forearms just thinking about it.

Before we took the field again after our pre-game warm-up, we were back in the locker room. It was time. It was time to put everything out of our minds and go compete in the biggest game we had ever been in as a team. Once again, I sat at my locker with a towel draped over my head and stared at the picture of Geno.

"THERE ARE NO FRIENDS ON THAT DAMN FOOTBALL FIELD!" I could hear him say to me over and over again. I kissed the picture on the glass and said to it, "This one's for you, Dad!"

We left the locker room and took the field together as we headed out into the blustery, frigid January night at Foxboro Stadium to take on the Patriots and looked our biggest battle of our lives dead in the face!

We lost that game 20-6. We gave them too many chances and didn't take advantage of our own. Our defense played an outstanding game. We held the Patriots to a total of 234 yards with Curtis Martin held in check with 59 yards rushing and Bledsoe and company with only 178 yards and no touchdowns. I had over ten tackles and tipped a pass intended for Ben Coates that our cornerback Aaron Beasley intercepted to stop a crucial drive early in the game. But it wasn't enough.

We made critical mistakes on offense and special teams. Sometimes that's just the way the ball bounces. You win as a team and lose as a team. And just like my dad said to me the year before, "You win some and you lose some."

Unfortunately for our team that night, he was right. No matter how much that loss stung, the Patriots were the better team that day and they deserved to win the game and represent the AFC in the Super Bowl. I had a little solace after the game knowing that I had played pretty well, but the amount of disappointment I was wrestling with was pretty indescribable.

Mike came down from the stands and I met him behind our bench as the clock read zero. I could see the look of disappointment written all over his face but he always had a way to put a positive spin on things.

"Dad would be real proud of you tonight, Tommy! You played your ass off!" he said to me.

"Damn, we were so close. I can't believe we couldn't win. We were right there!" I responded.

With that I looked to the sky, as Mike wrapped his arm across my shoulder pads, and said, "We almost had 'em. Didn't we, Dad?"

I gave Mike a big hug and thanked him for the letter and for coming to the game and told him I would call him later. I went into the locker room, got showered up, put my dad's picture back into my travel bag and headed out to the team bus. I got in and sat next to the window. I stared out into the wintry northeastern night as the site of the Patriots stadium quickly vanished over the horizon, not knowing if I would ever make it back to the magnitude of a game like that.

I felt like crap for the loss but had a sense of accomplishment once again. I showed that I belonged and that I could play in the NFL. It was something that Geno always knew I could do, and that meant everything to me. Although we didn't win, I knew deep in my soul that I did in fact win that year and it was all because of the man who had taught me how.

After we boarded our plane and took off down the runway at Logan Airport, heading back to Jacksonville, Mark Brunell sat next to me. As I glanced over at him, not knowing what to say, he looked over and stated with a smile on his face, "You know what, Tom? This really sucks and all, but you really proved yourself and had a great year!"

"Thanks Mark," I replied. It was all that was needed to be said. I really appreciated that from him. He was a star in the making and he didn't have to say that to me.

I shut off my overhead light and stared into space. I instantly thought of my father, and a sense of peace came over me. I knew he was proud of all that I had accomplished that year and I knew he had seen it all cheering me on with the Good Lord right by his side.

As the plane ascended into the night air, I leaned my head back and shut my eyes. And then with an all too familiar and perfect voice, I could hear Geno say, "You're just lucky it wasn't me out there tonight!"

Immediately I heard his big belly laugh in my head, and I whispered to myself, "I love you, Dad. I will forever!"

HIGHS AND LOWS AND
MEETING MY KRISTINA

During the last three years of my professional football playing career I went through a series of ups and downs. The offseason after the '96 season was spent having the time of my life, doing some traveling, and also giving back as much as I could. I had made a name for myself on the football field and off of it as well.

The route that I took to get to the elite level always made me feel very fortunate and it also kept me humbled and level-headed. Geno's upbringing had something to do with it too, of course. I knew what it was like not to have my dream fulfilled, so I wanted to make sure that I took it all in and gave back to the community as much as possible.

As I looked ahead to the '97 season, I was very determined to keep my position as the starting middle linebacker for the Jaguars and to continue to build my name on and off the gridiron. I worked as hard as I always had and was eager to prove myself once again.

Although the coaching staff had given me a lot of praise for what I had accomplished coming off the bench the previous year, they weren't exactly ready to hand me the starting job. They wanted me to go into camp and see if I could win the starting position outright. I had my eye on the prize, but unfortunately for me my opportunity didn't last very long.

I blew out the ACL in my right knee during the first week of training camp in 1997. We were practicing against the Tampa Bay Buccaneers down at their training camp and during a one-on-one pass coverage drill, I planted on my right foot and my knee gave out. It was devastating and even more surreal, like it was all a bad dream. I had never been really hurt like that before. It was scary!

I had gone into camp in great shape and was having a really good start. I was in a battle for the starting position at middle linebacker and things were going well. But, as the T-shirt says, "Shit happens." It was unfortunate and untimely. I had my knee reconstructed and sat out the entire season on the Injured Reserve list.

The team went 11-5 and made it back to the playoffs. Ironically, we went back to Denver and they whooped our ass, 42-17. Terrell Davis had a huge day. I was at my mom's house in New Smyrna Beach watching the game on TV and we got so fed up that we said "Screw it, let's go get a drink." We couldn't watch it anymore.

I rehabbed my knee that entire season and throughout the off season. I made it back to training camp in 1998. I was again informed that nothing was a given, not even a roster spot. If I couldn't perform up to the abilities that the coaches thought I should, then I would be let go.

I had a couple of setbacks with the knee early in camp, but finished strong at the conclusion and ended up starting four games for the Jaguars during that year. Again, we went 11-5 and made it to the second round of the play-offs until we got bounced out by the New York Jets, headed up by Bill Parcells and Curtis Martin.

I came back again in 1999, this time with the promise by Coach Coughlin to have a legitimate shot at winning the starting middle linebacker job out-right. I was ready to leave after the '98 season, to try my luck in free agency. I took a visit to the San Diego Chargers, but wasn't offered a contract. Coach Coughlin and I had a long telephone conversation shortly thereafter. After about 45 minutes of bantering back and forth, stating my case, and he his, I was told that I would be given a level playing field to win the starting job. That's all I wanted to hear in the first place. That was never the case prior to that conversation. You see, when a team drafts a player in the first couple of rounds and gives him big signing bonus money, that player is always given the upper hand to be the starter. It was very frustrating for a guy like me for I showed that I was just as good, or even better than the guy in front of me. By the time the 1998 season had ended, I had enough, and that's why I wanted to leave the Jags and try somewhere else.

I am so glad that I didn't leave, that Coach and I had that conversation. Call it fate, call it what you want, but I was destined to stay in Jacksonville, for reasons that will be told in a minute. I worked my tail off and looked forward to competing for the starting gig. I was two seasons removed from my ACL tear and was ready and determined more than ever to go into battle and regain my status as a starting middle linebacker in the National Football League.

I was in great shape heading into the 1999 season. I was 255 pounds and had increased my speed and agility. I felt as confident as I ever had been and was ready to go into battle for that starting gig. It was mine!

I was named the starter after the final pre-season game as we headed into our regular season. I had a great camp and was ready to rock! We were loaded with talent across the board. We were confidant as hell and knew that we had something special. I started the first two games of the year in which we beat the Steve Young led San Francisco 49ers and on the road against the Carolina Panthers.

Unfortunately for me, the last play of the Carolina game would also be the last play for me. We were up 22-20 as they lined up for a two point conversion after a touchdown. All we had to do was prevent them from converting and we would win the game. It was a pass play and I had the responsibility of covering a wide receiver. He broke to the outside and I planted my foot instinctively to turn and run right along with him, something that I had greatly improved upon throughout my time with the Jaguars.

Immediately, a shooting pain raced through my right foot and I went down on the turf. The pass went the other way and we ended up winning the game, but I had to be carried off the field as I couldn't put any pressure on the foot. It ended up that I had severed a tendon underneath my right ankle. That hurt like a son of a bitch!

It was an amazing irony too, considering that I had been in so many pileups throughout my entire football life, with my body contorted in so many different ways, yet I would get up without even a scratch. But both of my serious injuries had happened with no contact, just me running. Crazy, if you ask me.

I had to have my foot surgically repaired by a renowned foot surgeon in Chicago, Dr. Lowell Weil. He actually had to slice open the side of my foot, pretty much the entire length of it. The injury and the surgery hurt like hell. He later told me that my injury was so rare that my case would be later used in international podiatry conventions. It was the least I could do for the medical profession, right?

I spent the rest of the year back on Injured Reserve or IR as it was called. IR sucks. Sure, you're getting paid your salary and you do see your teammates during the year, but you are not really on the team. You're kind of stuck in limbo. The 1999 season was a tough one to watch. The team was great all year long except when we played the Titans. They beat us three times that year including the AFC Championship Game in Jacksonville. It was a tough way for the season to go down. We finished the year 14-2, but couldn't get to the big show. I didn't even feel a part of the team, though. I mean it's tough when you're not playing. At least I got to work out a ton and look towards continuing my career.

Sadly though, 1999 ended up being the last year of my professional football playing career. I was still only 29 years old and felt that I could continue on but the Jaguars and the rest of the league didn't see it the same way. I visited three teams as a free agent but to no avail. I was never signed to a contract again. My dream was over.

I was pretty dejected for a little while knowing that I would never play the game again. It happens to every football player, or athlete for that matter, when it's time to say goodbye to the sport you so love to play. Some people get to go out on their own terms, but most do not. That's why you always see grown men break down when they announce their retirement or have to walk away from the game, like I did. It's an emotional time.

No matter how your career ends, it's never easy. The hardest part of leaving the game is figuring out what's next. My whole life I had been a football player. What do I become now that my career is done? Who am I if not a football player? A lot of men struggle with that. It was another battle against a different kind of adversity for me.

Throughout my years as a Jaguar, I built a solid name for myself in Jacksonville, not only for my play on the field, but what I did off of it as well, whether it was being involved in charity work, or just being known as a good, approachable guy.

When the glory ends, all you have left is your name. And just like when my dad died, I couldn't use the way my career ended as a crutch. I had to battle back and find a new passion. I had to "adapt and improvise" and even get a little creative. I knew this, I couldn't rest on my laurels and I definitely couldn't make excuses or feel sorry for myself. I still had so much to live for and so much to accomplish in my life.

My dad would often tell me, "It's not where you've been, Tom, but rather, where are you going?" Those words of wisdom have always stayed with me to this day.

I look back on my football career and realize just how lucky and fortunate I was. All the way back to St. Mary's of Buffalo Grove, I have had people that have helped me along the way, to whom I am extremely grateful: Mike Flood and Murph, two of my first coaches; the coaches at Wheeling High School; Jack Bicknell and his staff at Boston College, especially Barry Gallup and Red Kelin; Steve Szabo, who turned into a great friend and a man who was instrumental in helping me get back to the gridirion; and of course, Coach Tom Coughlin, who gave me a chance of a lifetime to fulfill a lifelong dream. I will always hold him in high regard and with the utmost respect. I consider him my friend and wish him nothing but the best.

I often sit and reminisce about my football career, the ups and downs, the highs and lows. Although missing the Super Bowl by one game is still and always will be heart wrenching, the glory of achieving the ultimate dream, of making it to the top, the elite, the NFL, was incredible.

I beat the odds and won. Sure, I would have loved to have played a lot longer, but I wouldn't change it for the world. I played in a total of 53 NFL games, including 5 in the playoffs. I was a starter in 22 of those contests, including the 3 playoff games during our great run in 1996. I played in the biggest games, against the biggest stars. Not bad for an out-of-work line-backer prior to that. I proved that I did belong and that I could hang with the best of them. It was surreal, yet so phenomenal that words are tough to find to describe it. Those memories, though, always bring me back to the man who taught me everything.

Gene McManus was a true man. He wasn't perfect, but his principles of life are what our great country was built upon. His stories of overcoming adversity and persevering through trying times, especially his life and death situations, tell the tale of a man who lived such an incredible life. He truly was an American bad ass.

He taught me how to be a man in this world; a man who never gives up; a man who believes in himself even when people question his desires; and most importantly, a man who takes pride in his role of provider, protector, and as Daddy to his family. I wish every man, every person for that matter, could have the kind of relationship and influence that I had with my father. I will do my absolute best to pay it forward.

I can honestly say, I would have never had made it to the NFL if it weren't for my dad, but his impact on me carries way beyond the football field. His influence, his inspiration, his love and his story prepared me to believe in myself and make my own successes. He showed me what it takes to be a winner in life, and to be as great of a husband, a father, and person in this world, as I can be.

But this is not the end of the story. No, no, no. There is some really good stuff that I haven't divulged just yet. Sure, the way my football career ended was awful, but a ton of good came out of it as well.

All good stories must have a happy ending, and this story would not be complete without telling you about the predestined events that made my happy ending come to fruition. It all started to unfold right before my very last football season.

Pete Mitchell and I went our separate ways as roommates and we each got our own pad after the 1996 season. I rented a duplex a couple of houses from the beach. My landlords lived next door and we became really good friends. I had a ton of fun as I spent most of my time in the NFL as a single guy, living the single life.

I don't have to go into the whole thing of what it's like to be single and playing professional football. That would be the subject for a whole other book, but let's just say I had no responsibilities other than to myself, and I was able to do whatever I felt like doing, with whomever I wanted. I was also smart enough to know that half of it came my way because of my status as an NFL player.

After a while, though, the singles scene got real old. I had a good time, but I was alone more than not and I just got real tired of it all. All the singleness of being an NFL player and "living the dream" just wasn't attractive to me anymore. I wanted more out of my life.

I have only told this story to my closest friends and loved ones, but it is another true story and it is ultimately what this book is all about. As I had done my entire life, I lay in my bed one night and said my prayers. It was the summer prior to the 1999 season and my career-ending injury.

After my normal set of praise and prayers to the Good Lord, I prayed that I would find someone special. I was ready, truly ready, deep in my heart. I fell asleep that night and went about my business in the days and weeks that followed. A short while later, on the Fourth of July, I was invited by my landlords, to join them at a party down the street at the beach.

I obliged their invitation and looked forward to the party, as I usually did. After a lot of conversation and a few beers, I happened to walk outside the back of the house onto a second floor balcony, minding my own business, when I first laid eyes on her. Her name was Kristina and she was the cutest thing I had every seen. We said hello and small talked a bit. She was cool from the get-go, right off the bat. She had the whole "no drama" look on her face. You know what I mean? Some women you can just tell they are a little cuckoo. She was laid back, and just what I liked; hot, cool, and laid back. Bam!

But then things went terribly south. I ate something at that party that, let's just say, didn't sit too well with me. I had to get the hell out of there. I gave her some bullshit line and headed home. I found out that she lived at the beach, which at the time was a small community in its own right, so I figured that I would run into her again, soon. I never did get her number that day. I know, what a dumbass, right? Man, someone was looking out for me.

I didn't see her before I went to training camp that year. I was very focused on what I needed to do but I did think of her often. I went to camp for the 6-week preseason tune-up and on the first night out after camp broke I saw her again at a local hotspot in Neptune Beach, just east of downtown Jacksonville.

I had been dying to get out and get a release from the doldrums of training camp. Kristina, her friends, and I had a few drinks and ended up back at my place with me and some of my boys. We talked quite a bit and got along really well. She was really easy to talk to, like I had known her for years. I got her number and called her the next day. I picked her up for our first date and was just blown away. She was seven years younger than I was, at age 21, but extremely mature for a girl her age and cool, so cool. My good buddy Willy once described her as "even keel". He was exactly right. What a gift! You can high five me, fellas, at any time now.

All kidding aside, we had a great first date and hit it off. She was a well rounded, down to earth girl who came from a real good, close family. She only lived four blocks away and still lived with her parents. It was very ironic that I had never run into her before our first meeting since living in a small beach town, everyone pretty much knows everyone, but hey, timing is everything.

The next day I called her up and asked her if she wanted to go for a walk on the beach. We talked for over four hours. It was so easy. Plus she looked great in her bikini! We talked about everything: about her life and upbringing and, I told her the whole story about Geno, my mom and my family. That was it. I was hooked.

One day I walked into the locker room and was getting dressed when my good friend and old running mate, Brant Boyer, came up to me and asked, "You fallin' in love, Tommy? I don't see you out that much anymore." All I could do was smile. He knew it. It was written all over my face. I was done, cooked and happy to be there. He smiled, turned away, and just shook his head back and forth the whole time as he walked out the locker room. He would have to recruit another wing mate. They were good times my friend, good times.

Kristina and I had been dating for about three weeks when I got hurt with my nasty foot injury. It was my right foot and I had to have a cast on it and walk with crutches for eight long weeks, which added to my physical hopelessness. However, the Good Lord does work in mysterious ways.

It turned out that Kristina's dad was (and still is) a huge Jaguars' fan and I was one of his favorite players. I learned later on, that before I picked her up for our first date, she didn't tell her dad until right before I arrived as to who her date was. She said he would have driven her crazy because of his certain excitement for her. She also made him promise not to bombard me with football questions, which I wouldn't have cared if he had done anyway. I always loved to talk about the game, still do.

Well, when I got hurt, he told her that she needed to go over to my house and take care of me, to help me out since I couldn't drive. In fact, I could barely walk and I guess he felt bad for me. Well, she came over and, you guessed it, she never left! Even after I got my cast off, he asked me if I was going to bring her back home. I responded by telling him that he started this whole thing, and no, she wasn't coming back.

It gets better. Turns out she was a Jaguars' cheerleader for the past three years, while I was playing. I never knew it. Now, I know a ton of guys must have said, "Yeah, right!" But it was true. I didn't really know any of the cheerleaders, except for a couple. I never dated any of them so I was never introduced to her and never knew who she was.

Then it gets even better. One day she came over wearing this Pro Bowl baseball cap. My mind immediately started racing because I had this rule: I didn't date anyone who had dated a football player in the past, especially a Jaguar player. It was a rule I instituted with myself a long time before I met Kristina. Why? A locker room can be a very tough place. Let's just leave it at that.

It hit me like a ton of bricks because I already knew how much I was into her. She had been at my place for only two minutes when I inquisitively asked, "So, um, where did you get that hat?" thinking that some old boyfriend must have given it to her. She responded, "I went to the Pro Bowl last year!"

Now that totally freaked me out inside as I thought to myself, "Oh great, not only did she date a football player before, but on top of that, he's a Pro Bowler!" I must have had a real weird look on my face because the next thing she said was, "Tom, you do know that I was a cheerleader, right?"

"For who?" I asked, now even more screwed up.

"For Jacksonville, the Roar. The last three years. You didn't know that? My teammates voted me to be a representative for the Jaguars at the Pro Bowl after last season!" she announced.

"What? Seriously? Whew!" I said. I then suddenly grabbed her and gave her a big hug. "You scared the shit out of me!" I added. I eventually filled her in about my confusion and concern and she laughed her ass off.

We spent every day together, every waking moment throughout that football season. We had so many good times. She was all that I had asked for: someone special. I asked her to marry me right before Christmas up in Chicago, after four months of our courtship. And like the old cliché states, the rest is history! And it's still in the making! My prayers were answered that fateful summer night by the Big Man upstairs. I believe in my heart that Geno also had something to do with it. She is absolutely perfect, my gift from God.

As of this writing, we have been married eight years and have two beautiful daughters. Avery Ann is seven and Kelsey Marie, is four. We are also expecting our third daughter. Harley Mae is due in September (2008).

The running joke in our family is that I will have to go through the rest of my life telling my daughters that Mommy made it to the Pro Bowl but Daddy never even got a sniff of it! My father-in-law reminds me of that every chance he gets. Kristina's picture is even up on a Wall of Fame inside the Jaguars' stadium. I'm very proud of her. She's a wonderful wife and a fantastic mom. I always tell her that she's "The dream that saved my life!"

Although you may think this story is over, life's stories never really end. You have no doubt figured out that this book is about life and about love. It's about life's lessons, about believing and overcoming. But most of all, it's the story of a father and a son and the journey of their bond together that continues on today through three generations.

I learned so much from my dad and mom, through my upbringing and my faith, that I carry it with me every day. Geno showed me how to be tough and caring all at the same time. He was the embodiment of those two words. He showered my mom with love and brought us kids up to be loving, respectful, tough, and hardworking people.

More than anything else, I am so very proud to be the son of Gene McManus. I can't thank you enough, Dad, for helping me be the man that I am today. My only wish is that I will impact and inspire my girls as much as you have done for me.

Well, that's about it. I've covered it all, for now. What can I say, life's great! Make it great, I say, as great as you want it!

Wait a second. Hold up a minute. What about Joanie? I can't forget about our beloved Joanie. Joanie's great! She lives nearby, about five minutes away. I moved her up by us over six years ago. She's 77 years old and looks fantastic. She is a tough old gal and a sweet grandmother. We love her so much! With our new arrival due, my mom and dad will have a total of six grandchildren. We see her all the time and often reminisce about our Geno. Kristina has heard all of the stories about my dad time and time again, and our girls know all about their Grandpa Geno and what he did in his life. They'll know even more after they are old enough to read this book. I might have to give them a G-rated version, though.

You know it's funny. I often ask my mom if she would ever want to have, you know, a companion, a male friend to spend time with. After all, Geno has been gone for over 12 years now. That's a long time not to have anyone in someone's life. I always tell her and joke around that it would be fine with me, that I wouldn't be too hard on a guy if she did. You know what she tells me, every single time?

"Tommy! No one compares to your father!"

Doesn't that just say it all?

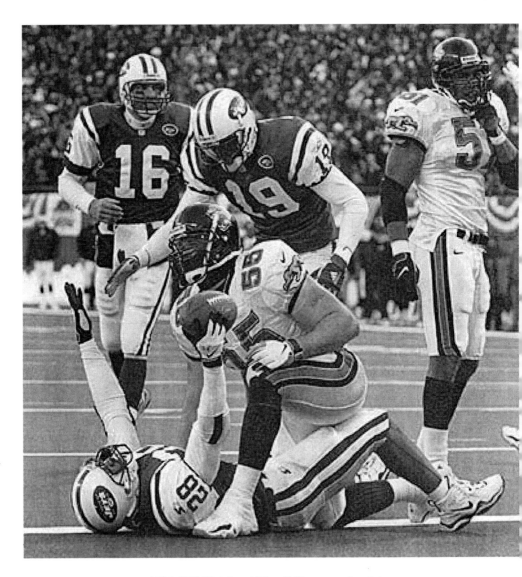

1998 AFC Divisional Playoff Game vs. the Jets